Who Stole My Church?

Other Books by Gordon MacDonald

A Resilient Life

Rebuilding Your Broken World

A Heart for the Master

Mid-Course Correction

Heart Connections (with Gail MacDonald)

When Men Think Private Thoughts

The Life God Blesses

Renewing Your Spiritual Passion

Restoring Joy to Your Inner World

Restoring Your Spiritual Passion

Ordering Your Private World

The Effective Father

Who Stole My Church?

What to Do When the Church You Love
Tries to Enter the Twenty-First Century

GORDON MACDONALD

THOMAS NELSON
Since 1798

NASHVILLE   DALLAS   MEXICO CITY   RIO DE JANEIRO

Published in Nashville, Tennessee, by Thomas Nelson. Thomas Nelson is a registered trademark of Thomas Nelson, Inc.

Published in association with the literary agency of Wolgemuth & Associates, Inc.

Thomas Nelson, Inc., titles may be purchased in bulk for educational, business, fund-raising, or sales promotional use. For information, please e-mail SpecialMarkets@ThomasNelson.com.

All Scripture quotations, unless otherwise indicated, are taken from The Holy Bible, New International Version (NIV). ©1973, 1978, 1984 by International Bible Society. Used by permission of Zondervan Publishing House. All rights reserved.

ISBN 978-0-7852-3049-6 (tradepaper)
ISBN 978-0-8499-2153-7 (special edition)

The Library of Congress has cataloged the earlier edition as follows:
MacDonald, Gordon, 1939–
    Who stole my church? : what to do when the church you love tries to enter the twenty-first century / Gordon MacDonald.
        p. cm.
ISBN 978-0-7852-2601-7 (hardcover)
    1. Church renewal. 2. Change—Religious aspects—Christianity. 3. Church history—21st century. I. Title.
BV600.M284   2007
262.001'7—dc22   2007031149

Printed in the United States of America
13 14 QG 0 9 8

To the five congregations who gave me the
opportunity to serve them as their pastor.

CLOUGH VALLEY BAPTIST CHURCH
St. Francis, Kansas (1964–66)

FIRST BAPTIST CHURCH
Collinsville, Illinois (1966–72)

GRACE CHAPEL
Lexington, Massachusetts (1972–84; 1992–99)

TRINITY BAPTIST CHURCH
Manhattan, New York (1989–1992)

CENTERPOINT CHURCH
Concord, New Hampshire (2003–07)

The title of this book, *Who Stole My Church?*, springs from a conversation a few years ago with a distraught man who felt betrayed by the church he had invested in for most of his adult years. From his perspective everything had changed—*overnight,* he said—into something that made him feel like a stranger in the place he'd always thought of as his spiritual home.

I listened to him describe what sounded like ecclesiastical carnage. Programs had been dumped, traditional music trashed, preaching styles and topics revolutionized, symbols of reverence (appropriate clothing, crosses, communion tables, and pulpits come to mind) thrust aside.

His anguish (and his anger) began with a young pastor who had been appointed with a challenge from the church's leadership to "stir things up with a new vision." His mandate: make the church grow like the Willow Creeks, the Saddlebacks, the Mars Hills, and all the other megachurches that have appeared during the last decade.

According to my friend, most of the church members—in particular, the older generation—had no idea what they were getting themselves into when all the growth talk began. Who would protest against, he asked, the idea of finding fresh ways to evangelize the unchurched? But what people expected was merely a fresh voice in the pulpit and a program or two imported from more successful churches.

Here's what I heard him saying. What he and his fellow church members had not anticipated was a total shift in the church's culture, a *reinvention* (a favorite word of mine) of ways to love God and serve people. What they did not see coming was a reshuffling of the church's priorities, so that *lost* and *broken* people rather than *found* and *supposedly fixed* people became the primary target audience. In summary: *virtually everything in the life of their church under new leadership became focused on reaching people who were not yet there.*

It was during that part of the conversation that my lunch partner finally said, "Our church has been stolen out from under us. It's been hijacked." His solution to the problem? To leave and search for another church that "appreciated" the older and better church ways his generation was familiar and comfortable with.

As I recall the conversation, my friend was less than delighted when he discovered that I wasn't completely sympathetic to his cause. I tried to find a kind way to say, "Get used to it," but I wasn't very successful.

My parting comment that day was something like this: "You need to think about the fact that any church that has not turned its face toward the younger generation and the new challenges of reaching unchurched people in this world will simply cease to exist. We're not talking decades—we're talking just a few years."

How many people of varying ages are feeling out of alignment with their churches today? Some of them think that their churches aren't adapting fast enough to new realities, and others think their churches have simply changed too much. Sadly, more than a few at both of these extremes address the "problem" by just dropping out. Some stick in there but take on the role of bitter critics, and they sap the strength of the community in their own way.

Here and there, however, are marvelous people who seem to understand that a church is not meant to be a club organized for the convenience of insiders but a cooperative where people combine together to grow spiritually, to worship the triune God, and to prepare themselves for Christian living and service in the larger world.

Every book can probably be traced back to a point in time when a fresh idea was birthed in the author's mind. That lunch conversation and the comment— "Our church has been stolen out from under us"—became the starting point for this book.

Preface

Many are the books on church change. Usually they are written from the standpoint and the instruction of the change agent, the leader (like my friend's new pastor) who has the responsibility to bring about something new. In this book, however, I decided to deal with the subject from the perspective of some of the people who are powerfully affected by change—the dear people in the pew who have to live with, and even support, the new ways.

My first attempt at writing about church change was abortive. I could not escape the feeling that I was writing one more dull book on an overworked subject. So I restarted my project, but in a way I'd never tried before. I decided to create an imaginary New England church in which there was a small collection of average people who were bumping up against change issues and resisting them.

Once I set these people in motion, I asked myself: *If I were to enter the story as I really am, what would I say to them? How might I engage with them and persuade them to take a fresh look at the realities in our world that do indeed require a new kind of church?*

My imagined people are all in their fifties and sixties. They are from the so-called builder and boomer generations, people who were once very much at the center of their churches and have now relinquished control and influence to others younger than they are. Once I had them all in their proper places in my mind, it was as if they took over the story and began to tell it for me. I just had to do the typing.

A story does not come out of thin air, of course. And there are places where this story borrows from my experiences as a pastor of more than forty-seven years in five different churches.

But those who have known me during the course of these years will waste their time if they try to match any person in this story with a real-life person. There simply is no connection.

The only real people in the story are my wife, Gail, and I. I put myself (with Gail at my side at times) squarely in the middle of this book, and much of what we say during the course of the story represents what we probably would have said in similar situations.

In this story I am the pastor of a New England church of a few hundred people. The church could be located in any of the six New England states, in any of the moderate-sized towns of the Northeast—but probably not Boston. The church in this story has no name, nor is it identified by denomination. Its official leaders—elders, for example—play almost no role in this particular story. Those who do play a role tend to be everyday, typical Christian church members. If you've done church for a lot of years, you'll recognize these types of people rather quickly in your own world.

While I'm offering disclaimers, let me add that the story leaves any number of issues dangling without resolution. There is one primary issue that I am concerned with in this book: *how do people face change when it threatens their comfort zone?*

My hope for this book is that it would spark dialogue among people of all generations who love the church. I would be grateful if the book would convince younger generations of church leaders to be more sensitive to the older generation and their thoughts. Conversely, I have a passion that older Christians would be led—if they read this book—to understand why many things about the way we have made church work must change and reflect new realities.

GORDON MACDONALD
Canterbury, New Hampshire

Acknowledgments

During the writing of this book I have discussed its progress with very few people. On the few occasions that I tried, I realized that no one had the slightest idea of what I was trying to do. Which is excusable because it's difficult to describe a book that is fiction but is also involved with facts of contemporary church life. Also, how do you describe a book in which twenty (or so) people do not really exist but two of them (Gail and I) do. Is there a name for such writing?

My lone companion in the process of writing was Gail, faithful wife of almost forty-seven years, who has been present and invaluable to me for all of my books. I never stop being grateful for her and the wisdom she brings to my life. She was especially helpful with this one.

Let me add a concluding word of thanks to my dear friends Robert, Eric, and Andrew Wolgemuth who represent me when its time to discuss the practical aspects of writing. They are always full of encouragement and insight.

And then an additional word of appreciation for the team at Thomas Nelson, Inc., that make a book happen in the physical sense. Thom Chittom, my editor, and Matt Baugher, vice president and publisher for Spiritual Growth and Christian Thought, quickly come to mind as having been a great help to me. I am grateful to publisher David Moberg for the opportunity to write for Thomas Nelson. And, of course, an author always beams in that wonderful moment when he or she holds the first copy of a book in hand and sees the cover and the title. I have Thomas Nelson art and packaging director Greg MacLachlan to thank for a moment like that.

A final note of gratitude to all the people who have been a part of the congregations I have served as a pastor. No one person in any of those churches is here in this book, as I've already said. But here and there I have described circumstances in church life that I have seen played out among these people whom I continue to love.

It Was a Dark and Stormy Night

I t was a dark and stormy night.

I am quite aware I have just launched this book with arguably the most unoriginal sentence in the canon of English writing. But the weather—dark and stormy—is the first thing that comes to mind when I remember that Sunday evening the Discovery Group had its first meeting.

A nor'easter had hurtled up the Atlantic coast that weekend, and when it slammed into our part of New England, it brought wind-driven rains that would have been eighteen inches of snow had the temperature been ten degrees lower.

While I would have much preferred to be at home that evening cuddled up with my wife, Gail, watching *60 Minutes* and the subsequent Sunday night football game, I was, instead, dodging puddles, sprinting across the unlit parking lot of the church where I have been a pastor now for three years.

Abandoning any hope of staying dry, I headed toward a side entrance to the church building. The door opened to a spacious room we call the Commons. Once inside I turned on the lights, hung up my wet coat, and began positioning two rectangular tables and fifteen chairs in an arrangement suitable for a group discussion. I expected to be joined shortly by fourteen or fifteen long-term members of our congregation.

There was no doubt in my mind they would all arrive promptly, if for no better reason than to prove that weather—be it hot or cold, rain or snow—never controls a New Englander. While people like us might consider canceling a routine meeting if the Red Sox were in a World Series game or the Patriots were playing in the Super Bowl, we would never permit a thing like weather to serve as an excuse for not showing up if we'd committed ourselves. Of this sort of perseverance we are very proud people.

You'd love our Commons. It's decorated in a New England motif. On the walls are framed photos of people of all ages in our congregation. The pictures are meant to underscore the message that we are an age-diverse family of people who belong to each other and to God.

As I waited for people to arrive, I tried to imagine the various directions the evening might take. Everyone was coming in anticipation of a candid conversation about some issues that had recently raised some tensions in our congregation.

The optimist in me wanted to believe that an hour or two of dialogue would settle everyone down. The realist in me, however, was nervous. I'm a reader, and I get around a bit. I was quite aware that the subjects most likely to come to the table that evening have been dividing Christians for some time. So it was probably wise, I thought, not to expect miracles.

Before long, rain-soaked, wind-blown people started coming through the door. Had you been there, you would have observed that we shared a common age range: late fifties to early seventies. Some of us exerted little or no effort to suppress the signs of the aging process. But others seemed reluctant to admit to their senior status and had turned to hair coloring, slimming clothes, and contact lenses. I'll admit to the contacts.

I think that your first impression of the group would have been that they were vigorous, spirited, even a tad on the crusty side. You'd have noticed rather quickly that they liked each other, in fact enjoyed being together. I also suspect that you would have quickly picked up on their New England Yankee accent—the one associated with "Pock yuh kah 'n Havid Yad."

All of us who gathered in the Commons that evening shared a common history. We'd been raised by parents who had persevered through the Great Depression and fought (or supported the soldiers) in World War II. We could remember a time when most homes had only one telephone, if any, and when an extension phone (once a common term) was considered a luxury. We could recall summertime polio epidemics, radio dramas, and President Truman. We had grown up afraid of communists, curious about UFOs, and envious of anyone owning a 1949 Ford with twin Hollywood mufflers.

Another thing we had in common was that we were all church people, Christian in our life commitment. All of us had years and years of history invested in organized religious life. And more than a few in the group—I was an exception—had been a part of this particular church since infancy. Several had married spouses they'd known since early childhood. One of the men, Winn Rilkey, liked to say—to the chagrin of his wife, Shirley—that, as infants, the two of them had often shared a crib in the nursery while their parents worshipped.

Two of those gathering at the table, Lillian Seamands and Yvonne Padula, had taught Sunday school classes for thirty or more years; a third, Ted Patton, was a former elder; another, John Sanders, the one-time chairman of a major building program; and still another, Stanley Baker, had been church treasurer for, it seemed, twenty zillion years. Some had been choir members (when there was a choir), and almost everyone would tell you that they had tithed for decades.

We were descendents of a passing Christian culture. We could swap stories of memorable Billy Graham campaigns. We often reminisced about our Saturday night dates at Youth for Christ rallies. And we were quite familiar with traditional church functions: midweek prayer services, Vacation Bible School, Watch Night services (midnight) on New Year's Eve, and sunrise services on Easter morning (6:00 a.m.) to which we were dragged by parents whose lives were defined by the church calendar.

We'd all been to summer camp, and we'd sung and even acted in Christmas cantatas. We'd memorized vast amounts of King James Scripture, prided ourselves in knowing the books of the Bible in sequential order, and competed in Scripture-knowledge contests on a local, regional, and even national level.

Our histories also included missionary festivals, prophecy conferences, and Bible exposition weekends. We could recall annual evangelistic meetings with guest evangelists who (in pre-television days) played musical instruments, put on magic shows, and produced chalk talks while they sang solos like "Throw Out the Lifeline."

Those who like to label the generations call most of us *builders*, sons and daughters of *the silent generation.* We builders have always been an optimistic bunch of people who have enjoyed starting organizations and programs, building buildings, and keeping things faithfully running and growing. We have always believed in steady-state church programs that function every week of the year. We also have a track record of persistent loyalty to those programs. Join the ushering team, for example, and you showed up fifty out of fifty-two weeks a year. The two off-weeks were for vacation. We did this because we were taught that Satan *never* takes a holiday; why should Jesus' people?

When the builders head off to heaven en masse (we hope), more than a few churches are going to be in trouble as they try to fill the holes we will leave behind. I'm talking about our financial giving record, our penchant for serving, and our overall organizational loyalty. You heard it from me first: we builders are going to be missed even if we don't ordinarily clap during contemporary worship services.

Back to an earlier comment. A good example of our generational habit patterns is the way we have given our money. We were taught from our earliest days that the standard for biblical giving was the tithe: 10 percent of our earnings. As children we brought our pennies and nickels to Sunday school. In our adult years when the income became more serious, we may have sometimes debated whether a tithe should be computed before or after taxes, but most of us remained committed 10-percenters.

These tithes of ours have always gone to the church, particularly to its general fund. If we builders gave to other organizations beyond the church, we considered that to be *extra* giving, "over and above," as we'd say. But that most important gift, the tithe, has always been sealed in a numbered offering envelope and dropped into the collection plate each Sunday.

As I also said earlier, whenever the church opens its doors, builders have always shown up. That is, until lately. Now something may be changing in our generational ranks. Faithful people who always used to be as dependable as the ocean tides on the Maine coast are beginning to signal a bit of annoyance with their churches. And their gifts and their faithfulness in attendance are beginning to fray at the edges.

All of these comments—some perhaps overgeneralized—are my way of sketching a picture for you of the kind of group that assembled in the Commons that dark and stormy night.

As I greeted each person upon his or her arrival, I felt a strange surge of both affection and apprehension in my heart. I really loved each one of these people, but to be honest, I was struggling to feel assured about their feelings for me. The next hour or two would probably confirm whether my growing "paranoia" was legitimate or not.

Again, some background—this time about my little world—might help. Churches tend to hire a pastor and tell him or her that they're in the mood for change. They want to get more up-to-date, they say, become more "outreach" oriented, more open to younger people. Then if any of that begins to happen, it's not unusual for some of the *same* people who hired the pastor to grow restive as they feel things slipping out of their control and migrating into the hands of others, usually much younger, who may be more energetic and hungry for innovative ways of doing church.

Pastors like me begin to hear comments like "The church is getting too big," or "What's he trying to do? Build an empire for himself?" or "I tell you, I don't know anyone around here anymore." We also could hear "We're larger in size but we're growing spiritually shallow," and "No one seems to know where this church is going anymore," or "Who's running this church anyhow?"

You might see a growing number of congregational "wars" over such issues as replacing pews in the sanctuary with individual chairs, placing coffee kiosks in the church lobby, relaxing membership requirements for involvement in certain church programs, or—this used to be a big one—abandoning the midweek prayer service.

Then there's the biggest of the most recent wars, which is characterized by comments such as, "This new music . . . this new kind of preaching—it looks like a slippery slope toward liberalism . . . or shallowness . . . or entertainment."

When comments like those start flying around the congregation, it is only a matter of time before the pastor may be headed out the door, heartbroken, bewildered, maybe even embittered. If it is not the pastor who leaves, then a lot of other people may begin looking for another church.

Thus the paranoia. I guess I found myself wondering more and more frequently if there was any chance that the case of the missing pastor might be *my* story in the not too distant future.

Back to Sunday night in the Commons. As we sat down at the table, there was some bantering about the weather outside. "Was last year's most memorable storm worse than this one?" And there was talk about our U.S. senator who might run for president. But it was all just warm-up conversation while everyone waited for me to take my place and start the conversation of the evening.

The specific reason for this meeting came out of an organizational meltdown that our membership had experienced in a congregational business meeting the week before. Our lay leadership had proposed a $150,000 initiative to upgrade the technology in our sanctuary and had assumed that it would get a slam-dunk endorsement from the membership. The leadership's wish list included a new sound system, theater-type lighting, and two new projectors and screens that would enhance the quality of videos and PowerPoint presentations.

If we had been a brand-new church with an eye on the twenty-first-century way of worship, we might have been proposing a technology package that was twice as expensive. But our leadership had been cautious and felt that $150,000 for our church was a ceiling of prudence.

To our embarrassment, we (the leadership and I) discovered that we had not done our homework when it came to assessing the congregation's feelings about even this level of sanctuary renovations. The people—some of them at the table this evening—who had spoken in opposition had dominated the discussion time. The result was that the initiative never reached a vote that evening.

Most people, supporters and dissenters, expressed themselves respectfully that night. A few did not. But there was a tipping point in the course of the meeting where the sanctuary proposal was forgotten and people simply began to vent their frustrations to the leaders about all the recent changes in the church. The exchanges between the leaders and people increased in intensity, and I finally asked the moderator for permission to speak. I proposed that we table the sanctuary upgrade idea until another time. In what seemed like a collective sigh of relief everyone said, "Aye," and headed for the door as quickly as possible. On the ride home that night, Gail and I admitted to each other that we were dispirited for the first time in our three years at this church. We'd never seen the people—people we really loved—act this way before.

How had we gotten to such an incendiary point?

During the last few years at our church, a new, younger group (many of them non–New Englanders) had moved into positions of responsibility, and when I'd come as the new pastor, I had tried hard to identify with them.

You might wonder why they had not called a person younger than I am.

Two reasons. I think, first of all, I'd been a "compromise" candidate who was somehow reasonably acceptable to both the younger and the older generations. To the older folks I was perceived as "one of them." To the younger I was a father figure who sounded as if he was reasonably in touch with today. In truth, many of the new families had moved here from other parts of the country and felt a bit fatherless. They felt safe with Gail and me and with the parental symbolism of our silver hair.

And the second reason? Today many younger pastors are not interested in a church like ours. They don't want to waste their time (as they put it) fighting tradition, unwritten rules, and change-resistant people. They'd rather start their own churches and make up the rules as they go along. That—to be blunt—was probably why this church ended up with me. (I once joked that people should thank me. My name had been so far down the search list that, had I refused, the next possible candidate would have been a monkey.)

Soon after I came to the church, the older people in the church discovered to their dismay that I would not be wearing a necktie while I preached and that I wasn't going to bring back organ music and hymnbook-based singing (which, by the way, had been dropped from Sunday mornings a year before I came). They couldn't believe that a man my age liked PowerPoint sermon presentations, small groups more than adult Sunday school classes, and children's play areas that looked more like Chuck E. Cheese's than the old institutionally gray, multiuse classroom.

During my first year or two, we launched some efforts to build healthier marriages and to learn how to raise kids with a faith that could make it in a secular world. We put an emphasis on building peer friendships that could offer strength and support from Monday to Saturday. And we set out to learn how to engage the surrounding community and find out who was in serious need of things a church could provide.

Most important, I was committed to pointing the church toward the outside world and getting it to see that the real action was what happened, not on Sunday in the church building, but between Sundays in the home, in the marketplace, in the school. There, not here, was where we would reveal the kind of Christ living in our hearts.

All of this meant that during the past three years, traditions and programs once considered untouchable had been reevaluated. Some programs were rebuilt and some were abandoned. Indeed, a new kind of church life was on the rise and moving steadily ahead—until that miserable business meeting a few days ago.

Now, with the clarity of hindsight, I could see that a dark tension between the generations had been growing for some time. I should have smelled it in the comments of younger leaders when the names of older members—some of whom were at this table—were mentioned. "Let them find another church," someone would say. "We can't let them get in the way when there are so many unchurched to reach," another would offer. And a third: "If they had their way, we'd be back to the doxology and a robed choir."

Given my age and years of pastoral experience I liked to think that, although I was a listener, I could not be pushed around and intimidated if I believed in something strongly enough. And up until now, I'd kept this age-diverse body of people together. But now I was becoming a bit uncertain. Had I pushed too fast and gone too far? Had I crossed a line and lost my ability to influence?

As I looked at the group around the table in the Commons, I thought about who wasn't with us. One couple—after more than thirty-five years in our church—had quietly moved their membership to another church in the city that was known for its highly (some would say *fundamentalist*) conservative culture. I'd met with them when I learned they were headed elsewhere, and they had told me that one of the better-known TV preachers had said a few weeks back, "If your pastor is not preaching against the sin of homosexuality, then you should find another church." And they couldn't understand why I, the lead preacher, wasn't more forthright about things like that. Didn't I understand that America was falling apart because people like me didn't take a stand? That's what the TV guy had said anyway.

My response—that I couldn't see condemning homosexuality from the pulpit as an effective way to introduce people, especially gay people, to the saving love of Jesus—didn't fly with that couple. And so they were soon gone to the other place and therefore weren't at this table.

I was aware of several other people who had been long-termers at our church. They'd just slowly slid off the edge of church life into . . . well, nothing. They didn't announce their departure. They just disappeared. Occasionally I heard they were staying at home on Sunday mornings listening to TV preachers.

A third group was missing. I call them *floaters*. Each week they study the religious section of the newspaper and pick the church that offers the most interesting program or sermon title. They go on Christian cruises, travel to special conferences and seminars, and show up at programs put on by traveling Christian celebrities who rent out hotel convention centers and arenas for special appearances. There's a lot of religious stuff to do out there if you have the money. There are many alternatives to local church life that weren't there before.

But, to their credit, here in the Commons on Sunday night were fifteen people who cared enough about their church to accept my invitation to talk. They *were* at the table, a bit nervous (they admitted to me later) as they wondered if I had called them together to scold them.

So the conversation began. And what happened in the next ninety minutes on that dark and stormy night opened the door to all sorts of insights that no one, beginning with me, could have anticipated. Let me tell you about it.

Yvonne Padula: widow, Wheaton College grad. Husband, Paul (doctor), died of coronary disease in 1997. Long-time Sunday school teacher. Loves traveling, cruises. Grew up in the church. Serious about photography. Will shoot pictures anytime you want. Speaks bluntly and takes no prisoners.

I began our meeting with words I'd rehearsed several times during my drive through the rain to the church: "I feel as if I've failed you." It was a good way to start because it clearly grabbed everyone's attention. And I wasn't trying to manipulate anyone—I meant what I said. I felt I had something to make right with them. The comment created an instant intensity around the table.

"I should have sat down with you long before the last business meeting we just had, and I should have sought out more diligently your feelings about some issues here in the church. I also should have been more candid with you about what the leadership and the elders were trying to do on an evening like that. It really bothers me that apparently you didn't feel consulted when this decision came up for a vote.

"Perhaps we could talk candidly this evening about your feelings and attitudes. Maybe you could explain to me why you said some of the things you said in that meeting."

The group didn't need much encouragement. Once they knew I wasn't going to be defensive, they told me everything that was on their minds and, perhaps, a little bit more than I was ready to hear. Beyond my initial description of the group, I'm not going to overload you with a list of names of those who were at the table. I'll let you pick up the names and something about each of them as we go along. In fact, why don't I let you thumb through the pastoral notes I've taken on each person I've come to know in the church? These are incidentals I've jotted down in a little black notebook I keep on my desk. I'll place one of these at the opening to each chapter.

Connie Peterson, not surprisingly, was the first to speak when I opened things for discussion. "Honestly, Pastor, I don't see why these new people feel that they have to change everything we have done for so many years. I never know anymore what to expect when I come to church. And, I'll be frank, if you want to know the truth, I can't get used to you not wearing a suit and tie. We were taught that you honor God by the way you dress in church."

We were only about six minutes into the evening, and I'd already learned lesson one about meetings like this: don't invite candor if you're a thin-skinned pastor, especially in New England. And I relearned lesson one several more times as the rest of the group seemed to take courage from Connie's boldness. I suppose the fact that I didn't flinch or respond to her comment about my Sunday morning attire signaled to everyone else that they could let fly.

"If it ain't broke, don't fix it. That's what I always say," John Sanders, the one-time building committee chairman, said. "These guys around here want to fix stuff that isn't broke as far as I'm concerned."

"They're worried about loudspeakers when what we really need," said Ted Patton, once an elder in the church, "is to get Wednesday night prayer service started again. Prayer meetings are the true test of how much a church loves the Lord. Why, we used to fill the whole sanctuary with people on Wednesday nights."

"Now really, Ted," Lillian Seamands retorted. "How many times did that happen? The sanctuary get filled for a prayer service, I mean. I can only remember the one time . . . when Cliff McGinnis was dying."

Turning to me, Lillian said, "Truthfully though, there used to be a lot more people come to midweek services on Wednesday night than come now."

Lillian, I had come to appreciate during my time at the church, was all logic, and she wouldn't let anyone—even me—exaggerate. Ted chose wisely not to debate with her.

I could see that the conversation was only warming up. *But*, I wondered, *was it warming up in a way that fit my objectives for the evening?*

"Someone else?" I asked.

"What bothers me is that we don't have Sunday school anymore," said

Yvonne Padula. "We used to have a wonderful Sunday school class. Called it the Home Builders. Connie, you and Lars were in Home Builders, weren't you?"

Connie nodded her head and said, "Now that room *was* packed every Sunday. I remember that Lars would always take up the offering for missionaries. We loved Elliot's teaching." Several agreed and told a few Elliot Coffin stories.

"Let's talk missions. I've wanted to say this for a long time," Ernie Yost interrupted the brief trip down the Sunday school nostalgia lane. His daughter, Amy, and her husband were missionaries in Colombia. "Missions is really going downhill in this church. The missions budget has been flat for years now. We used to have a missionary conference every year, and there would be several missionaries here from all sorts of places. There'd be pictures and stories and the young people would dedicate their lives to become missionaries. . . . We haven't had a missionary conference for . . . um, at least twenty years. I bet we haven't had a missionary speaker preach one Sunday morning for all those years either. This church just doesn't care any longer about getting the gospel overseas."

I knew that Ernie was having trouble coming to grips with the changing scene of missions in the larger world. But that, too, is another story. And I chose to let his words stand for the moment. I was there, I reminded myself, to listen.

"Well, if we're getting things off our chests—" Russ Milner spoke up, took a breath, and continued, "I wish there was more doctrinal preaching. How are these young people going to grow in the Word if they don't get some good solid teaching? I can remember when Pastor Collier preached through Romans verse by verse. Took almost three years before he got to the end—"

"That was the most mind-deadening collection of sermons I ever heard," Lillian interrupted, just as she'd done with Ted on the prayer service comment.

There was a lot of laughter when Lillian said that, and I got the feeling that more than a few were relieved that someone had said what they were thinking.

When the laughter subsided, Lillian continued. "Sorry . . . that just slipped out. But I agree with you, Russ. We need to teach these young people more Bible truth. I don't think they know their Bibles at all. They don't bring their Bibles to church anymore. They don't memorize God's Word like we used to. And I don't think they know any of the Bible stories." Now everyone—even Russ—murmured in agreement.

Then, for a moment, there was silence. It was almost as if everyone had run out of breath; they had to stop and think whether there was anything else that wasn't happening like it used to years ago. And in that moment I made a mistake. I asked a question—I guess I asked it just to fill the silent space: "What do you think have been the better moments you have had in this church? What are your very best memories? When did they happen?"

Want me to be honest? I really thought a few might talk about something that had happened in the last year or two—you know, during the years I had been there. I'm amazed, looking back at the evening, that I would have assumed this, but I actually thought they might forget about all that yesterday stuff and recall something that had happened during the past year or two. A sermon I'd preached, for example. Or last Christmas when we had such a beautiful Christmas Eve service, and everyone said it was the best ever. Perhaps they'd remember the day the congregation took up an enormous spontaneous offering for hurricane victims in the South. Or maybe someone would express delight in the housing project we'd undertaken with the Habitat for Humanity people.

I wasn't looking for compliments (well, maybe I was), but I was searching for any hint that the last few years had brought some gladness or satisfaction to them. I was hoping that they could revel in the fact that the church was going forward even though they were no longer in control. But I was wrong.

Their best moments? Let's just say that it went back to things that happened thirty years ago. Such as the weekend in 1972 when the president of Moody Bible Institute had come all the way from Chicago and preached a weekend Bible conference. Several remembered it well. Someone even remembered his Scripture text. One or two others described a citywide evangelistic campaign in the early eighties, and John talked about how the church had summoned all of its faith and energies to build our gymnasium in 1993.

Then this from Ted: "You know, it wasn't any one best moment. It was the singing we used to do . . . on Sunday nights. Anyone remember when Joe Lund was our song leader?" Everyone remembered. "The thing I miss most is the hymns. We don't sing them anymore. I miss 'The Old Rugged Cross' and 'I Come to the Garden Alone.' " Then, looking at me, Ted asked, "Couldn't we just sing some hymns again?"

Several weighed in with other favorites: "When We All Get to Heaven,"

"Since Jesus Came into My Heart," "When the Roll Is Called Up Yonder," "It Is Well with My Soul."

I made another mental note (but said nothing) that they had picked song titles that all came out of one particular musical era more than a hundred years ago. That era of gospel singing was reaching its end when they (we) were kids. None had mentioned the earlier hymns of Charles Wesley or one like "Crown Him with Many Crowns"—writers and songs from an even earlier time. They'd been nursed on a form of gospel music that had been around for, relatively speaking, only a short time and thought it was the only hymnody in the Christian movement.

Winn Rilkey, who is a floor manager at Home Depot, was sitting to my right, and he spoke up for the first time. "Yep, you're right. The old hymns had doctrine in them. These new songs the young people sing don't have any doctrine. As far as I can see, it's all about 'me.' And they sing the same lines over and over and over again. Sometimes I just want to explode. How are they going to learn the truth if they don't learn it in the hymns?"

Russ said "amen" to Winn's comments, and it was clear that both Winn and he were convinced that there was a serious dearth of theological content in contemporary church life.

"Couldn't you just make sure we sing at least *one* hymn each week?" Evelyn Moody asked.

"And couldn't we sing some of those songs without having to stand all the time? I don't think anyone knows how painful it is for a person my age to stand for a half hour—especially in the sanctuary where the floor is slanted," said Arlene Lewis.

Stan Baker began speaking the minute Arlene appeared to be finished: "I'm going to say it before someone else does. *I miss the choir.*" (There were several umms of apparent agreement.) "We had the best choir in town (more umms). And we had some great singers—Barbara O'Neil, for example. Ted Steele played the organ. They're gone now." (The supporting umms seemed deafening.) "Now," Stan said, "all we get is five people up in front with microphones stuck in their mouths . . . as if they're eating ice cream cones."

I thought the last comment unkind, but it was instructive to see things I'd never considered from someone else's point of view.

Moments passed as people around the table recalled various musicians from the past: soloists, trumpet players, someone back then who was extraordinary on the marimba, and a man who played the musical saw. (They had to explain this to me, and take my word for it, you don't want to know.)

Then Stan spoke up again: "What I really want to say is something about giving. These young folks don't give faithfully. They're driving all these nice cars and buying cabins up north . . . all this stuff. I'm on the counting team, and I've got to be careful about what I say. But I'm telling you"—and he almost whispered the next words as if he was afraid of eavesdroppers—"*they're not giving; they don't tithe.* When there are large offerings from them, it's almost always designated to a project or a program. But their giving to the general fund is pretty bad. I'm telling you, this church is going to be in trouble in a few years if it has to depend on the giving I'm seeing from the younger members."

For a moment I felt as if an undercover FBI agent was briefing us.

There was a heavy silence again as people processed what had been said. Outside the wind was blowing even harder and the rain was beating more violently on the windows.

The silence was broken when one of the women—Yvonne, who, I must admit, is a favorite of mine—looked at me and said with great sadness, *"All I know is that someone stole my church and I'd like to get it back."*

Yvonne said this with a severe determination in her voice. It was as if a precious thing had been taken from her life during a burglary. As if something of great sentimental value had been snatched away, never to be seen again. I sensed that she felt violated.

I was aware that almost everyone nodded when Yvonne spoke. And for another moment we lapsed back into silence. I was hard-pressed to know how to respond. My instinct was to feel totally repudiated. I felt as if she was saying that I was part of the band of thieves or at least the driver of the get-away car. For just an instant I had a terrible feeling that the group was telling me that I'd lost their confidence and that the sooner I resigned from being their pastor, the better.

I decided to break the tension by suggesting that we take a break. Some of us needed a glass of water. Some of us, given our ages, needed to go to the bathroom. And I knew I could use both—plus a few minutes to think. That last comment of Yvonne's had blown me out of the water.

During the break several found ways to approach me and affirm their affection. They feared that some of the things they'd said hurt me, and they wanted to reassure me that their comments were not personal. But despite their protestations, I couldn't help but take what had been said very personally. And I must tell you candidly, I was falling into deep self-doubt. This meeting wasn't supposed to be about me—but then again, maybe it was. This mess of feelings and divisiveness in our church was reaching a crescendo on my watch.

WHEN WE RECONVENED AROUND THE TABLES, I told the group how much I liked being with them. And I was being truthful. In spite of my bewilderment at their barrage of criticisms, I really did like them. They were good people. But how could I get my arms around this conversation? I was at a loss.

"You're not sorry you got us together?" Arlene asked. "I was thinking that you'd probably want to kick us out of the church now."

"No, Arlene," I said, "I needed to be reminded of the things you miss so much. But I do worry for you, because some of these programs are never going to come back. They were things our generation made happen in our best days. But now another generation wants to make other things happen. And we have to figure out how we can accept this and rejoice in their vision. In a sense they're just doing what we did to our parents. You don't think for a moment that our mothers and fathers liked all the stuff we changed, do you?"

That comment froze everyone for a moment.

"You know, Gordon's right," someone (I'm not sure who) finally said. "I can remember my father complaining that we were going to kill off the church when Pastor Fredrickson brought a TV camera into the church and started putting our worship service on cable. 'God never intended for a television camera to be in a church,' he'd say. He actually walked out one day!"

"Lots of people walked out from time to time," said Ernie. "Remember the first time Barbara O'Neil sang along with a recorded orchestra on the sound system? Whoo-ee! I thought old Cameron Coulter was going to have a heart attack. He was up the aisle and out the door in a flash. I was sure that he was never coming back."

Evelyn laughed. "Cameron was even more frosted when Pastor Kelso told him that he'd been the one to encourage Barbara to do it. But he finally cooled off and came back after a few weeks."

Stan said, "When you're the treasurer as I've been, you worry less about people walking out and more about people who show their unhappiness by withholding their giving. And we've had a lot of those in the past. They let you know real fast how they feel about things. They just stop giving, or they designate their money to a missionary and away from the church."

"I've done that," Arlene said. "I probably would have done it again if we'd voted to do that sanctuary thing last week."

"Not fair, Arlene," Stan said. "I know you've done it, because I've heard you talk about it before. But it's not right. You say you believe in congregational church government and majority approval, but the minute you don't like something, you take your money off the table."

Tension again. For a second I worried that Stan's bluntness had gone too far. I half expected Arlene to gather her things and head for the door. But she didn't. Apparently, she could dish out the truth as she saw it, and she could take it when someone else spoke to her blind sides. My respect for her grew.

Finally, Lillian broke the spell. "You know, I'd forgotten how my parents reacted when we did the singing Christmas tree thing—any of you remember that? They couldn't believe that we were not going to do the traditional Christmas nativity scene with the kids all running around in bathrobes."

Suddenly the group, even Arlene, forgot what had just happened and launched into a nostalgic recollection of the years of the "singing Christmas tree" in the church's parking lot. The choir, masked by pine boughs meant to look like a large tree, stood on rickety platforms (these were the years before lawsuits) and sang Christmas songs. It had been a novel and successful experience the first year, but a disaster the next two years when New England temperatures dropped into the subzero range. Within a few years the choir became little more than a quartet, and, mercifully, the tree was history. As each person added his or her part to the story of the singing Christmas tree, there was more and more laughter. Several around the table were laughing so hard they were near tears.

For a moment I lost control of the meeting. But it was, on the other hand, so good to see these people laughing. It aroused a fresh sense of love in me for every person around the table. I found myself wanting so badly to see what I could do to restore something of the church experience that Yvonne had said was stolen from her.

Finally I said, "I have a thought for you." They quieted. What came next was impulsive—an idea conceived within that very minute. In the weeks to come, I would look back on what I was about to say and wonder what on earth I'd been thinking.

Having gained everyone's attention, I said: "What if we were to meet on a regular basis for a while and talk about the church and why changes have to happen? I really think I could put your minds at ease about some things . . . well, a few things anyway. And I also think we could discover some ways to love this church better than we've been doing."

No one said anything, and so I went on. "You know, there's a harsh truth facing us. Most of us are not going to be here ten or fifteen years from now. We're either going to be in heaven . . . or Florida." Everyone smiled at this possibility.

"So unless you can promise me that you're going to be here regularly, serving forever, we have to figure out how to release this church into the hands of others and do it with enthusiasm. And that means we've got some thinking to do. I don't like seeing you so unhappy. But I also know that we have to deal with some new realities that will crush us if we're not careful."

Still, no one spoke. So, again, I filled the silence with a question.

"What do you think? Want to get together again?"

It was Arlene who spoke first. "I'm in," she said. "And if you want, I'll take care of any arrangements that are necessary to gathering us together." Looking around the table she asked, "You all in this with me?"

To my surprise everyone agreed and seemed to acknowledge Arlene's leadership. And at the same time I guess they accepted my leadership, believing that I was taking them seriously and that I might help them to understand some things they found terribly confusing.

In the one or two moments that it took Arlene to get everyone in alignment with my idea, I began to imagine what our get-togethers might look like. I said, "Next time we gather bring your Bibles and a notebook."

"So this is going to be a class?" John asked.

"Let's call it a venture in discovering our church, " I said, making it all up as I went along. "If you need a name, we'll call it the 'Discovery Group.' The next two or three times we meet we'll be doing some simple Scripture study before we get into other things. So hang with me."

Arlene insisted that we set a date, and it ended up being a week from Tuesday. I said a prayer, and we all headed for the door and the storm outside. Later, driving home, I realized that we never discussed that awful business meeting. Perhaps that was a good sign.

The rest of this book focuses on the things the Discovery Group learned as we met in the Commons or encountered each other in other parts of our community.

> **Winn Rilkey:** *Wife, Shirley. Home Depot manager. Good-natured about helping people fix things. A real visionary. Passionate about evangelism and church growth. Became believer while dating Shirley. Son is on pastoral staff at a Calif. church. Has associate degree from a technical college. Loves to go to Willow Creek Summit each year.*

Ten days later the newly formed and named Discovery Group met in the Commons. Everyone showed up, again, right on time. To my surprise Kenneth and Mary Ann Squires, relative newcomers to the church, joined the group. They had heard about our previous meeting from Arlene, who took the liberty to invite them without consulting me.

I was OK with the Squires (they're good people), but I did indicate to Arlene later in the evening that we ought not to invite anyone else. I have this little theory, I told her, that when a group exceeds fifteen in number, it loses its sense of intimacy.

When Connie arrived (she's usually among the first arrivals at any meeting) I asked her if she'd be prepared to give a brief prayer when we began. That was not a problem for her.

A word about Connie. She was one of the first people in this church whom I met when Gail and I originally visited at the invitation of the pastoral search committee. When we first became acquainted, Connie was still dealing with the loss of her husband, Lars, who had been killed in a tragic hunting accident the year before.

In that first year we knew her, Connie had been deeply involved in settling Lars's estate and selling the business that the two of them had built. I recognized that she was a very astute businesswoman.

Lars's death changed Connie, people said. When he was living, she tended to let Lars speak for both of them. But when she was left on her own, everyone saw new strengths and interests in her. I hadn't known her long when I picked up on three things of importance to her: a passion for photography, a deep Christian commitment, and a belief that Republicans could do no wrong. On any given day the priority order of those three could be shuffled.

I asked one of the men to add two more chairs for the Squires, and we all sat down. When I gave the signal, Connie prayed: "Lord, we meet in Jesus' name. We believe you're present with us. You know we're concerned about our church, and we ask you to help us to know your will and be obedient to it. You know I struggle with a lot of things going on around here. So help us all to understand what this all means."

I listened carefully to Connie's prayer, because a sincere prayer reveals a piece of a person's heart. What I heard was humility *and* openness. "Thanks, Connie," I said. "I appreciate your word *struggle*. It probably describes where a lot of us seem to be these days." She nodded in response.

I looked about the table and realized that everyone was anticipating the first thing I might say. It was clear that they were wondering where I'd start after last week's "venting." Would I try to offer a defense against the things they had said that evening? Would I launch into some sort of sales presentation about how they ought to be more supportive of the church program?

I'd given this moment—this beginning of a series of conversations—a lot of thought. And while my rehearsed opening sentence wasn't brilliant, I was at peace delivering it.

"All week long I've had Yvonne's comment rattling around in my head," I began.

Yvonne looked at me, startled, and interrupted me. "Did I say something wrong? What?" After twelve opening words, I was knocked off my script.

"Well, you didn't say anything wrong, Yvonne. But what you did say was a heads-up to me about the way we've been taught to think about the church."

"So what did I say?"

"You don't remember? I can't forget it. You said something like, 'All I want to know is who stole my church. I'd like it back.'"

Ernie said, "I remember what Yvonne said. I told Gretchen [Ernie's wife] about it, and she said she felt the same way."

I said, "Well, I suppose a lot of us could say the same thing. Maybe we all have the feeling that our church, at least the version of the church we like the most, has been hijacked." I was trying to create a sense of common cause among us.

Several people tried to speak all at once. They offered varying opinions about whether the word *steal* was the appropriate one to express what people were feeling. I pushed back at them and said that we should simply accept Yvonne's description for what it was. She'd said that she felt robbed, and her perspective was a good starting point.

Then Stan said in a voice loud enough to bring everyone back together again: "If the people who *stole* the church—Yvonne's word, not mine—are younger or newer people, then let 'em steal it. It's going to be theirs in a few years anyway. I vote we give it to them and go off and start our own."

Several people groaned, and Arlene suggested that Stan get a life.

Stan was probably going to be in the minority in this group, I thought. I've seen him in action before. He would often speak up and make off-the-wall comments that surprised everybody. He loved to say crazy things that got a reaction. I decided not to react and to stay as neutral as I could for as long as I could. So I returned to the idea that I wanted to put on the table this evening.

"Here's my problem," I said. "Yvonne said, 'Someone stole my church' . . . or words to that effect. Some have told us how Yvonne's comment has affected them, and we pretty much know how Arlene feels. So let me tell you what Yvonne's comment meant to me. And the best way is to tell you a little story."

Everyone repositioned their chairs so that they were facing in my direction. They obviously assumed that I was going to give some kind of a sermon.

"When I went to seminary almost forty-five years ago, the church in America was in tough shape. At least that was the impression of seminary students in my generation. There were books being published—every week it seemed—that foretold the demise of preaching, spoke of the irrelevance of the church, and even predicted that Christianity was on its way out. Many of us had graduated from colleges where we'd been involved in parachurch ministries—"

"Para-*what?*" John interrupted. "Never heard that term before."

"Oh, come on, John," Ernie said. "We talk about parachurch organizations in the missions committee meetings all the time. Everyone know what a parachurch organization is?"

Several people indicated that they weren't really that sure they knew either.

13

And I was relieved, because it was clear that Ernie's comment—almost like a put-down—had rattled John. So I just moved on as if everyone needed instruction about the difference between a church and a parachurch ministry.

"Parachurch ministries," I said, looking at John, "are organizations like Campus Crusade for Christ and InterVarsity Christian Fellowship. Youth for Christ is another parachurch ministry. The word describes an organization that is not a church but essentially does one particular Christian thing, such as evangelism or working with the homeless or counseling pregnant teenagers. Take Young Life as an example. It works with high school students and basically does one thing: points teenagers toward Jesus. A church, on the other hand, is a community of diverse people doing all kinds of things, such as worship, discipleship, pastoral care, children's work. It's supposed to serve people all the way from birth to death. Make sense?"

Everyone nodded. John in particular seemed satisfied.

"So a lot of us when we came to seminary were used to the parachurch organizations. Everything was about action, making things happen. There was a lot of vision, innovation, and strong fellowship. But when we left college and reentered the world of the local church we found things to be rather dull and uninspiring. In most places churches didn't seem to be doing much except holding everybody's hand.

"When we entered seminary we spent a lot of time jabbering about the ineffectiveness of most churches. We tended to be rather harsh in our comments. We loved to criticize the sermons we heard on Sundays. We were very critical of most laypeople. We got satisfaction out of saying that churches were like a football game: twenty-two players on the field in need of rest and fifty thousand people in the stands badly in need of exercise.

"Now here's the irony of all this: we were training to serve people like all of you here tonight, but in actuality we didn't really believe in you . . . well, sort of, anyway. We complained about your lack of involvement, lack of commitment. It didn't occur to us, by the way, that you all had day jobs, that your lives included a lot more things than just church life."

I could feel the stir of curiosity around the table when I made this last remark. But I kept on with my comments.

"I guess becoming a pastor was not high on our list of attractive options. Frankly, most of us thought that leading a congregation was probably for losers.

In our youthful idealism, we wanted to be part of something flashier that was full of action. We wanted to do something for God that made a significant difference. *Changing the world* became our motto. So we often talked about being street evangelists, or youth workers, or missionaries, or going back to those parachurch ministries that were so exciting. Anything but the church. We didn't see the church as interested or even capable of changing the world.

"Then one day a bunch of us were at a table in the cafeteria having lunch. The conversation was same-old, same-old . . . beating up on the church. And suddenly I was aware that someone was standing behind me. It was one of our professors. I guess he'd been eavesdropping.

"When I acknowledged him, he immediately said, 'Gordon, I'd like you to do something for me.' He stooped down and picked up a Bible that was on top of a stack of books I'd put on the floor beside my chair.

"He opened it and turned the pages until he found what he was looking for. Then he placed the open Bible in front of me and said, 'Would you read this for everyone, please?' He pointed to a paragraph in Acts, chapter 20, where Paul was saying what he thought might be his final good-byes to the leaders of the Ephesian church."

I stopped this story from my student days at this point and asked everyone if they would take their Bibles and turn to the paragraph I'd just mentioned.

Everyone did as I asked. They reached for their Bibles and in short order found the right page. This was a group who knew their Bibles, the New Testament anyway. Finding Acts 20 was no problem.

When they were all there, I said, "Now find verse 28. That's what the professor wanted me to read. Ernie, how about reading the verse for us?"

Ernie read, "Keep watch over yourselves and all the flock of which the Holy Spirit has made you overseers. Be shepherds of the church of God, which he bought with his own blood."

"That was the verse the professor wanted me to read," I said when Ernie finished. "When I'd read it that day, he said, 'Think you could read it again?' And I did. So Ernie, how about reading it again?"

Ernie read Acts 20:28 a second time: "Keep watch over yourselves and all the flock of which the Holy Spirit has made you overseers. Be shepherds of the church of God, which he bought with his own blood."

Then I continued: "After I'd read the verse twice, the professor asked me, 'What are you hearing the text say?' And I'm going to ask you guys the same question: what are *you* hearing the verse say?"

Everyone in the group stared down at their Bibles. No one really wanted to be the first to speak, so there was an awkward silence. And then Connie broke it—her voice a bit tentative.

"I think Paul wanted the leaders to take special care of themselves and the people of the church."

"Good," I said. "The professor would have liked your answer. That's pretty much what I said to him. Now talk about what term Paul used when he spoke of leaders."

"He called them shepherds," Mary Ann Squires said.

"And what do you know about shepherds?"

"That they're responsible for the protection and the health of the sheep?" she answered in that tone of voice that sounds more like a question than a statement.

"And who are the sheep in this text?"

"The church . . . in Ephesus." Two or three people said this more or less at the same time.

"So, about that church in Ephesus," I said. "Whose church is it?"

They looked back at the text, and Clayton Reid finally said, "God's church."

"Why did you say it's God's church, Clayton?" I asked.

"Because he bought it," Clayton answered.

"Bought it? For how much?'"

"With his blood . . . Jesus' blood actually." That was Lillian, and you could detect some impatience with my deliberate questioning.

"Again, that's exactly what I told the professor," I said. "He had asked me the same questions I'm asking you. And I was just as uncomfortable answering them as I think some of you are right now. Want to know what he asked next?"

"Umm," several answered.

"He asked, 'What does that tell you about God's attitude toward the church . . . this flock of sheep . . . that *you're* supposed to shepherd?' I remember the moment well. Here we all were, at a table in the middle of the seminary cafeteria, lots of noise around us. But at our table no one was moving. This professor had posed a thunderous question to us . . . to me."

I was impressed that, as I told this story from my seminary days, the people who were gathered with me in the Commons were just as quiet, listening just as carefully to me, as that original group of students had been when listening to the professor. In both cases people seemed to intuit that a very important insight was about to burst forth from somewhere.

"I remember pausing for several seconds," I told the group. "The professor was obviously nudging me toward some kind of mind-changing insight, and I wasn't yet sure I was ready to go there.

"'*What does that tell you about God's feelings about the church?*' he'd asked. Suddenly the answer I knew he was looking for came to me, and as the words formed within me, I realized that I was about to rebuke myself—and all the other students around the table who had been complaining about the church. Finally I broke my silence and gave him the only answer that made sense to me: 'God sees the church as *precious . . . valuable . . . important.*'"

As I recounted the story to this older generation group, I let my voice drop to an almost dramatic quietness as I spoke out those last words: *precious, valuable, important.* There was absolute silence except for air coming through the ventilation ducts in the ceiling. Just as the group of students around the table in the seminary cafeteria, we too sat silently around the table in the Commons for a moment.

Finally I said, "I remember that student group processing this idea about God and the church—just as you're doing right now. With just a few words the professor had forced us to deal with a profound thought. But he wasn't through. He had one more thing to say. 'Perhaps you gentlemen need to think a little bit more before you talk so disparagingly about something that God cherishes so much that he gave his blood for it. And perhaps you need to ask if the church doesn't have a lot more going for it than you've thought about.' And then he walked away."

Having finished the story of that day in the seminary cafeteria, I sat back in my chair and waited to see what it might have meant to the group. To my right was John, to my left, Lillian. I could almost hear their minds weighing the implications of the story. And that was probably true of all the others. No one spoke, and no one looked around. The best I could figure was that everyone was recalling how many times they too had spoken harshly of the church—our church in particular. Perhaps they were feeling just a bit of the same embarrassment I'd felt so many years ago. Who was I—who was anybody—to ridicule this expression of God's treasure, the church?

Finally, Clayton broke the silence. "You know, you're reminding us of something we've all known. Of course it's God's church just as the man said. But it's something that's easy to forget. I mean, you put a lot of work into a church . . . you give money . . . you're there every time the doors are opened, and the next thing you know, you're thinking the church is more yours than God's. Any of the rest of you feel like that?"

Several people nodded in agreement.

"Clayton's right," Arlene said. "Fact is, we've all been taught that Jesus gave his blood for each of us . . . me . . . you. But you almost never hear anyone say that Jesus gave his blood for the church."

"So what's the bottom line here?" Ted asked. "That no one is ever supposed to criticize the church?"

"No," I responded. "In its physical or visible expression, the church is full of human beings—we are a good example—who make lots of misjudgments. If we don't have some system of checks and balances that comes through frank conversation, even criticism, then we're going to be in trouble. But I think the point is this: we probably need to make real sure that when we do criticize our leaders or a ministry or even the church itself and where it's going, *we do it with great respect and only with the intention that the church be everything God wants it to be.*" I said this last part slowly and in such a way that no one could miss the message.

The next thirty to forty minutes were spent talking about our church and its history of struggle and factiousness. Most of these people were veterans of various church wars. They had sharp memories, and some of their stories were not pretty. Admittedly, there were some funny stories that relieved the heaviness of the darker tales, but overall I had a feeling that the group was now revisiting the church's long story with just a bit of sorrow. They were suddenly seeing past realities in a fresh light—the light of God's investment in the church.

They recalled the names of some who had left the church as the result of disputes and criticism. It was not hard for them to remember a couple of recent pastors who'd resigned and, their spirits crushed, left the ministry. And they described a few business meetings that, someone said, were more like nightmares than anything else.

When there was a break in the storytelling, Clayton said: "To be truthful with you, there are a lot of times when I just don't feel safe among most Christians, especially in this church."

"What are you saying, Clayton?" I asked.

"I'm just saying that you never know when someone has a long memory and has been holding a grudge. Or they're ready to fight you to the death on a political or doctrinal issue. There are a lot of things I never talk about around here."

"I can tell you that it was a long time before I felt safe in this church," Winn broke in. "Matter of fact, when I first came, I wouldn't have lasted very long here if Shirley hadn't made it abundantly clear that if I didn't attend church with her that would be the end of our dating."

Everyone laughed at Winn's comment, and then they simply lost it when Evelyn said, "Shirley always was a strange kind of evangelist, and look what it got her: Winn!"

Winn continued after the laughter: "You all know I go to some of these megachurch conferences"—he named several annual ones held across the country— "because I need to get pumped up with vision. I don't get that around here. I'd lose heart if I didn't get out to some other places. You should see how they welcome strangers like me and make you feel like a million. You know, last month when I went to that evangelism seminar, there was a young woman out in the parking lot with a yellow sticky pad. As I parked my rental car, she came up and handed me a sticky-note with the location of where I'd parked. She said, 'Sir, keep this handy in case you forget where you parked after the session.' She'd written 'MM-14' on it. Now that's how to make people feel a part of things!"

We'd all heard Winn tell this story several times in the last few weeks. It was one of many tales he imported from other places. Listening to Winn made it seem as if innovative things in churches only happened west and south of the New England states. But he had a point to make. No one was doing that "sticky-note" sort of thing around our church.

Clayton, who like Connie is single, waited until Winn had told his story. Then he said, "I meet people all the time who are moving into our city. [Clayton, by the way, is a real estate broker.] They want to know about schools, shopping malls, libraries, the whole nine yards. I always want to tell them about my church, but, you know, I usually don't. And I guess it's because, even though I love my church—I really love all of you—sometimes I'm embarrassed about it. I just fear they're going to be disappointed if they come. Are they going to see real Christianity here? Or are we just a bunch of people running a Bible club, more worried about what's in it for us than for someone looking for something better than what they've got?"

Two or three people around the table confessed that they sometimes had the same thoughts when it came to inviting people they'd met to come to church. They didn't know that others felt the same way.

Then Yvonne spoke up. And when we all looked at her, we saw wet eyes.

"Let me tell you what God is speaking to my heart right now." We were listening carefully, and I had the feeling that the success of this evening, and maybe even the future of these discussions, hung on what Yvonne was about to say.

"A while ago the pastor told us about a moment in his life when he was forced to face his lack of love for the church. I have no doubt that he loves it today. But I'm not sure that I have loved the church in the right way. I'm not sure any of us do. And in a sense we've proved that by dredging up all the stories we've been telling about the past. Not one of us has told a story about the times when we've been enriched by this church.

"Last week I said, 'Somebody stole my church. I want it back.' And I was wrong. It isn't *my* church. As Pastor said, it's God's. He owns it, and I never thought of that before. I should have known better. Now, our church is changing, and I can see that. But maybe God is doing the changing. If anyone's stealing the church, it's him. He's stealing it back because we haven't been doing a real good job with it. So I think we need to keep on talking together and asking if God isn't dealing with us at heart levels we've forgotten about."

Just when I thought Yvonne was through, she began again.

"Winn, I've heard you tell that story of the girl with the sticky pad two or three times. But tonight I really heard what you were saying for the first time. It would never have occurred to me that I should do that. Who knows? Maybe Jesus would be the one doing the sticky pads if he were in our church. Anyway, I'm going to pray that God will take 'my church' back and make it his.

"Now that doesn't mean I don't have a lot of questions. And it's very hard . . . very hard [her voice broke] for me to see some things I've loved so much disappearing." Turning to me, Yvonne said, "So if you want to keep these meetings going, I'll probably push you hard on some of the things that are going on around here. I'll try to understand, but you need to know that it's hard for an old girl like me."

Evelyn, who had been quiet most of the evening, reached over and put her hand over Yvonne's. It seemed a gesture of solidarity and affection, all at once.

A couple of people around the table thanked Yvonne for her candor. Stan said something like, "We needed to hear that." And Winn added, "I promise I'll be a little more careful with my words at the next meeting."

When the evening began ninety minutes earlier, Connie had prayed, "You know I struggle with a lot of things going on around here. So help us all to understand what this all means." I had the feeling we'd taken a first step in the direction of receiving an answer to that prayer.

I suggested that we end the evening with another prayer. I did the job, and the minute I said, "Amen," Arlene (ever the organizer) made sure we were all committed to meeting the next Tuesday. Everyone was. Russ, who owns a fast-food franchise, offered to bring some apple and cherry pies if someone else would make coffee. Arlene said she'd arrange it.

After the guys broke down the tables and stowed the folding chairs in the closet, we all went out into the night, each with his or her own thoughts about our church—God's church—that all of us loved and cared for so much.

Russ Milner: Wife, Debbie (she struggles with depression). Owns a Burger King franchise. Great business instincts, very entrepreneurial. Bible conference junkie, favors doctrinal teaching. Son in drug rehab. Wants to start a prison ministry.

After Tuesday night's Discovery Group meeting, I went home and tried to describe what had happened to my wife, Gail. I found it hard to represent the ethos of the evening and ended up saying several times, "You just had to have been there—" My excitement derived from the experience of seeing some people my age and older open themselves up just a little bit to the possibility that they had some thinking and listening to do.

The rest of my week filled up with staff meetings, conversations with our budget committee, and planning sessions with the missions people who were laying the tracks for their annual missionary festival. On Saturday morning I gave a talk at a men's breakfast and then dashed over to an indoor soccer game in which our granddaughter was playing. Add to this Sunday sermon preparation (or cramming), a hospital visit, dozens of e-mails and phone calls, and you have an idea of a typical week for me. It's all good stuff to do, please understand, but a lot of it deters me from getting out and engaging with unchurched people in the larger world. That always troubles me.

Sunday services seemed to go well. On Monday I presided at a funeral. And then Tuesday evening was staring me straight in the face again.

When I arrived for this third meeting of the group, I found the ever-conscientious Arlene already in motion. She'd asked Kenneth and

Mary Ann Squires, the newest, and so far, the quietest people in the group, to come early and help her set things up. Our makeshift conference table was already in place, and Mary Ann was arranging a small bundle of flowers as a centerpiece. Kenneth was busy getting the last of the chairs into place.

Off to one side I saw Russ setting out a couple of pots of coffee, the necessary flavorings, creams, and sugar, some cold beverages, and a box of apple and cherry pie desserts from his fast-food restaurant.

I had asked Arlene to e-mail or call (not everyone in the group does e-mail) everyone a couple of days ahead of our meeting to remind them that Bibles would be important for this session. So when everyone sat down a few minutes later there were enough copies of Scripture on the table to stock a bookstore.

"We're going to get off to a slow start tonight," I said. "I want us to do a little climbing down into Scripture, and I want to drain a few Bible verses for everything they have to offer. So hang with me."

Ernie Yost was designated to kick off the evening, and as soon as I nodded in his direction, he launched into his prayer. I keep forgetting that when Ernie prays out loud he always lowers his voice and speaks with agonizing slowness. It leaves people—at least me—squirming with impatience. Tonight was typical.

"Dear Lord . . . I know I've looked forward to this evening . . . and I pray . . . that everyone else has too. All week long I've been thinking . . . about how to love the church . . . like you love it. I've realized . . . that it's not that easy. Forgive me . . . for all the critical things I've said . . . and help me to see the church like . . . you see it. Please . . . help us to learn something new tonight, and please help us to . . . to . . . to be better Christians."

Silence—ten to fifteen, maybe twenty seconds, of silence.

Had Ernie ended his prayer? Who knew? He hadn't said amen, so we all remained motionless with our eyes closed. I thought about murmuring, "Ernie, the meter's running." But of course I didn't.

Then Ernie started up again: "And Lord . . . we need a revival in our church. We need people . . . to see the importance of preaching the gospel . . . in all the nations."

A word about Ernie. He rides a restored Indian motorcycle that is unbelievably loud, and it (both the motorcycle *and* its racket) makes him the envy of quite a few men in our church. If the outside temperature is above forty, you know that Ernie will be on his bike. And you'll hear him blocks away if he's coming to church. How, guys are always asking, did Ernie get his wife, Gretchen, to agree with his buying the *Indian?* And they also want to know how he got her to climb on and ride with him.

Ernie's prayer continued: "Lord . . . we need young people who will hear your call to be missionaries and evangelists . . . and preachers. So Lord, give us a wonderful evening . . . In Jesus' name, amen." And Ernie was finished.

"Thanks, Ernie," I said. And then I looked around to make sure everyone was ready to begin. "Last week some of you mentioned a few people who walked out of church services because they were upset. Any more stories like those?" I asked. There was a bit of think-time, and then a few heads began to nod. Yes, they could remember other times.

"John Colter was a walker," Clayton said. "Usually it was because he was upset about the music. He thought it was too loud; he didn't like canned music behind singers; and he went up the wall when worship leaders tried to get us to clap while we sang."

"My father walked out of church one morning when he discovered that they'd taken the American flag out of the sanctuary," Yvonne said.

Yvonne had grown up in the church. After graduating from Wheaton, she'd returned home, married a doctor, and raised three children. Now she was a widow who loved to go on tours and take lots of pictures. "We had a new young pastor—can't remember his name. . . . He didn't stay long . . ."

"Mark Shapley," Connie said. "Nice young—"

"Yes, Shapley. Thank you, Connie," Yvonne said. "Pastor Shapley called on my father and tried to tell him that American flags didn't belong in a sanctuary. But my father wouldn't hear of it. So he stayed away until the pastor left, and the day after his last Sunday, my father came to church and put the flag back. It's been there ever since."

Everyone chuckled at Yvonne's story.

"My mother never walked out permanently," Clayton said. "But she could get steamed about lots of things, and when she did, she simply dropped out until she cooled off. She'd stay home. She'd stay home and watch Billy Graham."

"So it sounds like almost all of you have seen people close up who have had real angry moments in church," I said. Again, the nods.

"How did you feel when you saw someone leave angry?"

A few around the table volunteered one-word answers. "Embarrassed." "Confused." "Disgusted." Someone quietly said, "Envious," and that brought laughter from all of us.

"Could you imagine a moment when Jesus might have walked out?"

Clayton asked, "When would that have been? Are you talking about when he kicked all the money people out?"

"No," I answered. "Another time."

There being no other comment, I continued: "Look up Matthew, chapter 23, in your Bibles." Everyone began turning the pages. Connie got there first. She was incorrigibly competitive whether it was a Yankee–Red Sox game or getting to a page of Scripture before everyone else.

"I've got it," she said. "Which verse?"

"Why don't you read verses 37 to 39," I said. "Read verse 37 with frustration in your voice."

"Frustration? OK." She began: "O Jerusalem, Jerusalem, you who kill the prophets and stone those sent to you, how often I have longed to gather your children together, as a hen gathers her chicks under her wings, but you were not willing—" She strung the words out and did a good job injecting the appropriate feeling into the reading. She made us feel the frustration.

I interrupted Connie and said, "OK, Connie, read the next words slowly, and if you can, put a little anger into your voice. Read the words as if you are really appalled."

"What makes you think I can sound like that?" Connie asked with a grin.

"Just do it, Connie."

And she did. "Look, your house is left to you desolate. For . . . I . . . tell . . . you," Connie was spitting out the words with considerable dramatic effect, "you . . . will . . . not . . . see . . . me . . . again . . . until . . . you . . . say, 'Blessed is he who comes in the name of the Lord.' "

"Go on, Connie, into the next chapter."

"Mad or frustrated?" she asked.

"Normal," I replied.

"Jesus left the temple—"

"OK, stop!" I said. And she did.

25

"Let's pull these lines apart and see what Matthew was describing. No opinions until we know what Matthew was saying. So, what are you hearing in verse 37?"

Silence. Everyone was looking at verse 37, but, as usual, no one was sure they wanted to be the first to respond. So I looked at Ted, knowing he would not be rattled if I called on him, and asked, "Ted, you got a thought?"

"Well, he certainly isn't complimenting the city. Sounds like he's saying it's not a safe place for prophets."

"Good, Ted," I said. "Anyone else want to add to Ted's comment?"

Russ: "Jesus is saying that he always wanted to gather people around him like a mother hen protects her chicks."

Then Lillian spoke up. "I'd never noticed before how Jesus uses the picture of a mother hen to talk about his feelings for Jerusalem." Lillian was more outspoken than any other woman in the church about how often women seemed to be second-class citizens in our church. It was typical of her to point out anything that emphasized a woman's perception of things.

"OK," I said. "So we have Jesus speaking in rather undiplomatic tones. He's calling Jerusalem an unsafe city for prophets. The people, he's implying, don't want to hear God's voice, especially if it's a rebuking voice. And then he's saying that he's longed to engage them with mother-like love. You cool with that, Lillian?" She nodded.

"So what does he say next?" I asked.

"Want to know what I hear?" It was Kenneth Squires, and this was the first time he'd spoken in the group.

"Go ahead," I said.

"He's telling them that he's fed up with them and they can have their temple— or house, as he calls it. They've run it corruptly for too long, and he's out of there."

"Is there a key phrase, Kenneth?"

Kenneth looked back at the page and, after a pause, said: "Yeah. I think it's 'left to you desolate.' He's saying that the temple is going to become like a desert . . . or a bombed-out building. And he's saying that he wants nothing to do with the place anymore."

"I'd like you to think about this. The Son of God is condemning the temple. As Kenneth said, 'He's out of there.' What would make him do that?"

Several in the group began to speak out quickly.

"It's all about dead religion."

"It's a system where a few people are getting rich and others are getting poor."

"Didn't Jesus say something about it not being a place of prayer anymore?"

Others added ideas, but they were essentially the same as these. I waited until everyone had a chance to add to the dialogue.

Then I continued. "Now I'd like us to watch very carefully what happens. Winn, could you pick up the reading in chapter 24? Start right back at the beginning where Connie left off."

Winn was embarrassed. He'd already closed his Bible and had to find the book of Matthew and the right chapter again. When he found it, he said, "Chapter 24? OK, here it is. Jesus left the temple—that's where you wanted me to start, isn't it?" I nodded yes.

"Jesus left the temple and was walking away when his disciples came up to him to call his attention to its buildings—"

"Winn," I interrupted, "could you push the pause button for a moment, please?" The group all looked at me, and I said to them: "Look at that sentence carefully, and use your imaginations. Put yourself into the scene. What's happening here?"

"Well, Jesus is walking out . . . like you said," Evelyn offered. "And—" she looked back to the Bible to make sure she had it right, "and the disciples are following him? It seems as if they are, anyway. And they want him to look back at the buildings."

"Why do you think they'd want him to look at the temple buildings? He'd seen them plenty of times." I got the feeling by their reaction that these veteran churchgoers had never really looked at this story, much less tried to figure out what was going on.

Now Mary Ann Squires, who, like her husband, Kenneth, had been very quiet until now, spoke up. "I don't think they're asking him to look at the *buildings*, but they're really asking him if he has forgotten how important the buildings are. I mean, good grief, this *is* the temple, and Jesus has walked out of it and said he wasn't coming back."

I was impressed with Mary Ann's answer. As far as I was concerned, she'd nailed the point.

"Great, Mary Ann," I said, "let me push you a bit. If you're right, the disciples were shocked at what Jesus just said. I suspect they even thought he'd gone over the top. I mean, you could get killed for saying something like this—'your house is desolate'—because what he was really saying was that the temple was, religiously speaking, bankrupt . . . God was not there any longer."

Mary Ann immediately came back at me: "I don't think the disciples see it the same way. I mean . . . all their lives they have looked at the temple as the center of their faith. They would have gone there regularly, wouldn't they? At least those who lived in the area. The temple was the center point of all their religious life. And now the Lord is telling them that the place is no good anymore. I think they're really upset and confused . . . and maybe angry that Jesus has said such a dangerous thing so publicly. He could get them all killed."

"Mary Ann, you've got it!" I looked around the table and said, "Now again, get right inside the Scripture if you can and become part of the story. For example, you and I are among the disciples. Jesus has just told us that our 'church'—let's call it that—is corrupt, out of date, not doing its job anymore. For three years Jesus has visited the temple—at least once a year—and tried to speak like a prophet into the mess. And now finally he says, 'I'm out of here. I'm no longer going to connect with this place.' And, what I'm hearing him say is, 'I'm actually going on to other places.'"

Everyone was quiet as they took in this thought. I think a few of them had done what I had asked and were visualizing the moment just as Matthew had described it.

"Winn, still got your Bible open? Read the next verse, would you?"

Winn read. "'Do you see all these things?' he asked. 'I tell you—'"

"Winn, forgive me," I interrupted. "Question for you: what were the disciples pointing to?"

Everyone looked back at the words.

"Buildings . . . buildings," several said.

"So what did Jesus point to?"

"Things—" Stan said. "I never saw that before. The disciples saw buildings, and Jesus only saw *things.*"

"I just wanted you to see how important words can be . . . Winn, go on. I won't interrupt again."

"'Do you see all these things?' he asked. 'I tell you the truth, not one stone here will be left on another; every one will be thrown down.'" Winn looked at me as if to ask if I wanted him to go further. And I made a sign with my hands, the old T-sign meaning "time-out."

"Watch how things have devolved in a matter of four or five lines. From *house* to *buildings* to *things* to *stones*. And from magnificent buildings to a heap of nothing but stones. That's how quickly, in Jesus' eyes anyway, something powerful, beautiful, important can become worthless. And here's the kicker. I think Jesus has been saying this to churches ever since. Nothing, temple or church, can assume that it is going to last forever. As far as Jesus is concerned, a church is not a building, not an institution, not an organization. A church is people—little more! It's a living thing, and it only gets to live as long as it's doing the right things. And when it stops doing the right things, Jesus is— what's our term?—*out of there?* As far as he is concerned, it's no more useful than a pile of stones.

"Now let me pose a question to you. You don't have to answer." I paused for effect and then asked, "What if someone you love and trust stood with you in our front parking lot and referred to our church building as nothing more than a pile of stones?"

There was—I can only call it—a powerful hush in the room. I don't think anyone in the room had missed the point. Were they beginning to wonder if their church qualified for this description of a pile of stones?

Ted was the first to break the silence: "So I think I know where you're going with this. You're telling us that a church can die . . . that Jesus might stop coming, or, if he came, walk out. That's something to think about . . . in fact, to even worry over."

"That's exactly what I was hoping someone might say, Ted. It's something to think about. You were once an elder of this church. You know how delicate things can get in the life of a church at times." Ted was nodding his head in agreement with me. "I'd like you to think about the things that might turn Jesus off about a church and make him walk out of it in the same way that he walked out of the temple."

The rest of the evening's dialogue took off from there. Everyone around the table, it seemed, had a story to tell of some church here or there in New England that was—in their opinion—dead or dying. Their stories were about the misuse of money, the sometime failure of leaders, conflicts over every imaginable issue that led to divisions and splits. The stories seemed endless and depressing.

I am a pastor with a lot of mileage on his resume, a person who thought he was impervious to surprises. But as people talked I felt a suffocating cloud of sorrow come upon me as these people described all the ways that churches, once filled with hope and vitality, could commit an ecclesiastical version of hari-kari.

If Gail had been with me that evening, she might have chided me for letting the stories go on too long. She would have been concerned that the evening might end on a downer. But my heart told me that we could survive this conversation. And my instinct was to let my friends around the table conjure up strong, unavoidable, mental images of dead or dying churches. I could see the value of gaining a sense of horror about what can happen when a church turns sour.

When we reached our lights-out time, I made a closing comment: "I had one goal for this evening. To get you to think exactly as you're thinking—about what kills churches. But there's something else that can kill churches, and no one's mentioned it. And that will be the topic the next time we sit down here. Before we meet again, I want you to read Matthew 24 and get acquainted with it. We're not going to spend a lot of time there, but there's something Jesus said that I think is very important."

Again as I had the week before, I prayed the ending prayer: "Jesus, thank you for your courage. It's an example to us. I pray that we'll not forget what we learned from these very few lines in the Bible. Help us to think clearly about what happens when well-intentioned people lose their way. Amen."

I chatted with one or two people for a few minutes and then grabbed my Bible and coat and headed out the door and into the parking lot. As I walked toward my car, I realized that I'd been the first to leave. And when I drove away I could see through the window into the Commons. No one else in the group showed any sign of being ready to leave just yet. The conversation was still going on . . . without me.

John Sanders: *Married to Whitney, builds high-end homes. Chairman of last building committee. Very protective about church building. Converted during high school years. Loves boating and fishing. Interested in end-times and prophecy themes. Quick temper.*

On the next Tuesday evening, after an early dinner with Gail, I headed toward the church for the fourth Discovery Group meeting. All day long I had felt a strange sense of apprehension about the meeting and now it seemed to increase. I kept trying to trace it back. Where had this nagging feeling come from?

I knew that during the past week I'd felt a strong sense of satisfaction about our last meeting. It seemed as if others in the group felt the same way. "When I was in the worship service this morning, I saw the church in a whole new light," Stan had said to me on the phone Sunday night. And Lillian had sent me an e-mail on Monday expressing thanks for the Tuesday night meetings and saying that she was doing a lot of fresh thinking. During the week, two or three others in the group had commented to Gail how glad they were to be included.

Then, as my mind sorted through things that might be the source of my uneasiness, I recalled an encounter with John Sanders at the door of the men's room on Sunday. I'd greeted him and said, "Sure hope you're enjoying the Discovery Group."

I remember thinking that his response seemed distant, almost dismissive. "I'll talk to you about it sometime," he'd said and then turned and walked away.

An exchange like that can leave a pastor distracted. To be honest I probably had been seeking a word of praise that all of us were doing something especially good on Tuesday nights, but John hadn't delivered. Instead, he'd made an oblique comment that could have meant several different things. What might have been bothering him? Was there something about our last Tuesday night conversation that had rubbed him the wrong way?

It's strange how positive messages can be trumped by one message (just one!) that leaves you hanging. *The power of words*, spoken or unspoken. Do most people have any awareness of how they can either build or tear down another's spirit by the way they say things? This is why leaders long for thicker skin. As a friend said, "Pastors have feelings too."

You may recall that the Discovery Group arose out of a brainstorm in the middle of what was meant to be a one-time Sunday night meeting. In that moment of enthusiasm, when I proposed a series of weekly conversations, I had no long-range plan or curriculum in mind. I was just giving vent to what seemed a good idea.

Now, four weeks into the process, I was living with the pressure of delivering what I'd promised. No regrets, understand, but preparing for each session was not a small burden. I knew, however, that once into it, I couldn't afford to squander this marvelous opportunity to dialogue with earnest people who wanted the best for their (God's?) church but who had a difficult time knowing the difference between that and their own self-interest.

I determined that my preparation would be done with a single three-point objective: *to help a group of "influencers" adjust to the inexorable force of church change, to grow in the process, and to be guides to others in need of the same experience.*

Arriving at the church, I locked the car and headed for the door that opened into the Commons. The meeting was to begin in about twenty minutes. Tonight my plan was to walk the group through a brief history lesson that traced the theme of sudden and massive change. I was very much aware of the burden to make the subject interesting enough to stir imaginations.

When I make presentations I like to first seek out the historic frame of whatever the issue may be. I become curious about where an idea has come from. Who first conceived and described it? What were the conditions in which the idea was birthed? How has it stood the test of time? And how have things changed through the years?

Our subject on Tuesday nights was the nature of change itself. If I could get the group to see that there were other times in history when people had to face big changes, then perhaps they might understand a bit better the times in which we live.

Everyone was already there when I arrived. Arlene had everything under control. Ernie, Winn, and Connie had been appointed to set up tables and chairs. Lillian was the designated "coffee lady," and John had been tasked (I was glad for this) with providing refreshments. He'd passed the responsibility on to Whitney, his wife, who was known for her "killer" cakes. Result? A huge carrot cake waiting for the midevening break.

Yvonne was the opening prayer (I'd asked her on Sunday), and at 6:58 p.m. precisely, she took charge. She herded everyone, including me, toward the table and commenced her prayer.

You could tell that Yvonne had given her prayer some thought. She had a habit of accenting certain words she wanted you to especially hear by giving them a distinct tone of voice.

Yvonne began, "You are *Lord* of the church, our Father, and we are *privileged* to be part of it. We give thanks that the church is Christ's *beautiful bride,* that He has paid the highest price for it. We want our piece of the church to be all you want it to be. And we want it to be a place where Jesus would be proud to be present . . . *and never leave.* Forgive us if we sometimes get in the way of what you want to make happen here. And we ask you, O God, to help us to *listen,* and *learn* . . . and *act* with responsibility. Through Christ our Lord, we pray these things. Amen."

Whenever Yvonne prayed there was a respectful silence, and tonight we listened to every word with the sense that here was a person with lots of experience in conversing with God.

Incidentally, I didn't include the part of Yvonne's prayer where she thanked God for my leadership in the group. Let's just say that she helped dissolve a bit of the uncertainty I'd brought into the room with me. If only church people knew how little it takes to reinforce a pastor's spirit.

After thanking Yvonne for her prayer, I said: "Tonight I want us to begin in the book of Matthew. But we probably won't stay there very long. I'm going to test how much you love me, because I want to offer you . . . well, a history lecture. So belt in."

Stan immediately put his hands in his lap and made a clicking sound as if he were doing just that—belting in. I saw Clayton roll his eyes in mock dismay. Connie offered that she loved history and was just finishing a new biography on St. Patrick.

"So let's reconnect with Matthew 23 and 24," I said, and everyone opened their Bibles. "Last week we read about Jesus exiting the temple rather dramatically to the horror of the disciples. You'll recall that they tried to argue with him over the implications of what he'd done, but he pushed back with a startling statement. Let me paraphrase it. 'Do you see all this? This temple is coming down; it will end up as a pile of rocks.' So we talked for a while last week about whether this might be the condition not only of the temple but also of churches that lose their way."

"That story has bothered me all week," Stan said. "Every time I passed by a church that seems to be dying, I wondered when Jesus might have walked out."

Lillian: "You know, I had it on my mind during church last Sunday. I imagined Jesus sitting somewhere in the sanctuary—probably up front—while the service was going on and suddenly getting up and walking up the aisle and out the door. I'm like you, Stan. I thought about it a lot."

"Well," I said, "It sounds as if we're really into Matthew 24. Terrific! John, think you could read a few lines for us?"

"You going to keep telling me to stop?" he asked in a tone of voice that could be interpreted as dry New England humor or as a warning shot across my bow.

"I love the power," I responded. "So yeah, I'll probably do just that." It was a stupid thing to say, and I should have corrected myself immediately.

John began: "As Jesus was sitting on the Mount of Olives, the disciples came to him privately. 'Tell us,' they said—"

"Ur, sorry, John, but mind stopping?" John still had his mouth open to read the next word. He stopped, but I detected a speck of irritation.

"What word did John read that sticks out as worth talking about?"

"Well, given what little he read, it has to be the word 'privately,' Connie said. 'Privately' suggests that no one else was around—this was a secret conversation."

"Well, no wonder they'd keep it private," Ernie said. "Didn't someone make the comment last week that you could get killed for bad-mouthing the temple?"

"OK," I said. "You guys are all over the idea. The key word is 'privately.' This was a quiet conversation that had to be off-line. Just keep that in mind."

I turned to John and said, "Want to go on? Sorry I interrupted you."

John read again without responding to my apology. "'Tell us,' they said, 'when will this happen, and what will be the sign of your coming and of the end of the age?'"

"Thanks, John," I said. "Any wild idea as to what this question is all about?" I asked the group. No one jumped to answer. I wasn't surprised, because I've found the disciples' question rather perplexing myself. I've always wondered how some people can preach and write about this particular Scripture text as if they've got it all figured out. I certainly don't.

I said to the group, "Here's my take on this. I think Matthew loaded into one single question all the confusion the disciples felt. This conversation on the Mount of Olives happened just a short distance from the temple, just outside the walls of the city. I've been there, and I can visualize the twelve disciples (if Judas is present) and Jesus sitting there on the hillside and looking down on the temple in all its beauty. I imagine the disciples about to have collective heart attacks over Jesus' prediction. They want to know how, when, and why Jesus thinks the temple is going down. For them this is a massive 9/11-type *change*—if you please—and they'd never anticipated it. For them the temple was the most permanent thing in the world. That make sense?"

There were some nods. Not a lot, but some.

"John, mind picking up the reading again? We can't read the entire chapter, but I'd like us to get the flavor of some of the first things Jesus said to the disciples. Notice, when John reads, that the Lord didn't really answer their questions. Rather he talked about a set of historic conditions and their need to get ready for them."

John began to read again: "Jesus answered, 'Watch out that no one deceives you. For many will come in my name, claiming, *I am the Christ*, and will deceive many. You will hear of wars and rumors of wars, but see to it that you are not alarmed. Such things must happen, but the end is still to come. Nation will rise against nation, and kingdom against kingdom. There will be famines and earthquakes in various places. All these are the beginning of birth pains.'"

"Let's pass the reading over to Lillian. Take the next paragraph, will you?"

Lillian said OK, adjusted her half-moon glasses, and began reading: " 'Then you will be handed over to be persecuted and put to death' . . . oh my!" she said and shook her head. " 'At that time many will turn away from the faith and will betray and hate each other, and many false prophets will appear and deceive many people. Because of the increase of wickedness, the love of most will grow cold, but he who stands firm to the end will be saved. And this gospel of the kingdom will be preached in the whole world as a testimony to all nations, and then the end will come.' "

Lillian sat back and said, "It's been a while since I read those lines. I've forgotten how violent this all is."

"Is this what they call prophecy?" Mary Ann asked me.

"Yes, you'd have to consider it that. Jesus was speaking with foresight. He saw things in the future that no one else could see. There is always a question: was he talking about things that have already happened since he said them or about things that are yet to happen? There are different opinions on that question."

"So what's the take-away for us?" Lillian asked.

"I wanted you to see one example of the Lord bracing his disciples for some wildly turbulent moments in history. These men are going to have to be masters of change, but most of them have come from backwater communities where everything stays the same; nothing changes except rock-hard poverty and lots of suffering. But now they're headed toward the front line of a kind of revolution in a very dangerous world where they end up laying down their lives."

We talked for a few minutes about all the things that were going to happen to the disciples during the next few years after the Mount of Olives conversation. They'd preach the gospel of Christ in the streets of Jerusalem, defend themselves in front of the top religious leaders of the city, face prison, bring Gentiles into the movement, and help launch a worldwide effort to propagate the faith. In the end, they'd end up as martyrs.

"How do you think most people cope with the kind of changes these men were going to face?" I asked.

No one answered. And I suspected that their reluctance to respond was rooted in the realization that such a discussion would get too close to the situation in our church.

After some silence, Ted grinned and said quietly, "Very, very carefully." That was the best I could get out of anyone. I pushed on.

"I'd like to spend the rest of this evening and probably next week talking about the history of change in the Christian movement. What I'm hoping we'll see is that Christians have frequently been forced—here's a new term for some— to *reinvent* the ways they do church life. Note I said, 'do church life,' not reinvent their core beliefs.

"Anyone familiar with the word *reinvent?*" A few said they were. But for the others I said, "*Reinvention* simply means that you take a look at something you've been doing the same way over and over again and find a new way—a totally new way—to do it that fits the world you live in now. For example, when Henry Ford mass-produced the automobile so that everyone could buy one, it could be said that he *reinvented* transportation.

"What you're seeing in this Scripture is Jesus preparing the disciples for the fact that the early church is going to be a reinvented movement whose purpose will be to reach out to the larger world with a freshened message about God's love and salvation.

"When you read the story of the early church, you learn that the base of this new church life would not be the temple. The base would be the houses where people lived and the places where they worked. And preaching would not happen on religious property but in the streets. And the preaching itself would not be done by certified religious 'professionals' [I made the quote sign with my fingers], but by plain ordinary people like you and me who spoke the language of the street. And while the Lord didn't say all that right here, he was no doubt visualizing all of this happening in the coming years when these men would go into the world to make disciples."

"Interesting," Lillian said. "I never thought of any of the things going on in Acts as necessarily different. But you're saying that everything changed."

"Everything! The message, the people preaching it, and the way they organized to make it happen. And then if you read on in the story, you see them having to change their ways over and over again. For example, when the first Christians faced serious persecution from the temple leaders, many of them were scattered across the countryside and—guess what? The church started spreading because, wherever they went, they talked about Jesus. And the result was that

Gentiles began to hear this new gospel and were drawn to it. So now what do you do if you thought this gospel, this so-called good news, was only for Jews?

"That alone had to be a terrible shock to the first Jewish Christians. They probably thought at first that this new Christian thing was going to be an ethnically pure movement. Now they had to find a way to accommodate Gentiles? Read a few chapters further, and you discover that they were having to accommodate pagan people far, far beyond Jerusalem, and now the question became: do Gentile men have to be circumcised as if they were good Jews? And the answer, in a word or two, is no, they don't! But none of that went down easily at all.

"In one sense you wonder why they were so surprised when all of this happened. Jesus had told them that they would end up preaching in Jerusalem, Judea, Samaria, and the rest of the world.

"And that's the thing I want most to impress upon you this evening. These men were always facing new realities and having to make adjustments. The Lord had warned them, but they didn't fully comprehend his words until they were right on top of each situation."

"Good thing this didn't happen in a place like New England," Winn said.

"I'd like to suggest that if you think New Englanders struggle with change, it's nothing like what people struggled with in those days. I don't think we have any idea what they went through as this constant state of reinvention went on. And if they had resisted these changes, there would have been no Christian movement."

I talked about other great historic moments when the church had to open itself to reinvention. We talked about Paul's innovative missionary strategy of church planting. And we talked about what effect the emperor Constantine had on the church when he legitimized Christianity and made it the official Roman religion a few centuries later.

"Ask yourselves," I said, "what you would say if you lived in Constantine's day and you awakened one morning to find out that Christians no longer needed to worship in secret. Suddenly you and your fellow believers could own property, talk about your faith openly, and argue your convictions in the public square. Would you consider that good news or bad?"

We had a fun few moments debating whether the Christian church was stronger when it was considered illegal or when the emperor embraced it.

I recounted the story of St. Patrick and his creative ways of bringing the gospel to Ireland in the late fifth century. We spent a few minutes talking about the thirteenth-century St. Francis and his way of breaking away from organized religion to advocate a fresh understanding of Jesus and his love. Again I asked them to consider whether they would have supported or opposed men like Patrick and Francis who reinvented the way the world would hear about Christ.

Finally I brought up Martin Luther's name and the reformation he sought that exposed the Roman Catholic Church in its lowest moments of institutional and theological corruption.

"Martin Luther came along in the late fifteenth century and stood up to everything in the organized Christian church that was institutionally and theologically destructive. Think of it, in his lifetime he saw a whole new way of church life spring up across northern Europe. Much of what he accomplished was made possible by the movable-type printing press invented by Johannes Gutenberg. The printing press—one of the greatest inventions of all history— made it possible for people to read Luther's thoughts. Without Gutenberg's invention, there probably would have been no Reformation."

Again, I asked everyone to consider whether or not they would have agreed with Luther, or if they would have joined those who opposed all changes in his time.

We talked about this string of life-changing events in the church and how each change reflected situations unique to that particular time. And I could sense that most in the group were beginning to see how important it had been down through the centuries for congregations to make changes appropriate to the situation in which they lived.

There was only one person at the table who seemed disquieted about our conversation, and that was John. He grew more and more silent as the evening passed. Was he simply bored, or was he perceptive enough to look ahead and see where all this was going? Did he understand what others in the group had not yet fully perceived: that if you accept all of this, you're going to have to ask yourself, *And what kind of changes will be demanded of me in my life and in my church?*

"Before we have to quit, I want to cover one more great moment in the history of church change. It occurred in England in the 1700s. You're all familiar with John Wesley, right?"

Everyone seemed aware of the name. Some more than others.

"Wesley came along at a crucial moment in England's history, the mid-1700s. The poor were losing interest in the organized church to a considerable extent. It seemed to them to be a place only for the privileged classes. Many of them—especially the men—were moving away from small towns and villages and finding work in the emerging factory towns of England. In just a generation or two, a huge percentage of the English population relocated into urban centers. But here's something important to think about: the church, for the most part, *failed* to follow them there.

"That became the basis of a challenge and a vision for John Wesley. If the church refused to go to where the poor working people were, then Wesley would break with accepted practices and go there himself. To the shock of change-resistant churchmen who would never preach outside of a fully certified church building, Wesley began to preach the gospel of salvation to people, particularly men, *where they worked.* He traveled incessantly. He was up early in the morning, and if necessary he was in motion late into the night. He went anywhere people would give him a hearing. Sometime in the near future we'll talk about his brother, Charles, who stood with John and gave the Christian world a whole new way of singing.

"The result? Wesley and his people laid the carpet for an incredible revival in England. And it was a revival that sprang up among the poor and the working classes. When the established church chose to ignore them, Wesley organized everyone into what he called societies, not unlike local churches. And he further broke the societies down into small groups of twelve to fifteen people that he called bands and classes. Suddenly there was a remarkable small-group movement that continued for more than a hundred years, and, in some places, goes on today."

"Here's something John Wesley wrote," I said as I fingered through some old notes.

Our societies were formed from those who were wandering upon the dark mountains, that belonged to no Christian Church; but were awakened by the preaching of the Methodists, who had pursued them through the wilderness of this world to the Highways and the Hedges—to the Markets and the Fairs—to the Hills and the Dales—who set up the Standard of the Cross in the Streets and Lanes of the Cities, in the Villages, in the Barns, and Farmers' Kitchens etc—and all this in such a way, and to such an extent, as never had been done before, since the Apostolic age.[1]

"Now that's an example of what happens when someone looks at their world with fresh eyes and asks, 'What has to be done to reach out to lost and struggling people and bring them the love of Jesus?'

"So here's the bottom line of all of this. Down through two thousand years, you have only one unchanging thing in the church: *the gospel of Jesus that calls people to forgiveness of sins and to participation in a community of people who want to serve each other and go forward to make a statement about God's love in their worlds.* But the ways in which people organize themselves to actualize this one unchanging thing is changing all the time. Almost nothing can stay the same for long if you want to connect with people and introduce them to Jesus Christ."

For the next little while everyone around the table asked questions and commented on the resilience of the Christian movement through the years. Winn, whose daughter is a missionary and who has made several trips to Latin America, emphasized that he had seen all sorts of experimental ways of doing church in other cultures. I hadn't expected that from him, but it merely served to strengthen the case I was trying to make.

When I looked at the clock, I saw that it was nine fifteen. I'd made an earlier commitment that we'd end these meetings each time at nine. But the vigor of our discussion had been such that no one noticed the time. Even when we had taken a moment to pour some decaffeinated coffee and pass around pieces of Whitney Saunders's carrot cake, people had returned to the discussion as quickly as they could.

"Let me end the evening with a quote that's attributed to Jack Welch, the former CEO of GE," I said. "Welch wrote somewhere, 'When the rate of change inside an organization is slower than the rate of change outside an organization, the end [of that organization] is in sight.'"[2]

Someone asked me to repeat the quote, and I did. More than a few people said, "Mmm. . .," as if they were deeply impressed with the insight. I could tell that they wanted to react to it, but I told them that we had to quit and would have to save further discussion until next week.

Yvonne said, "Well, I prayed that God would give us the power to listen and learn, and I, for one, feel that my prayer has been answered. I have to tell you all that I've been letting my age speak too loudly to me. There's something here I have to deal with. I'm beginning to realize that I want the church to be a place of safety and comfort. But Jesus was saying to those disciples that serving him would be a call to danger and discomfort. Somewhere along the line I forgot that."

There was a provocative silence around the table. Several people told Yvonne that they agreed with her.

"You guys finding this useful?" I finally asked. There I was again—seeking the compliment, reassurance perhaps, that this was getting us somewhere. There were lots of nodding heads, John's the exception.

"Well then, next time let's talk about changes in the world that we might be going through now and what that means to our church." We prayed, cleaned up the room, and headed for the door. Well, John and I headed for the door. Most of the others kept on chatting.

When we got outside, John and I went in separate directions. We exchanged "good nights" but nothing more.

From my pastoral notes:

Evelyn Moody: Intensive care nurse, dry humor. Graduated U of Connecticut. Married to Philip who never attends church. Converted in her early 30s. Deep concern for abused women. Great reader.

L ater that week Gail and I stopped by Borders to pick up some books she'd ordered. Book lovers that we are, we succumbed to the temptation to separate and wander the aisles for a while. I headed for the biographical section, Gail, ever the grandmother, to the children's lit section.

I was thumbing through a new book on Lewis and Clark when I felt a tap on the shoulder. It was Evelyn Moody from the Discovery Group. She'd seen Gail and me come into the store and wanted to say hello. There were the usual how-are-you greetings and a comment or two about the book in my hand. When Gail saw us, she came over.

Evelyn has been an intensive care nurse (night shift) for more than twenty years at our local hospital. I asked her one time why she'd never played her seniority card and moved to daytime hours, and she told me that she preferred working at night. ("It's a much quieter shift," she said.) But I suspected there might be other reasons.

Most of us at church have never met Philip, Evelyn's husband. She had told me that he had no interest, whatsoever, in her faith. Nor had he any desire to socialize with her church friends. If you phoned Evelyn at home and Philip answered, you got a cold reception.

It's pretty obvious that Evelyn's marriage is far from a nourishing one, and that, apart from her job and church, she lives a rather solitary life. Evelyn and Philip have no children, and I've never heard of anything they do together.

If asked, I would describe Evelyn as a rather deep person, thoughtful, and certainly committed to following Jesus. I once heard her tell the story of her spiritual journey. Years ago she'd gone to a weekend women's conference with a friend, and she heard enough to convince her that committing her life to Jesus and his way was a sensible thing to do. Spiritually, Evelyn never looked back after that weekend. She joined a small-group Bible study; she became an avid reader of substantial Christian literature (C. S. Lewis comes to mind); and over time she became an advocate of any church activity that challenged people to go deeper into their faith.

Among our church people Evelyn is appreciated not only for her faithfulness but also for her great sense of humor. I would bet, however, that much of Evelyn's humor is driven by her desire to cover a sadness she feels about her disappointing marital life.

"Can I treat the two of you to some coffee?" Evelyn asked. It was one of the few times when neither Gail nor I needed to be somewhere during the next hour, and we happily accepted Evelyn's invitation.

"I want to tell you how much I'm enjoying the Tuesday night group or whatever *you're* calling it," Evelyn said when we were seated at a table. "Gail, you've got to show up sometime. The group would love to have you."

We both thanked Evelyn, and Gail assured her that she'd join me on the first Tuesday she had free.

Evelyn said, "I might as well tell you the truth. That first Sunday night when you got us together, I came feeling rather defensive. I figured you were going to scold us because some of us had gone to that business meeting to vote against the sanctuary changes. But you know, you surprised me when you said you were trying to understand how some of us might be feeling. Now we're into these Tuesday meetings, and I've enjoyed the conversations so far."

Gail said, "You seem awfully tired to me, Evelyn. Are you OK?"

"Oh sure. I'm fine. Maybe I'm down just a little bit." There was an awkward pause and then, "It's been kind of a bad morning . . . until now when I saw you two. I worked all night, and when I came home my . . . you've never met Philip, my husband, either of you; he doesn't come to church. He resents my going more than once a week. For some reason he chose the few minutes we had together this morning to let me know what he thought of my going to the Tuesday evening group. When I told him I intended to keep going, well . . . he just wasn't very happy. Enough said about that."

"I'm so sorry," Gail said. "I've seen sadness in you more than once and wondered if you were dealing with something like that at home."

"You've probably figured out that he and I live fairly separate lives. Whenever I can, I try to get into his world and show interest . . . unless he tells me to scat. I'm going to have to miss next Tuesday's meeting because his company is having a dinner. He doesn't know it, but they're going to recognize him for being there for thirty years. I really have to go with him. If I'm ever going to get him to come with me to church someday, it will be because I do my best to enter his world whenever possible."

I assured Evelyn that she was making the right choice.

"Well, I'm going to miss being with you guys, because I love history. And I enjoyed hearing about how churches and Christians have changed over the years. I so wanted to be there when you talked about where the church is right now."

Gail said to me, "Why don't you tell Evelyn what you're planning to say? We've got some time."

I couldn't believe Gail said that. I don't think she had any idea that I hadn't given any thought at all as to how I was going to organize next Tuesday's meeting. Anything I might tell Evelyn would come straight off the top of my head.

But Evelyn leaped at Gail's suggestion. "I've got time; I don't have to be anywhere. I'll sleep this afternoon. So tell me where you're going on this change thing."

So I took my best shot. At least it would give me a chance to clarify my thoughts in advance of more serious preparation.

"OK," I said, "but you'll have to understand that I'm not as organized on this as I'd like to be. Last week we picked a few places in history where the world was changing, and leaders in the church had to respond."

"Yes, the things in the early church. And I remember St. Patrick and Martin Luther. And then there was John . . . John—?"

"Wesley," I said.

"Yes, Wesley. He was the one who did all his preaching outside of the church buildings."

"Not all of his preaching . . . but you get the message. What you see happening with John Wesley and now with all the generations that followed him is an effort to export the gospel beyond church walls in all sorts of ways and to all sorts of different people. In the next hundred years or more after Wesley, there was this incredible stream of Christians who found every creative way in the book to bring the gospel to non-Christian people. D. L. Moody is probably one of the best-known—"

"Sure, I've heard of him," Evelyn said. "Isn't Moody Bible Institute named after him?"

"Exactly. He started it. And he conducted huge evangelistic meetings in England and in America. He was probably among the first evangelists to appreciate the use of music to prepare people to hear the sermon and to make decisions for Christ. Some Tuesday night we'll have to talk about that.

"About the same time—the mid-1800s—there was also an incredible couple in England named William and Catherine Booth who founded the Salvation Army and did all sorts of innovative things to bring Christ to the poorest of the poor. Within a few decades their work expanded all over the world.

"But in both situations—Moody and the Booths—there were many church-based Christians who were brutal in their opposition. They couldn't find anything good about the new ways these people were going about things. They remind you of those original guys in Jesus' time who held on to the temple with their lives."

"I just can't imagine that," Evelyn said. "Who would have attacked the Salvation Army? I see their people at the hospital all the time."

"Evelyn, the chances are that the three of us might have disapproved of the Booths if we'd been living then. We've got to face it. There's no way of being sure that we wouldn't have been among those who were totally opposed to the changes these people introduced: Moody with his music, the Booths with their bands and uniforms and service projects for the poor. It was too off the wall for the tastes of many people who find security in sameness. Too many of us opt for the status quo in almost every part of life and faith. We go with the familiar and we resist the new.

"By the end of the 1800s there was an explosion of all kinds of ground-breaking organizations that were formed to push the gospel out into the world.

For example, the YMCA reaching out to young men, the Student Christian Movement involving university students, and the Bible societies that wanted to get the Bible into the hands of everyone. Missionary organizations of every kind began popping up because Christians became aware of the many people who had never heard the name of Jesus.

"Then you get into the twentieth century, and the Christian movement was engulfed in a slew of technological and scientific changes that seemed to affect almost every aspect of life."

"Like what?" Evelyn asked. "Give me some examples."

"Well, there were mass-produced automobiles, the first airplanes, the phonograph, and movies and radios. Country roads started getting paved, and homes were electrified. And so you look back and ask, What did this do to the way churches did their thing?"

"And what did it do?"

"Take automobiles and improved roads," I said. "They made it possible for people to become more choosy about what church they'd join. Before cars you pretty much had to settle for what was in your neighborhood. And you probably stayed at church for most of the day—which is good news and bad news— because one trip back and forth by horse and buggy or by walking was enough. But when the automobile appeared you could go a farther distance to a church that was more preferable. I suspect that caused a lot of congregations to begin thinking about how they could attract more people.

"Then soon after came things like the radio, and before long Christians began to hear preaching on religious programs from long distances, and their access to the first celebrity preachers and musicians began to grow. By the time you get to the days of television, Christians were getting pretty sophisticated about what good preaching and entertaining Christian music was all about. I've often wondered if radio and television haven't contributed to a lot of the dissatisfaction that you see in church life. It's hard for a small church to match the stuff people hear and see during the week on radio and TV.

"But you know there are other kinds of changes that have profoundly affected the church during the last fifty years, changes that we live with every day and probably do not appreciate in terms of their impact.

"Take reliable birth control methods, which came of age in the 1950s," I said. "That's changed our overall society as much as anything in many thousands of years. And the church has felt the impact in a powerful way."

"You can't be serious."

"I am serious. Reliable birth control provided women with the chance to redefine themselves and their role in society. They could now control the reproductive process and determine if they wanted to be mothers or not. And if they wanted to be mothers, they could say when and how many times they wanted to birth children. And if they preferred to have a career and forgo motherhood, they could do it.

"Within a generation there were enormous numbers of women entering the workforce and challenging men for career positions. Many women began to reinterpret their life contributions in terms of monetary value. In other words, many of them no longer wanted to spend their lives doing things that didn't generate an income. In a way I don't have a problem with that. But it did deal a serious blow to a necessary kind of labor that is done purely out of love and the spirit of servanthood.

"For many years churches depended heavily on the volunteer labor of women. Now that source of energy has dried up for all practical purposes. So how have churches responded? They have started paying people to do things women used to do for free. Again, I'm not being critical; I'm just saying that this is the way things are. And it's meant change.

"Let me add one more thought while I'm on a roll here. The change in the role of women has had an enormous effect upon men. And a huge number of men are going through a kind of crisis trying to figure out what *their* role is, now that women have moved into almost every job category that used to be exclusively male. And by the way, there are a lot of churches that haven't faced up to this yet. They believe that women have no place in church leadership, and they're probably going to lose the loyalty of young women who see no future for them in those congregations. That's a consequence that we're just beginning to realize."

After a refill of coffee, Evelyn, Gail, and I discussed the women's issue for a short while and Evelyn admitted that she hadn't given this enough thought. That fascinated me, because Evelyn was a lifelong career woman.

I asked Evelyn if she'd thought about the impact that the interstate highways had upon the church, and she seemed surprised that I'd raise this issue.

"Well, think of it. Before President Eisenhower decided to network the nation with high-speed, restricted access roads, people's travel was somewhat limited. But when the interstates became operational, people no longer gave a second thought to traveling twenty-five or more miles to shop at malls or go to the movies or even to go to church.

"This could be one of the key reasons we have megachurches today. Now people can drive long distances to a church campus that provides every kind of ministry imaginable for their families. Take away the interstates and we would lose most of the megachurches overnight. There would be sizable churches only in the center of cities where people can use mass transportation.

"We're also living with some dramatic social changes," I said to Gail and Evelyn. "In my earliest days of ministry, I could assume that most people who came into the church—Christian or non-Christian—came out of reasonably stable family backgrounds. They were dependable, somewhat faithful people who knew how to make relationships work. But now things are very different. A pastor has to assume that most people coming toward the church, for whatever reasons, are bringing enormous personal problems caused by dysfunctional family backgrounds. So now we have support groups, counseling ministries, and a million books about personal problem solving. Enormous amounts of a pastor's energy are taken up wrestling with the fallout of a society that is unraveling.

"Here's another reality. We have a growing single-adult population the church never had before. Young men and women are more career conscious than any other generation. And they're struggling—far more than we ever did—to make decisions about marriage and family commitments. So they wait and wait for the perfect mate, until they have lots of money, and until they've seen which way their career is going to go. Result? We have large numbers of unmarried adults in the church, and we have to have a way of including them in church life. I don't preach about marriage half as much as I used to, because a large part of the audience finds it irrelevant to their interests.

"It even gets more practical than that. Singles bring more cars into your parking lot. They're inclined to be more loyal to a larger Christian network of churches and organizations than they are to their local congregation. So one week they may be on a ski trip with Christian singles from other churches, and another week they're away for a conference or a mission trip. You can't build a traditional church ministry like you and I used to know on patterns of involvement like that. Something's going to change."

"I've just never thought of all these connections," Evelyn responded.

"Understood. But these are the kinds of things that church leaders begin to live with that force change in the way we do ministry among people. Wesley and the others weren't the only people who had to look at the new realities and ask, 'What do we do now?'

Evelyn sipped from her coffee cup as she thought about our conversations. Then she said, "I think I hear you saying that we old fogies who like things to stay the same make it difficult for you."

"Evelyn, you're anything but an old fogy. I'll take several more like you any day. But, yes, pastors and church leaders have to think harder about how things get done and not be afraid to try new things if we really want to reach new generations. We're reading pretty reliable statistics that tell us that a frightening percentage of teenagers are dropping out of churches as they approach their twentieth year. We know that most churches that number between two hundred and five hundred are not growing. And we also know that the complexities and busyness of general life is reaching a point where people simply "X" out anything on their schedule that doesn't add value or significance to their personal experience.

"And you know what? I haven't even started to tell you where the big, real big, changes are coming from."

"Oh my. What now?"

"Well, we've not even mentioned the most monumental change in our time—namely the computer, digital technology, and the Internet. These are not gadgets that are going to come and go. They are impacting everything—the way we think, the way we organize ourselves, the way we communicate. I could go on and on. And the question that keeps me awake at night is, how will all of this affect the church during the next fifteen years? I know I'm speculating when I say this, but I firmly believe that the church of fifteen years from now—at least the church that works—will look totally different from the church we attend today."

"So where am I likely to see this happening right now?" Evelyn asked me.

"Look at the way we teach the basic elements of Christian thought and life. Let me give you an example of what I have to think about every week when our worship team designs a worship service or I prepare a sermon. I know that there will be up to five different generations in the building on Sunday. In a church our size, they all crowd into the same room—the sanctuary, and they expect to have a worship and a teaching experience that fits their unique generational experience.

"Each of those generations has a preferred kind of music. Each listens to sermons differently. Take our children and young people. They're used to not only hearing words, but also having the words accompanied by something visual. And they're used to lots of action as they learn. Tell them that they have to sit and listen to a monologued sermon for thirty or more minutes, and they'll be incredulous. They rarely *ever* listen to anyone talk nonstop for thirty minutes. So why would they do it in church?

"Even adults are becoming that way. Have you noticed how CNN presents the news? A newscaster speaks; there is action on a screen behind the speaker; and at the same time there are little messages, ten to fifteen words each, that crawl across the bottom of the screen. And, if that's not enough, you're getting stock exchange averages in the lower right-hand corner. That's a lot of information going into our heads all at once. Do you really think that the average person who lives in that world during the week is going to continue to be content listening to a thirty- or forty-minute sermon, often communicated by a very average speaker, each Sunday morning?"

"So that's why you are doing that PowerPoint thing with your preaching? And the videos and the interviews?" Evelyn asked.

"Sure, and I feel light-years behind the curve. Oh, by the way, that's why the leadership wanted to upgrade the sanctuary with all that technology. Because if we fall behind in how we communicate, we stand to lose our youth and our children. And we need to be as passionate about bringing them to faith as Jesus was when he hoisted them into his lap to give them a blessing."

"I'll think about that," Evelyn said.

"But while we are into this, here is one more idea, and then we'd better wrap this up. None of us have any conception of how much the Internet is going to impact the church. I think the whole world is in the process of reorganizing around the information and communication that the Internet makes possible. Before 1993, let's say, almost none of us had ever heard of the Internet. Then, bang! Within a few years almost every one of us sported an e-mail address. We no longer send letters, we send e-mail. We're learning how to "google" people so that we know something about them. We have Wikipedia to get information on almost anything. There's eBay to buy and sell. We make our travel plans on Expedia or Travelocity or other sites. We buy our books on Amazon, used books on AbeBooks. We blog, we send photos of our grandchildren, and we download our music to our iPods. *All this within a matter of three to four years.*

"Now what does this mean to a church? It used to be that you had to go to the church to get your information. That's one of the reasons we built what we call sanctuaries. They were safe places to hear preachers give us information.

"But now, thanks to the Internet, we can get that same information to come to us wherever we are. Christians can download sermons and Bible studies by the bushel. They can get into chat rooms and connect with other Christians around the world. You can be part of a small group that worships at home and then tunes in via the Internet to get a live sermon from the communications center of our church or others across the world. You can be in Berlin on a business trip and access your church's last worship service at three in the morning because you're suffering from jet lag and can't sleep. There is no end to the possibilities.

"And this is all leading to something they're calling the multisited church. Now one church can plant several others but keep them all networked together with technology. Each of the congregations may meet separately, worship separately, and then gather to listen to the same pastor preaching—over an Internet connection. And this is only the beginning of things that technology is making possible."

The more I rambled, the more Evelyn poked and prodded me with questions. And I could see her growing less resistant to what I was saying and becoming more fascinated.

And then Evelyn said, "I'm feeling stupid. I work at a hospital that has put all these changes that you're describing to work in health care. And I use all this stuff every night. All our medical equipment is digital. All our record keeping is computerized. I mean, everything is so different from when I started in the seventies. Everything!

"And here's a thought. I've never had a patient tell me that he wants to go back to the old ways of doing things. If our new technologies are going to save his life, he wants me to hook him up to them. So why do you think we embrace these changes to save our lives in the hospital and then resist them in the church when they're designed to save somebody's soul?"

"Perhaps," I said, "you're just like me and a lot of other people. We resist change in the church because it seems like the only safe place left in this world where a 'yesterday' still exists when things seemed simpler and more manageable."

"So that's why we're seeing more and more money in the church budget for new gadgets?" Evelyn said.

"Evelyn, I heard a younger generation pastor say that if he had three hundred thousand dollars to start a church, he'd put the first two-thirds of the money into sound, lighting, and visual technology. He'd rather do church in a warehouse and have state-of-the-art technology."

"I think some people in our Tuesday group would die if they heard that."

Just then my PDA chirped, reminding Gail and me that we had to get to another appointment. So we thanked Evelyn for the coffee, and I told her that she'd be missed at the next meeting. And we went our separate ways.

> ***Clayton Reid:*** *Real estate—highly regarded in the real estate com-*
> *munity. Wife died last year, cancer. Estranged from his son. Sports*
> *fan. Came to faith when his daughter, Olivia, got into church*
> *youth program. Is he dating?*

I talked with Clayton Reid just before our first worship service the following Sunday. I asked if he would pray at the beginning of our next
Discovery Group meeting. He stonewalled me at first, saying that he
didn't do "out-loud praying." I told him that I didn't want to be pushy,
but asked if he would consider writing a prayer ahead of time and simply
reading it for us. After a bit of hesitancy, Clayton finally relented and said
he'd give it a try. And then he added, "You're the only one I'd do this for."

When Tuesday night came, the start of the meeting was delayed
because Arlene's designated setup team—Yvonne, Clayton, and
John—had to search the church for our tables. Someone had "borrowed" them and then left them in the wrong place. When everyone
was finally seated, I explained Evelyn's absence, outlined my hopes for
the evening, and then turned to Clayton for his prayer.

Clayton pulled an index card from his shirt pocket, said, "Shall we
pray?" and began reading. I could tell that two or three around the table
were startled, maybe even uncomfortable, when they realized Ted was
reading from a card and that he was "praying" with his eyes open. Like
me, they'd been raised to believe that prayer was supposed to be "from
the heart" (as we liked to say it). Back then a lot of us had been
taught—wrongly, of course—that only "liberals" and Catholics read
prayers and prayed with open eyes. So I was tickled to have put
Clayton up to this. It was a tiny, tiny step out of the box—for Clayton
and others.

His prayer? "Heavenly Father, your Son, Jesus, once said, 'Come to me all you who are weary and burdened, and I will give you rest.' All of us are weary from a day of work. And some of us are burdened with great cares. So we come to you asking for Jesus' rest. We pray that you will guide our pastor and give him great wisdom in leading us. May we have open minds and hearts to learn from what he has prepared. I thank you for him. And I thank you for all my friends around this table. I pray this in the name of Jesus. Amen."

I thought Clayton's prayer was terrific. And I knew he was serious when he read that many of us are weary and burdened. Clayton had lost his wife, Teresa, about a year ago. Cancer. He had taken her death very, very hard, and I suspected that he was referring to himself when he spoke of those needing Jesus' kind of rest.

Clayton and Teresa had raised two children. The youngest, a midlife baby, had dropped out of college a few months ago when he was cut from the football team in his junior year. Absent Teresa's calming influence, Clayton had not handled the situation well at all. And now father and son were estranged just when they needed each other the most. I believed there was a lot of pain deep down in Clayton's heart.

After our exchange about him praying on Tuesday night, Clayton had confided in me that he had taken Sara Hughes, a single woman in our church (divorced, I think) out to dinner the week before. He was a bit bashful as he told me that it had been a wonderful evening, the first time he'd felt truly happy since Teresa had died. I think he was concerned that I'd think he was being disloyal to Teresa's memory, but I assured him that I could not be happier for him. And once he heard that, he said that he'd invited Sara to go with him to the Patriots game next week.

Clayton's prepared prayer finished, I picked up on the subject of great changes in history and how they had affected the Christian movement. After reviewing the history I'd covered last week, I said I'd like to talk about the era of change I believed we were living in.

"Evelyn told me we were in for quite an evening," Arlene said. "Evelyn got her own private lesson the other day from the pastor and Gail. Doesn't seem fair to me," she teased. "Shouldn't we all get—"

"Evelyn had the winning lottery ticket," I kidded back. "Besides, she bought Gail and me flavored coffee. I don't see any of you offering to do that." Lots of laughter and several invitations followed.

"Well, let me tell you what the three of us talked about." I then talked about automobiles, mass communication, some of the societal changes in the past years, and the digital revolution. With more time and the advantage of more preparation, I also talked about some things that we'd not had time to discuss.

"Are any of you familiar with the name Peter Drucker?"

Stan, who had been a finance executive for one of the state's larger companies, immediately said he was. "I thought you only read spiritual books," he teased. We had a friendly interchange, and I continued speaking to the group.

"Somewhere in the early nineties, Drucker wrote about great changes in history:

Every few hundred years in Western history there occurs a sharp transformation. We cross . . . a 'divide.' Within a few short decades, society rearranges itself—its worldview, its basic values, its social and political structures, its arts, its key institutions. Fifty years later, there is a new world. And the people born cannot even imagine the world in which their grandparents lived and into which their parents were born.[1]

"Drucker probably had only limited knowledge about the Internet or what it would become when he wrote this, and there's no way that even he could have imagined how our lives would be changed since then.

"But he's talking change—big change—language here, sudden bursts in history of tumultuous change that overwhelm every person and institution, not unlike an avalanche of snow. Businesses, schools, governments, all institutions, families, even churches—everyone feels the effect in one way or another. Here's the important thing: once that burst of change begins, nothing stops it. You might resist it for a while or simply hope it's going to go away. But finally you capitulate to it. As Drucker said, 'A new world exists.'"

Clayton said, "I can tell you that there's a new world in my business. It's powerfully affecting the way we sell houses. My clients get on their computers and take virtual tours of one house after another and never leave wherever they are. Today I talked with a couple who live in California about three houses they've studied in detail . . . on the Internet. It's as if they've been in the houses. The wife already had lists of all the colors in the rooms of each house, and I've been able to show her—

remember she's three thousand miles away!—what each of those rooms could look like if she painted them in different colors."

That got Russ's attention, and he spoke as soon as Clayton finished. "Our whole business is computerized. As soon as anyone buys a cheeseburger, the people in Chicago know about it, and our supplier automatically knows that his truck should have one more piece of meat, a bun, and whatever else you put on a cheeseburger for tomorrow's delivery—all done over a satellite hookup. And you won't believe this, but when someone orders stuff at our drive-in window . . . you know the menu board where you pick your poison? They think they're talking to someone behind the counter in our building, but they're actually talking to an order taker in Indianapolis about seven hundred miles away, believe it or not, who sends the order to a computer screen at our food prep table."

During the next fifteen minutes, various people in the group told stories about how computers and the Internet were affecting their lives at work or at home. Ernie mentioned that his daughter and her husband and their children talked to him and his wife, Gretchen, regularly. And, he emphasized, it wasn't just voice communication. The computers were equipped with a camera, and everyone's face could be seen when they connected each week. Winn said that he could swear that the airline reservation agent he'd talk to this afternoon was somewhere in India. Everyone tried to trump the last story with one of his or her own.

I sat back and let the stories roll on. The group was convincing itself that Drucker was right.

Finally, I spoke up. "There's a man by the name of Joel Arthur Barker who makes presentations to businesspeople about how businesses have to reinvent themselves in a time of furious change. He uses the popular term 'paradigm shift' when he talks. Paradigm is similar to the word *worldview*. It describes a way of seeing and organizing things.

"Barker said, 'When the paradigm shifts, everything goes back to zero.'"

Mary Ann leaned forward. "And what in the world does that mean?"

"It means that an organization, a church let's say, that was considered to be the best of the best at one point in time is likely to lose most of its advantage when there's a massive historical change or, as Barker puts it, a paradigm shift. If that organization doesn't take the changes seriously and ask what they mean and make suitable adjustments, it will find itself losing ground to its competitors, maybe going out of existence. In fact . . . let me take it a step further. It's not just *suitable adjustments*, it may mean *total reinvention.*"

"So what are you saying when you talk about total reinvention?" she asked.

"Well, reinvention means you start all over again, in effect. You examine everything you do to see if it still works and ask what you should change to make sure everything works better under the new conditions."

"Isn't that what got the railroads in trouble years ago?" Kenneth asked. "Somewhere I read that they didn't take the airplane seriously. They viewed themselves as runners of railroads rather than movers of freight and people. If they had reinvented themselves and diversified into the airplane business, they could have been the primary 'movers' of just about everything. They weren't perceptive enough to see that one day the airlines would virtually drive their passenger business into the ground."

"That's a great example, Kenneth," I said. "Here's another one. Xerox could have dominated the market on the personal computer years ago, but it sold its patents because it didn't believe that there would ever be enough popular demand for computers. So it stayed in the photocopying business."

Everyone was listening, and someone mentioned the old story about the absurdity of making state-of-the-art buggy whips after the automobile was mass-produced.

"Hey," I said. "What I was hoping we'd come to see is that this kind of thing can also happen in the Christian movement. Let's talk about the Jewish temple again for a moment. We've talked about how the temple was a powerful religious institution at the peak of its importance when Jesus came on the scene. And then, overnight, well, three years after Jesus had gone public, you have this Pentecost event where common people surged out into the street speaking the biblical faith in a fresh new way. The first day thousands were converted to Jesus. In a matter of days there were thousands more. And the temple leaders had nothing to do with it. In fact, they felt seriously threatened. Instead of asking, 'What are we missing here?' they tried to keep doing business as usual.

"Within a short period of time—for example, between twelve and twenty years—the Christian movement was beginning to scatter all over the world. And it couldn't be stopped. The dominance of the temple was broken when the Romans destroyed it, and the Christian way began to spread. It was a decentralized movement; it was in the hands of common people; and it struck a chord in the hearts of countless people. Within a few decades it grew strong enough to subvert the Roman Empire. That's the power inside one of these things Barker and others call paradigm shifts."

"And you're saying that the same thing can happen today . . . to a church." This was John, tilting back his chair, looking at the ceiling as if he were trying to wrestle with the implications of what he was hearing. The way he said it made me realize that this was not going down easily for John. I credited him for being at the table, but I picked up occasional signals that he might rather be some other place.

"Yeah, when one of these big historical change periods is under way, better keep your eyes and ears open. It could pass you by just like the change described in the book of Acts passed the temple by."

Connie spoke: "So let's say we're in one of these big—what do you call it?—para—?"

"Paradigm shift, Connie," I said.

"Paradigm shifts . . . let's say we're in one. What will be different when this one is over?" Connie asked.

"Let's start with what's different already, the stuff we already know. You think for a moment and tell me what's changed in the world since . . . let's say . . . 1960 . . . when most of us were in our twenties."

There was a moment or two of silence and then the contributions began to flow.

Lillian: "If we're going to think back to the sixties, we have to remember the madness that swept the country. Many of us grew long hair, demonstrated against the Vietnam War in the streets and on college campuses, and pretty much made the president's life miserable. So I guess our generation started rebelling against tradition."

"That's when the civil rights movement gained real momentum," Ted said. "The marches, the demonstrations, the riots. I'll never forget when Martin Luther King and Bobby Kennedy were killed. We're a pretty different country today."

"There was the women's movement," Lillian said. "People like Bella Abzug, Betty Friedan. A lot of women became very angry. Women began to demand equal rights. Evelyn said you talked about that the other day."

John added, "Don't forget Watergate. It shook us to the core. I can still see Nixon standing at the door of his helicopter when he left the White House."

"There was the gas crisis in the early seventies, and Detroit never recovered from the stupidity of making big cars." I think Ernie said that.

"Hey," I said, "there is an example of an industry that didn't get the message. There was real change in the air—people wanted cars that didn't guzzle gas, and Detroit kept turning out big cars. Advantage—the Japanese. I think Detroit and some churches have a lot in common."

Kenneth: "What about the Berlin wall and the defeat of communism?"

And Yvonne: "Well, you add to that what's going on in China—"

"India too," Ernie said.

I jumped in: "If we're going to talk about the global situation, just remember that America is the first single superpower the world has really had since the Roman Empire, and that's not as healthy a situation as one might first imagine. In a sense it means that the whole world finds creative ways to keep nipping at our edges. Little alliances crop up here and there and now and then—all testing American power. And Americans aren't necessarily handling this very well."

That comment brought a little bit of feedback from Connie, who tends to react to any seeming criticism of America.

"I want to get back to changes that *we're* feeling . . . right here where we live," Stan said. "Sometimes I feel as if my whole world is in a state of shock. I can't turn on the television without being bombarded with profanity, sexual innuendo, and violence. All around me it seems as if families are falling apart, marriages ending. Even right here in our church."

"Children don't know the Bible anymore," Yvonne (a former Sunday school teacher) said. "No one memorizes Scripture anymore, knows the books of the Bible, the stories—"

An avalanche of complaints and observations followed. I was trying to take notes, scribbling as fast as I could.

Clayton: "They're all too busy. Everybody's into sports. Kids doing e-mail. I heard that everybody's got a cell phone, and they're sending messages to each other all day long."

Russ: "Few people working very hard . . . undependability . . . people take jobs and quit in two weeks . . . show up late for work . . . want rewards, few responsibilities."

Kenneth: "Young people living together for years sometimes before they marry, . . . if they marry. Going into debt to buy luxuries we postponed buying for years."

Ted: "Who prays anymore? Prayer gatherings have dwindled. Even the pastor is on to other things on Wednesday nights."

Ernie: "Can't believe how few people care about missions anymore. Hard time getting people to come out to hear visiting missionaries."

Yvonne: "The younger generation likes having children in programs but is reluctant to serve on the various teams that run children and youth ministries."

Finally, I broke in: "Now look, you guys. Stop and listen to what you're saying. You're all finding ways to describe this period of highly charged change we've been talking about. You're feeling the pinch of it at work, where you live, here at church. Remember, I suggested to you that when there is one of these massive changes that Peter Drucker talked about, everybody begins to think differently, organize differently, and, as a result, live differently. I'm going to keep on using those same words over and over again. All of these things you're frustrated about—some of it is actually good news and some of it is bad."

"Let's hear some good news," Connie said.

"Well, would you be surprised if I suggested that there's a revival going on across North America?"

"A revival?" Several said this all at once in a surprised tone of voice.

"Yes, a revival. In the largest sense there's a spiritual revival. People are finding it easier to talk about spirituality, about evil, about powers, and believing. You wouldn't have heard these words in polite company thirty years ago. But now you hear it all the time. For example, many of Oprah Winfrey's shows center on spiritual matters. And people are listening intently to everything she and her guests say. Think about all the TV shows during the past few years that have featured angels, stories about so-called miracles, even the programs and soap operas that feature New Age stuff such as witches, paranormal activity, psychics. If there is a revival, let's just agree that a lot of it isn't Christian, but there is, nevertheless, a new openness to spiritual issues."

"I'd never have thought of that as a revival," Connie observed. "A lot of that stuff is off the wall. It's creating terrible confusion."

"I hear you, Connie," I said. "But what it all suggests is that people are asking questions about realities that are beyond the purely materialistic. They are feeling disillusioned about the promises that science and technology have made and not delivered on. They're feeling the growing inability of once dependable institutions and systems to protect us and guarantee the good life. So they're turning to the world of the spiritual as an alternative. It's not unlike Bible times."

"What do you mean by that?" Ernie asked.

"In Bible times people had a strong conviction that what you couldn't see, the invisible things, was, maybe, more real than what you could actually see. They really believed in powers and magic. That's what Paul was saying when he said to the Ephesians: our battle is not with visible things (like human beings); it's with things we cannot see, powers in the air and systems that are bigger than us. It was Paul's contention that if you didn't have the power of the stronger Spirit, the Holy Spirit, you wouldn't be able to survive a world full of spiritual influences that had evil intentions.

"Our civilization has just come through a period of about two hundred and fifty years where non-Christian people rejected (or at least thought they rejected) any notion of spiritual reality. Most 'smart' people said that spiritual stuff was a figment of the imagination, the religious leftovers of prescientific times. We now refer to this period as *modernity*, a time when increasing numbers of people rejected the idea of faith and became convinced of the importance of the individual making his own way in the world. There was, they said, a scientific explanation for everything. Given enough time, we would find an answer to every question, a solution to every problem. It was really quite an arrogant view of life. And it had some powerful implications for the Christian movement."

"How would it have affected Christians?" Ernie asked.

"Well, you can see the effects of modernity in Christian teaching. The emphasis upon the individual became reflected in the heavy emphasis upon a so-called 'personal relationship' to Christ. Our Christian vocabulary has tended to be all about Jesus and *me* rather than Jesus and *us*.

"Even Bible teaching and preaching began to sound as if you can figure out every little mystery in the Bible. Many different theological systems have tried to pretend that they can explain everything. You hear very little emphasis on the idea that there may be some great realities that God has no intention of explaining to us. He wants us to worship and serve and stop trying to figure out every little thing."

"You're saying that individualism is wrong?" Russ asked.

"Not wrong, Russ, but individualism is only a part of a bigger reality. You are not totally an individual, Russ; a large part of who you are has to do with your community, the people with whom you live. They are influencing who you are and how you think all the time—know it or not. And you're influencing them. No, we're not merely individuals. We're that plus a lot more.

"And you see signs that people are struggling with the effects of individualism. Young people running in groups and gangs, people finding all kinds of ways to connect in chat rooms on the Internet, at places like Starbucks, in a thousand different interest groups, such as motorcycle clubs and various sporting activities. Go to the soccer field on Saturday morning and look at the parents gathering on the sidelines to watch their kids play. They're connecting in much the same way a church group might come together. They want relationship.

"Some of you are familiar with the term *postmodernism*, and perhaps, some of you are not. Some think *postmodernism* is the successor to *modernity*. *Postmodern* is the word people tend to use when they describe the collapse of modernism and whatever is taking its place."

Lillian, who is a schoolteacher, said, *"Postmodernism*. The word gets kicked around school quite a lot, but I am never fully sure any of us knows what it really means. And don't tell anyone I admitted that."

"I'm not sure I'm your guy when it comes to explaining it like a scholar," I said. "I can give you some pretty good book titles on the subject, but I'm not confident that I can clear away the fog. I can say this much: postmodernism begins with the idea that there are no fixed, stand-alone truths. Rather than this thing called truth coming from beyond ourselves—as Christians believe about God's revelation—the postmodernist claims that truth is really only what *we* see or experience from our perspective. And when enough of us see or experience something in a similar way, then whatever that is becomes truth for us.

"Whatever truth is, it's personal and social, according to the postmodernist. It's not something revealed and binding and universal.

"This is a scary thing for Christians, because we believe that there are certain things God has said to us in creation, through the writers of Scripture, and through Christ that comprise *truth*. And a lot of us were trained in the so-called modern era when the accepted theory was that if you could explain the truth about Christ clearly enough, people would abandon whatever they believed and embrace what you preached. In a strange way we became guilty of a kind of a conceit among many so-called Christians. We said to the larger world, 'We've got *the* truth; you don't. And the sooner you hear what we've got to say, the better off you'll be.'

"So in the latter days of *modernity* we put our 'truth' into persuasive sales presentations like the *Four Spiritual Laws*, and we assumed that you could pull someone through those laws, and when they got to the end of the fourth law, they would say, 'That makes perfect sense; I'll give my [whole] life to Christ.' And this could happen theoretically in the space of fifteen minutes or in an evening, such as at a Billy Graham rally. I want you to think about that for a minute. We actually have thought that you could get people to reconsider their entire life organization in the space of a few minutes and make a decision that would redirect their entire lives, to the end of time. Incredible as it seems, it worked for a period in history—particularly in our generation.

"But what happens when people begin to say, 'You've got Jesus? Well, I'm glad for you; you're into something great for yourself.' *Yourself!* Hear that? *Yourself!* And then they say, 'I'm into Buddhism, and you know what? I'm just as happy as you are.' Sooner or later (if you haven't already) you're going to run into someone who says they have *the secret*. And what you're going to hear is a bundle of ideas that sounds awfully close to biblical faith attached to a bit of Hinduism and some New Age ideas. *But it's all about a basic faith in yourself rather than faith in Jesus.* It comes very close to God language, but which god? Now in postmodern times, *you* are God. Everybody has a customized 'faith,' and each individual's version is considered as valid as someone else's."

Lillian interrupted me (which was good because I was talking too much anyway): "I hear what he's saying every day at school. I hear it from teachers; I hear it from students. And I'm amazed at how quickly it can grow on you and affect your view of things. When I first became a Christian, I really wanted to convince everyone of what I'd seen. But now I find it easy to just shut up about my faith in Jesus and settle for the idea that it's every person for himself."

Two or three others around the table agreed with Lillian. What startled me was their admission that each of them thought that he or she was the only person thinking that way.

"Well," I said, "what do you do when no one wants to argue about or debate matters of faith and belief, but want simply to enjoy a good discussion? We're living in a period when many people think that evangelism (persuading people to Jesus) is actually offensive and ought to be banned if possible—certainly in public places. And what they're saying is that you have your truth and I have mine. Now let's get on with figuring out how we're going to solve the health-care problems in our country."

"How do you lead people to Christ, then?" Kenneth asked.

"Now there's a good question, Kenneth. *How do you do it?* In fact, have you noticed how few people are coming to Christ these days in our church? In my opinion, that's because we've been trying to convert people the old way, a way that doesn't work any longer. People aren't feeling guilty about their sins, and they're not interested in hearing about forgiveness because they don't feel the need to be forgiven.

"And furthermore, as I've tried to emphasize, they're not impressed with our truth because they've got their own truth that they believe to be just as good."

"So what are you telling us? That there's no more evangelism?" Ted asked.

"No, I'm not saying that at all. But there may be new ways to evangelize and to do church. The old way is becoming obsolete and ineffective."

"That's pretty depressing," Mary Ann said.

"Not if you're like Paul," I said. "When he ventured out beyond the world of Jews and began mixing it up with Gentiles and pagan-oriented people, he found new and fresh ways to explain who Jesus was and why people should organize their lives around him. He simply reframed the gospel and put it into terms that made sense to the people he was with. 'When I'm with Jews,' he said, 'I talk like a Jew. And when I'm with Greeks, I talk like a Greek. I am all things to all people.' In other words, he flexed with the new realities. He didn't compromise the core of the gospel a bit, but he certainly found new ways to talk about it. And he flexed with the new realities he found in every town. His ultimate objective: whatever it took, he was going to show people what a Christ-centered life looked like and why the power of Christ was stronger, greater than all other powers. And he was successful in making it happen."

"I can tell that you don't think our church is doing that," said Stan. "Am I correct?"

"The truth?" I said. "No, we're not doing it very well. And I'm at fault as much as anyone else. I have a lot of strong ideas about this, but I probably haven't been as candid as I ought to be, because I have fears that if some people knew what I thought, they'd write me off."

"Write you off?" Connie said.

"Quite a few pastors who are much better leaders than I am have been written off because they dared to talk about these things. Status quo thinking that is grounded in yesterday is rather difficult to change. Much easier to get rid of the messenger than face the fact that the way we're doing things is not working anymore."

It was time to end the meeting. I knew that the last several minutes of discussion had been very sobering. Some were thinking—perhaps more deeply than ever before—about these things and trying to sort out their deepest reactions. Others were struggling. And as far as I could see, no one was struggling more than John. Everything about his body language told me that he wasn't "buying."

We prayed, picked up around the Commons and left the building. Clayton walked with me to my car and said, "Thanks for getting me to pray tonight. First time I've ever done that. I know it was a short prayer . . . I can't say all the nice words Ernie says. But it was a good experience for me to get quiet at home and put a prayer on paper." I could have hugged him.

As I drove home I worried that I might have gone too far with my comments. Perhaps I'd dug too deeply into some of the issues that more than a few Christians find it preferable to avoid. And then I allowed my imagination to take over, and before I drove into our driveway, I found myself worrying about my job.

The next morning—after a restless night—I wrote in my journal:

Discovery Group last night. The conversation went well most of the evening. But I may have said some things that people weren't ready to hear. Lillian was into it with both feet. She's in a world every day that forces her to think about these issues. On the other hand, John seems to be hardening. Ernie is probably wondering where in the world I stand on some things. I think I'm beginning to understand why the younger guys prefer to start churches. I sometimes think that changing one is impossible.

Ernie Yost: Son of pastor. Wife, Gretchen. In middle management at Blue Cross. Would love to have been a preacher. Is there guilt about not following his father into ministry? Daughter, Amy, and family in Colombia as missionaries. Sensitive about all aspects of church outreach. Graduated Houghton. Rides an Indian. Serves on mission committee.

A couple of days later, I came into the church office area and saw Ernie's wife, Gretchen, talking to Diane, our church business manager.

Very casually, I sauntered over in that direction and, getting closer, said hi. Gretchen said a "hi" back, but there was a hint of coolness in her voice. Something was bothering her.

"I've enjoyed having Ernie as part of our Discovery Group, Gretchen. Sometime you ought to come along with him."

"I don't think so," Gretchen said. "I'm not sure if Ernie will continue in the group."

"You're kidding. Why not? Something wrong?"

Gretchen looked at Diane, then back at me, took a deep breath and said, "Ernie was upset when he got home the other night. He thinks you may be changing your views on some things—"

"Like what, Gretchen?"

"Apparently, you said that evangelism is out of date . . . that no one accepts Christ through the *Four Spiritual Laws* anymore. And, you know . . . Ernie has this heart for the lost. . . . He's always wanted to see people coming to Christ. . . . So your comments . . . I don't know . . . I wasn't there. But it sure sounded as if—"

"Why don't you come down to my office?" I said. When we were seated in my visiting area, I said, "Gretchen, that's not what I was saying at all. I was trying to help the group see that there come times when the way we talk about the gospel to people has to change . . . because people—especially younger people—are hearing things differently now."

"That's hard for me to accept," Gretchen said.

"How did you come to Christ?" I asked her.

"Youth for Christ. I was in junior high, and my best friend's mother used to take us to the Saturday night rallies they had at the city auditorium. One night they showed a movie about a boy and a girl who ran away from home. When the movie was over, they gave an invitation, and I went forward and received Christ. When I went home that night, I knew I was a Christian."

"Are they still doing those rallies?"

"No, as far as I know they haven't done them for years."

"How come?"

"I don't know. I guess kids stopped coming. There was too much else to do on Saturday nights—"

"So they stopped giving invitations like the one that brought you to Christ."

"I guess."

"Your daughter, Amy, and her husband in Colombia. Do they do rallies?"

"No."

"Invitations?"

"No."

"Well, what do they do so that they can introduce people to Jesus?"

"They open their apartment to neighbors and people they meet on the street. There are discussions and Bible studies."

"So how do people become Christians?"

"Well, it just seems to happen as people get into one group or another. Gretchen said that sometimes it takes months, maybe longer, but one by one people come to faith. You never really know when it happens or if it's going to happen at all. But one day someone simply says, 'The other night I asked Jesus to come into my life.'"

"But that's not the way you came to Christ, is it?" I asked Gretchen.

"No, it isn't."

"And that's the main point I was trying to make the other night. People are coming to Jesus in different ways. The methods are changing. Many people don't make a change on the spur of the moment after watching a movie . . . or even reading something like the *Four Spiritual Laws*. They want to spend some time getting to know the kind of people who have been following Jesus. Nowadays, relationships often become the pathway to Jesus. People take time to see the genuineness of your life. They want to know if the gospel really works. And that's what's going on in your daughter's apartment. People are being drawn by her hospitality, by the qualities they see in her marriage with your son-in-law. They experience generosity, care, Christian love. And once they feel that they belong there and they feel comfortable with the people, they begin to listen to the stories of Jesus. You don't have to persuade them, coax them, sell them. They just—and you never know when it's likely to happen—cross the line and begin organizing their lives around the love and lordship of Jesus."

"Did you say this to Ernie the other night? Because he didn't see it that way when he told me about the meeting."

"No, we didn't get that far. It's possible that I didn't do a very good job of explaining myself. I can see where Ernie might have gotten the wrong idea. I'll have to talk to him."

"Well, I wish you would," Gretchen said. "He was pretty worked up . . . even the next morning. You know Ernie. He thinks everything in the church should be about missions and evangelism."

PROCRASTINATOR THAT I AM SOMETIMES, I resisted calling Ernie all day long. Conflict and debate are not my game, and I don't really enjoy having to argue my way through to a point I really believe in.

Ernie's father had been a pastor, and I suspect that Ernie felt more than a little pressure to follow him into the pulpit life. Ernie never explained his reasons, but after he'd graduated from a small Christian college, he took a few business courses and went to work in the health-care industry. He's been with an HMO ever since. You'd not call him a wildly successful man if you're looking for material assets, a corner office, and a private parking space.

But to his credit Ernie has kept his family together over the years. He has—Gretchen was right—been faithful to the themes of missions and evangelism. And their daughter, Amy, along with her husband, Bart, has been a missionary for sixteen years now. And I'd say they're good missionaries; they seem to always be adapting to the Colombian culture and finding creative ways to connect with Colombians. You can tell that they love what they do and the people with whom they do it.

Nevertheless, Ernie can be a bit difficult sometimes. If you listen to him on church matters for very long, you'll learn that he thinks there's never enough money in the budget for missions. We never have enough meetings where missionaries are recognized and prayed for. Not enough, anyway, to please Ernie.

It would have been easy for me to simply avoid calling Ernie. But he solved my problem; Ernie called me that afternoon on my cell phone.

"Gretchen thinks we need to talk," he said. I wondered to myself if men would ever talk if the women in their lives didn't push them as Gretchen had obviously done.

"Yeah, I hear that you're a little ticked off at some things I said the other night."

"I'm past it, I think," Ernie responded.

"Hey, how about breakfast in the morning? I'll buy."

"Sounds good," Ernie said. We picked the time and place for breakfast and said good-bye.

I CALL IT MY CONDO TABLE. It's in the rear of the restaurant where things are quiet and conducive to the kind of conversations pastors have with people. The restaurant staff knows me pretty well, because I show up there two or three times a week. They are aware, for example, that my first cup of coffee is always caffeinated, black ("leaded") and the subsequent cups are decaffeinated, black ("unleaded"). And they know that my normal breakfast is fruit and an English muffin—toasted, never grilled. In some areas I am unchangeable.

I was at my table the next morning when Ernie drove up to the front of the restaurant on his Indian motorcycle. A minute later he was seated across from me. When Michelle took our orders, I simply said, "The usual," while Ernie ordered the number 2 special.

As we waited for our food, we talked about our families, some rumored layoffs at the HMO where Ernie worked, and the new Japanese pitcher the Red Sox had just acquired.

Then with our breakfast served and a prayer of thanks given, we got into the matter that seemed to have bothered Ernie on Tuesday night.

"Ernie, I don't think there's anyone in our church who has stronger feelings than you do about missions and getting the gospel out to people. I want you to know I really admire you for that, and I respect your opinions."

"Appreciate that. Thanks."

"So let's go back to the other night. What did you hear me say? And why did it bother you so much?"

"I think you told the group that times are changing, that our church needs to change. And we're not going to challenge people to accept Christ anymore? I guess that made me realize that if that's how you feel about witnessing to people, then it won't be long before you don't think missions are important either."

"Ernie, how long have we known each other?"

He said something about it being three years or whenever I'd come to the church as pastor.

"Do you really think I would give up on the importance of people making choices to follow Christ—here in our town or any other place in the world?"

"Well, it's hard to believe you would."

"I'll never stop believing that every person in the whole world should come under the influence of the love of Christ. No, let me rephrase that . . . *the saving love of Christ.* I'm not the greatest evangelist around, but I can tell you that there's no greater thrill than to be part of a conversation where someone makes a choice to follow Jesus."

"But the other night you said that we're not going to do that anymore."

"Ernie, friend . . . what I said was that *the way* we talk to people about Jesus may have to change. Remember Paul's words: 'When I'm with Greeks, I talk like a Greek, and when I'm with Jews, I talk like a Jew.' We have to make sure that we're speaking into the lives of people in a way that they can hear us. No point in answering questions they're not asking. And no point speaking to issues they don't care about."

"But you said the four spiritual—"

"Let me see if I can explain it this way. There was a time when the majority of the population had a base of thought that was influenced by biblical themes."

"Meaning—"

"Meaning that, for example, you could use the word *sin,* and people knew what you were talking about . . . even if they weren't disturbed about it or didn't think they were sinners. They still respected the subject and understood that sin was about something that was wrong between people and God.

"There was a time when most people at least respected the Bible, even if they didn't believe it or know much about it.

"The four spiritual laws worked rather effectively in a world where most people respected the idea of God, the Bible, and the cross. Believe it? Probably not in many cases. Respect it? Perhaps. So if you could take the ideas of salvation and put them in a presentation that made sense to a person, you had a pretty good chance of getting a hearing. Maybe even agreement that this was right and that they had to give serious thought to following Christ. And it was not unusual to see a person pray a simple prayer right then and there. And you'd walk away feeling good about having led a person into the presence of Jesus."

"Yeah," Ernie said. "We saw a lot of that happen in college. Not so anymore."

"Well, that's the point, Ernie. Now we have a couple of generations of people in this new historic period, as we've been calling it, who know nothing—*nada*—about the Bible. They have no sense of God whatsoever. Jesus is little more than a swear word or a character mentioned in *The Da Vinci Code.* The notion of listening to a twelve-minute presentation from a stranger and giving one's life to Christ, as we like to say it, seems almost ludicrous to them.

"Add to that all the impressions they have of Christianity today, and you have a totally different ball game. People do not come to faith in Christ today because the words make sense—"

"Why do they come to Christ, then?" Ernie broke in, his words signaling a bit of agitation.

"They start in the direction of Christ because they first see him in you . . . then, later, in the words."

"I'm not sure I see the distinction."

"During these couple of decades, relationships have become increasingly important in terms of what one might or might not believe. People do not trust words. They've seen that words can be made to do anything you want them to do. The important thing is the word giver. How well do you know him or her?

"Let me give you an example. John the Baptist pointed out Jesus to two of his disciples. They became curious and began following him. John had called him the *Lamb of God,* and they found that hard to resist. So they followed because they wanted to see what a *lamb* of that kind looked like.

"Jesus noticed them following and challenged them, 'What do you want?'

"They said, 'Where are you staying?' I think they were really saying, 'What do you do all day?'

"So Jesus said in effect, 'Come on along and you'll see.'

"The two of them found where Jesus was living, and they spent the remainder of the day with him. I think there's an important message here. Jesus didn't ask people just to swallow his words, but he asked them to spend time with him and see what he was about. At that time the world was cluttered with people who claimed they were the Messiah. If Jesus were to stand out from among them, it would be because people like John's disciples observed his life. Did his *life* match his words?"

"OK," Ernie said as he lifted his coffee cup to his lips, "where's the difference between now and a few years ago?"

"Let me restate it. The difference is this. We're in a new era where people want less of your carefully scripted evangelism sales presentation and more personal demonstrations of your genuineness, your authenticity. They want to see evidence that what you believe has legs—that it does something. They're not impressed with suits and ties, with empty ceremony repeated over and over, and with people who talk big but don't deliver on their promises. Rather, they're drawn to untrained voices in music, torn jeans, passionate emotions, and real stories. Fail there, and you lose them. Show your heart and you win them."

"So what are you suggesting?" Ernie asked. I could tell he was still feeling discomforted by some of these ideas.

"Let's talk again about Amy and Bart and how they became missionaries. When they decided to go to Colombia, what was the first thing they did after they got out of school?"

"They raised support."

"Yes," I said, "but what else did they do?"

Ernie thought for a minute and then said, "Oh, they had to go to language school."

"Language school. Why?"

"Because they didn't know Spanish."

"Why? Why not go down to Colombia and just start preaching?"

"You crazy? We both know the answer to that. What's your point?"

"My point is—and I said this to Gretchen—that your daughter and her husband spent a huge amount of time preparing themselves to fit in with the Colombian culture. They learned the language, chose a place to live among the people they wanted to influence, and adopted customs that would show the Colombians they really loved them. They went all the way, didn't they? Just as Jesus went all the way from heaven to earth and became a human being. Why not halfway? Why not just half a man?

"And, Ernie, why didn't your daughter simply say to the Colombians, we'll come halfway and you come halfway. In fact, we'll meet, let's say, in Costa Rica."

Ernie laughed.

"Ernie, if you believe in evangelism, you have to go all the way . . . all the way . . . to meet the person you want to influence to Jesus. You get involved in their lives to such a depth that they see your realness, your authenticity. And then, in a moment that only the Holy Spirit can arrange, a wonderful transaction happens. You may never know the moment it happens. You may be there when Jesus enters their life; you may not be."

"What you're saying is that evangelism in big stadium meetings may not happen much longer. That a lot of evangelism is going to be done quietly, almost unnoticed."

"I guess I really believe that," I said.

"But there are still big rallies, aren't there?" Ernie asked.

"Yep, there are. But more and more, if there are people going to them who don't know Jesus, it's only because someone who does has invited them. And the two go together because there's trust in their relationship."

"So where is this taking us?" Ernie asked.

"Here's a key word: *belonging*. The new church has to throw open its doors and go out into the community and engage people in their worlds, and when possible, throw open its doors and invite people in to share experiences that are hospitable and welcoming. In every transaction, the people of Christ have to create an environment of belonging."

"Don't we do that now?" Ernie queried.

"Not really. We tend to project a message that begins with *believing*. Believe like us, hold our values and our ideas, and we'll accept you. Dress our way; speak our language; sing our songs; and we'll accept you—then you'll belong.

"Sometime pick someone you know who is as far from church and God as can be. Ask them if they'll do you a personal favor. Ask them to come to our church as a stranger. Warn them that you won't even say hello to them. And then ask them to take careful notes of every impression they have—every impression from the moment they get out of their car to the moment they return to it. Then sit down with them and ask what they experienced. If they're honest, you're going to get blown out of the water with how strange an experience it is to come to church if you're an outsider. There's very little *belonging* in most churches until you *believe*. And even then you may have a problem."

"Yes," Ernie responded, "doesn't the Bible say that when Paul became a Christian they wouldn't let him in the church?"

"Yes, that happened. But it's hard to blame those guys. Paul had a reputation for killing people, putting them in prison. Who could trust that he wasn't just gathering names? It took real guts for Barnabas to vouch for Paul and convince the leaders in the Jerusalem church to accept him. But, and you've put your finger on it, Barnabas had to say to Paul, 'You belong to me,' and to the church, 'He belongs to us.'"

"So you're saying that if our church is going to be evangelistic, it's going to have to change?"

"You got it. If it doesn't know how to connect with unchurched people and create an environment of genuine belonging where people can really develop trust relationships, kiss evangelism good-bye."

I picked up the check and paid it, and Ernie and I left the restaurant. My car and his motorcycle were parked right next to each other. "See you next week at the group," he said.

Lillian Seamands: Single. Public schoolteacher—math. Masters, Plymouth State. Came to faith in InterVarsity. Active in teachers' union. Also SS teacher for years. Serious walker; has climbed all New England mountains over 4,000 feet. Strong feelings about women's issues.

When the next Tuesday rolled around, I wanted in the worst way to cancel the evening Discovery Group meeting. A bad cold, twenty-five inches of snow, or a pastoral emergency would have provided a convenient excuse. But I wasn't sick; it was a beautiful day; and no one, as far as I knew, was in trouble. The truth was that *I just wasn't ready for another church meeting.*

Perhaps I was suffering from "overnight burnout," an occasional dark-spiritedness that hits church leaders when the perception is that nothing is going right.

My gloomy mood began on Sunday morning when Loretta Cassens (age: north of seventy-five) fell and was seriously injured in the church parking lot. Seeing Loretta, whom everyone loves, driven away in an ambulance shocked us all. A few minutes later I learned that the worship team had fallen into conflict about how to handle a worship song, and one of the musicians lost his temper, unplugged his guitar, and walked out. Little did I realize that the morning's meltdown had just begun.

Many of our younger families were gone because it was a three-day weekend followed by a week of school vacation. It seemed as if everywhere I looked there was nothing but gray hair.

Just as the first worship service began, the power went out in our part of the city, meaning that we were without sound, lights, and ventilation. I convinced everyone to push ahead with songs most of us knew by heart and which we could sing without electric instruments. Prayers, Bible readings, and the sermon, of course, were delivered with loud voices.

While preaching during the first hour, I found it hard to concentrate because two families brought infants into the service who seemed bent on competing with me with coos and cries. It would have been a terrible morning to preach on Jesus' words, "Bring the little children to me."

My second sermon was no improvement on the first, and by the end of the morning, I felt terribly discouraged.

On Monday morning Sunday's memories were reinforced when I found the attendance and financial statistics in my box. Giving totals were poor, and attendance was down 8 percent from the previous week (our head usher loves statistics). Later in the morning our weekly staff meeting was dominated by a discussion on Loretta Cassen's accident and how we had all responded to it. I did not have the will to guide the staff into more uplifting conversation.

My gloomy outlook was further fueled on Tuesday morning when I received a call from Phil Rickets, one of our top church leaders, saying that he and his wife (both physicians) would be moving to Beijing, China, where they were going to establish a medical education program sponsored by Harvard University. I'd known about this possibility for months, but now it was reality. I knew that Phil was thrilled with the opportunity, and on the phone I pretended to share his excitement. But I was instantly brokenhearted. I could think of ten other people in the church whom I would have been glad to send to China. Losing Phil and Jennifer was a real blow to me.

By Tuesday night I found myself thinking how nice it would be if Gail and I could just hop on a plane and head for . . . let's say, Bermuda. That might be far enough away to escape the events of the past two days. But Bermuda wasn't possible. So I was left to console myself with a reminder that there were pastors all over the world who suffered from problems that dwarfed mine. "Get off the pity-pot," is one of Gail's favorite expressions, and I kept repeating the words like a mantra as Tuesday evening neared.

Entering the Commons that evening, I found everyone standing around. Arlene, away for the week, had apparently forgotten to appoint a set-up team, and, so far, no one had taken responsibility to get things arranged. I learned there would be no refreshments, because Clayton, who was supposed to provide them, had written down the wrong date on his calendar. Then when Mary Ann checked the cabinets, she informed us that we were out of coffee.

Would "Sunday" never end? For some reason I recalled the guitar player who had walked out on Sunday morning, and I secretly envied him.

I asked Stan if he could rally the troops, and he did. Soon we had the tables and chairs arranged. Clayton, acting a bit sheepish, found a couple of pitchers of water and some cups. And our evening started.

Minutes earlier I'd asked Lillian to pray, and when I called on her, she began: "Dear heavenly Father, our church could be dying, and we need your guidance. We pray that you will help us to lead more dedicated lives and do what needs to be done to make the church flourish again. I pray for Loretta that you'll heal her and bring her home from the hospital as soon as possible. We also pray for an encouraging evening. Amen."

Encouragement? *Where in the world,* I asked myself, *would we find encouragement after a prayer like that? Take a note,* I said to myself. *Teach people what a kick-off prayer is supposed to sound like!*

Before I could say anything, Lillian spoke again: "Maybe I shouldn't have said that our church might be dying in my prayer, but that's the way I felt after Sunday morning. Everybody seemed so lifeless, and I just had the feeling that we'd lost our joy." And looking directly at me, she said, "You seemed so down, Pastor. I had the sense that you were terribly disappointed in us."

Russ raised his hand as if asking permission to talk. "I had the same impression. It was just one of those miserable days when you go home feeling worse than when you came. I got to church just after Loretta fell, and seeing her lying on the ground took the starch out of me."

Clayton jumped in. "I don't remember many Sundays like that. We all seemed to lose it, didn't we?"

Yvonne said, "Things have changed. Remember a few years back when the choir loft was full, and the ushers had to put chairs in the aisle to cope with the overflow?"

"That was when we had one service, Yvonne," Stan said.

"Well, the ushers weren't very organized Sunday." This was John speaking. "No one was outside helping the older people out of their cars, and that's probably why Loretta fell. That wouldn't have happened a few years ago."

Connie shook her head. "What happens to churches anyway? We used to have such excitement around here. We couldn't wait to arrive on Sunday morning, to see what surprise was being cooked up somewhere around the building. We've lost a lot of that spirit."

"Don't get too down on us, Connie," said Stan, trying to play the role of the optimist. "Lots of people were away for the weekend, and it was just us old guys."

Connie seemed not to pay attention to what Stan said. Looking in my direction, she asked, "Is that what you've been trying to say to us in a nice way? And are you saying that something is missing in our church and it's all our fault?"

There was a powerful silence at the table as people awaited my response. It was clear that those of us who'd been there on Sunday were all struggling with doubt.

In my mind I scrambled for an appropriate answer to Connie's question. There was a part of me, an angry part, that would have liked to say: *Yes, Connie, it is your fault. You've all stood in the way of every effort to bring this church into the twenty-first century.* But that would have been a terribly unfair and unwise thing to say. And it would have devastated everyone needlessly.

So instead of giving vent to my emotions, I said, "Let's not talk about blame or fault. Let's just keep going back to the question, *What does God want for this congregation for the next several years?*"

Even though I would have preferred not to have this meeting, I had prepared some thoughts for the evening. I'd intended to discuss more about historical changes and their effects upon the Christian movement in the past, but there was something about the spirit at the table that made me decide it would be better to return to that subject on another occasion. Tonight, it was clear that we needed to go in a different direction. In an instant, I rebuilt my presentation.

"I want to try out an idea on all of you tonight," I said as if I'd been planning this all along. "I've never put these thoughts together in quite this way before, but I have a feeling that I might provide us with some talking room as we try to understand what could be going on in a church like ours. Are you willing to let me think out loud with you?"

Everyone indicated a readiness to listen, and so I launched into some thoughts that had been forming in my mind during the past weeks.

"If you want a title for the evening, try this: 'The Shelf Life of a Church.' I'm interested in the question, How do churches and organizations and marriages and even friendships sometimes start out with such freshness and then, later on, go stale?"

Mary Ann said, "All of us would like to know the answer to that question."

I began: "I'd like to propose that all human relationships or organizations have a similar beginning that is based on the discovery of a need or opportunity." I tore off a piece of paper from my writing pad and wrote "need, opportunity" at the top. Those who were taking notes, everyone except John, wrote the same words.

"I put these two words—*need* and *opportunity*—at the top because they represent a realization on the part of some person—a founder, for example—or some group that there is something that has to be accomplished. There's a problem that awaits a solution or an opportunity that has to be seized. There's a product that needs to be produced. Or there's a church that needs starting.

"As an example, let's take the city where we live. Years and years ago someone came to the realization that there was a need for a certain kind of church in this city, a church with convictions and structure like this one. Whoever that person was must have defined the need in such a way that it excited the imagination of some others. Now let me emphasize that the need this person defined could have been there for some time. But it was necessary for just the right person of influence at just the right time to get others to see what was possible. Looking back, we would say, of course, that God was in the process from beginning to end."

Winn, who had written a brief history of the church a few years ago, spoke up at this point: "I can tell you exactly what happened. There were no churches in this area that adhered to baptistic principles and had a strong evangelistic purpose. And that interested a pastor of a church over in Portsmouth. He visited here several times—coming on horseback actually—and each time he contacted Christians to see if they shared his concern."

"So what you're saying, Winn, is that the Portsmouth pastor was the man God used to raise the matter of need, and soon there were others who agreed with him."

"Right," Winn said. "Before long the pastor was coming here once a month and leading prayer groups of about twenty or twenty-five people."

"OK, Winn. You've described what I mean by need or opportunity," and I pointed to the top of my piece of paper. "And now you're getting into what is going to be my second key word for this evening: *vision*." I wrote it down under "need," and everyone else did too.

I continued: "Now it may sound as if I'm playing games with words, but need and opportunity—when they're defined correctly—lead to this second word on the list: *vision*.

"Vision represents the moment when someone—maybe even the same person who first articulated the need—says, 'this is what we should do about the need.' Winn said that the need was for a baptistic and evangelistic church in our town. Then he said that a group got together for prayer. What happened next, Winn?"

"Somewhere along the way, the people in that prayer group said, 'We need to get that church started . . . right here.' I've read descriptions of those meetings written by people who were there. You would not believe how much they came to believe in the vision. They were convinced they were right in the center of God's will."

"There was a need," I said, "and then a vision—a church that was baptistic and evangelistic and planted right here in this community."

Ted interrupted: "You're suggesting that the people who started our church only got in motion when they felt gripped by *both* a sense of need and a vision. OK, but that's more than a hundred and fifty years ago. Why is it important today other than that it's a nice story?"

"I think it's important to periodically revisit both the original need and the corresponding vision to see if they still form the basis of the church's present existence. Is there still a faithfulness to the original dream, or has it been forgotten? And if forgotten, why? Remember the words in the book of Revelation? 'You've lost your first love!'"

"Of course it's possible that a church or an organization might conclude that the original need has been met and the vision has been realized. Then—close up shop! Get on with something else.

"I guess it's also possible that the need has morphed or changed into something new and different. That might mean a new or upgraded vision. Again, if the need has changed, then the vision has to change. And someone needs to say this in such a way that everyone understands it. *There is no longer the same need as once existed when this thing began."*

"So what's the next word on your list?" Ernie asked.

"After *need* and *vision*? How about the word *initiative*?" I asked. "Not a very electrifying word, but it's the best I can come up with. *Initiative* describes the first experimental efforts that make the vision real. After all the talk about a need for a church here in our town and all the praying and dreaming that formed the vision, there had to be a moment when someone said, 'Let's do it.'"

"Yep, and I've read about that moment too," Winn said. "The first official church meeting was a worship service, and it was held in a home about three blocks from here. The house has been rebuilt a couple of times since, but it still looks pretty much the same as it did back then."

"OK," I said, "let's review the process. A need generated a vision. The vision generated an initiative. Somebody did something. In this case it was as simple as gathering together for worship and seeing if things clicked." I wrote *initiative* on the third line of my sheet of paper. And everyone else, except John, did the same on theirs.

"I can almost guarantee two things about those early days. There was great excitement, and everyone—everyone!—was involved. There were no spectators.

"Now in the normal process of an organization's shelf life, the initiative is a tryout time, and everyone watches carefully. And if something doesn't work right, it's changed immediately. And that's really important to remember. Nothing except the vision is sacred at this point. No one ever says, 'But we've always done it this way.' If something doesn't work, it's changed.

"Furthermore, the group that's involved is usually pretty small, and everyone has a chance to be heard. And that's why the excitement—everyone feels a part of things.

"I'm sure that most of us here have had a chance to help start something. A club, a team, a ministry here at church. You could even include starting a marriage in this way. Remember the excitement of planning to get married?" Several heads nodded, but no one spoke.

"You're listening too hard," I said. "Talk to me."

"I guess I'm not used to all this analysis in church life," Russ said. "We used to do these things without a lot of thought . . . or so it seemed. Maybe I didn't know all the things leaders were discussing when I was young. But it's interesting. You realize, don't you, that you're describing the way I got our food business off the ground? The marketing people in our franchise chain helped us locate a place where there was a need for a fast-food store. There's your need thing. Then, I guess the vision thing came about when we agreed and began to imagine what the business could do and how big it could get. Then we reached the initiative point, as you call it, by building the store, recruiting and training a team, and opening the doors."

"Russ, you've described what's going on perfectly," I said. "Now let's say the initiative is a good one. Not perfect—but good. We tweak it, we do the best we can to perfect it, and we come to a point where we're convinced that we have something that works and works effectively and efficiently. So what do you think happens next? Anyone?"

Silence again.

Then, Russ: "In my world it means that you begin hiring more people, training them, staying open more hours, maybe even think of a second store."

"Terrific. That's what I'd call a *program*, Russ." And I wrote that down in a rather dramatic fashion so that everyone around the table would follow. *Program* represents that point where you have tested your key initiative and you know that you can do it over and over again with the same results.

"A Sunday school program is a great example. Anyone know how it got started?"

No one seemed to know.

"In the very last part of the eighteenth century, a man by the name of Robert Raikes became deeply concerned about the number of desperately poor children running the streets of the city of Gloucester. These were kids with no hope of education or character training. If they were neglected, they would become a danger to themselves and to the community. For Raikes that smelled like a *need*. His *vision* was to start a school that would meet on Sunday when the children were not pressed to be at work. The *initiative*—opening a single school—was so successful, that he and his people had almost two thousand kids involved within three or four years.

"When word about this got around England, people began to replicate Raikes's Sunday school in other cities. So the initiative became a *program*—something repeated over and over again in different places. It was phenomenally successful.

"Organizationally, a church is a bundle of such programs. Many of them are simply imports of ideas first tried in other churches."

"How long can programs last?" Lillian asked.

"Indefinitely, I suppose. *But only as long as they continue to meet the need and fulfill the vision.* If they stop doing that, they have to be modified or euthanized. Russ can tell you that in business this is done all the time. If a program or a process isn't profitable, it's cut immediately, ruthlessly. And if it isn't, the business heads for trouble. Finally it goes bankrupt. Russ has probably made these kinds of decisions any number of times."

"You betcha," Russ said. "I can tell you about different kinds of sandwiches and salads that we were sure would sell. And when they didn't, we cut them from the menu instantly. There was no hesitancy. You can't be sentimental about something that doesn't sell, even if it was your idea. And while you may be a bit more charitable in the way you handle things, you have to make similar decisions about employees who aren't doing what you hired them to do. That's the necessary part of business that isn't fun."

I acknowledged Russ and said, "Unfortunately, in the church, we have a more difficult time dealing truthfully with programs. We don't spend enough time asking, 'Why are we doing this?' and 'What is the intended outcome when we do that?' So we often keep programs going long after they have stopped being effective, just because we're comfortable with them and we're reluctant to try new things."

"I'm not sure I'm following you," Kenneth said. "Could you give me an example?"

"OK. Remember, I'm coming off the top of my head this evening, and I may get myself into trouble. I don't expect some of you to like what I'm about to say, but since you've asked, Kenneth, I think the traditional church choir is a good example of a program that may have outlived its time in many congregations." I'd said it. And I could feel an instant tension around the table. After all, I was talking to several long-term choir members.

But I was in too deep to stop now. "People are working and commuting longer hours during the week. Most parents now choose to stay home on school nights with their kids rather than go out. More and more people are drawn to small groups in the church. And, finally, in most churches the congregation does not want to be entertained; they want to sing.

"I should add that music tastes are changing and new generations are really not into choirs any longer. So what happens? The program called 'choir' runs out of energy. Or it remains populated by a small group of people who love it whether it gets results or not. Some of you probably don't want to hear it, but the choir is one example of a program that had a long shelf life but is now unprofitable."

"You're right," John said abruptly, "I don't like hearing that."

I got the immediate impression that John wasn't interested in the logic of what I was saying. He just didn't like what I was saying—period. I acknowledged what John had said and suggested that we agree to disagree. John couldn't even look at me.

"Let's go on," I said. "From *program* we move to *institution*." And I wrote "institution," on my list.

"An institution is essentially a bundle of programs that have worked reasonably well over a long period of time. But now things get complicated. The leaders devise strategies and policies to keep the programs going in the desired direction. They acquire space or build buildings where everything can happen. They recruit and manage staff—salaried and volunteer people who will do the work. Remember these three words—*strategy, space,* and *staff*—because they are at the core of what makes an institution. Your *strategy* is how you animate your vision and resource your programs. *Space* refers to where the vision and programs take place. And *staff* indicates the people who make everything happen. Every time you toggle one of those three things, the other two are somehow affected. In other words, a larger strategy means more space and more staff.

"Now if the institution works reasonably well, it can get larger and larger, more and more complex. And that's where problems begin to grow. If we're not careful, institutions breed a kind of politics and internal conflict. And if leaders are not alert, people become more interested in running the institution than in getting the results defined by the need and the vision. Institutions tend to take on a life of their own, and if you're talking about a church, it's not unusual to see something that appears to be very busy but does little to bring people to God and help them grow and serve in Christian ways."

Ernie asked, "A couple of weeks ago when you talked about the temple in Jesus' time, you were describing something that had become an institution, right?"

"Sure. Look at what happened to it over a period of time. It became less and less a holy place and more and more a moneymaking operation with a religious face on it. It became a political hotbed of intrigue and even violence. Remember Jesus' words? 'This was supposed to be a place of prayer [the need and the vision], but you've turned it into a den of thieves [the institutional outcome].' Several generations seemed to forget the original need and vision of a place where God was center of all things."

"And that happens to a lot of churches, doesn't it?" Arlene asked. "They become institutions?"

"If they are not careful, that's exactly what happens," I responded. "You end up serving the institution rather than it serving you. Someone likened an institution to a big factory where they deliver trainloads of resources at the door marked Receiving. Then you hear all the roaring noise of machinery from inside. But at the other end of the building where the finished product comes out, you see something the size of a peanut. And you ask, 'What in the world was going on in there? Why so little outcome after all those resources and all that noise?'

"So it's true. You can have a church with a million programs, none of which are doing anything but keeping people busy. Your energy gets bogged down in procedures and paperwork, in business and staff meetings, in rules and policies. More and more people are hired just to keep the institution running. But all that joy you had during the days when it was all about *initiative* oozes away."

"You think we're in the institutional phase at our church?" Stan asked.

I was quiet for a moment. I said, "Before I answer that, there's one more word on my list. Let's look at that first before we go to your question, Stan. The word is *tradition.*"

"Oh, oh," Yvonne said. "Welcome to New England."

"*Tradition* is a stage of shelf life where people do certain things over and over again but have no idea why. They've lost their memory of the original need and vision. You could say they've become addicted to institutional life and keep doing things over and over again without really asking why. And to stop doing those things would be like going through withdrawal. Church-wise, it's the moment when the insiders—the folks who have always been there—see themselves as more important than the people outside the church whom we were supposed to be reaching."

Finally, Arlene spoke: "Is that why last Sunday was such a downer? We were just going through the motions. We let some bad moments, empty seats, even a power outage control our moods and attitudes. We couldn't adapt to the conditions, and we were mad because we couldn't do the regular things."

We talked about that for a few minutes. I suggested that we stop and ask God to forgive us for our attitudes and loss of confidence. Yvonne volunteered to lead us, and she prayed a magnificent prayer.

"Is that the end of the list?" Stan asked when Yvonne finished.

"No," I said. "There's one more thing to add."

"And that is—" Stan said.

"Reinvention," I said as I wrote down this final word. I did not write it at the bottom of the list but between the words *program* and *institution.*

I held up my page and pointed to the placement of *reinvention.* "It's right about here that you go back to the drawing board and ask, 'Are we still confident that we know the needs and the vision that speaks to them?' Right here you push the reset, and start again—even if it's painful, disrupting, and a bit threatening."

Stan leaned forward across the table and studied the list. Everyone sensed he was going to say something, and so we waited. And then he spoke, "Do you realize what leaders are being asked to do if you're right?"

"What?" I asked.

"They're supposed to make a fresh start at just about the time that everything in the church is going right. Because right here," Stan pointed at the space between *program* and *institution,* "is the only place on the line where things are likely to be running smoothly. And you're saying that this is the time to take new risks and try new things."

"Yes, that's what I'm saying."

"Can that really be done?" Yvonne asked.

"I honestly don't know, Yvonne. I think each church has to determine whether or not it prefers traditions to the work that Jesus said we were supposed to do—"

"Which is?" John asked.

"To turn our eyes out the front door into the larger world and see who needs to be touched with the saving love of Christ. Our founders did that when they met together in that house a few blocks from here. And we have to ask ourselves if we're willing to pay to do the same thing now."

"But," John asked, "what do you think we should be doing that gets the same results they were going after?"

"What I have in mind is giving a new generation a chance to do what we did when we and other generations were young. Encourage them to figure out new ways to get back to reaching out into the city around us and showing people who Jesus is and what he wants to do in peoples' lives."

There was a reflective quietness. And then John broke the silence: "So this is your way of getting us to agree with everything the leadership wants to change. We're supposed to stop having church like we've had it for years and do it their way. And even help pay for it?"

"Yes," I said. "If those are the ways you want to describe it, then yes. That's what I'm hoping you'll do."

"I don't think so," John said.

Soon after, the meeting ended. I think I was glad that the meeting had happened. But I'm not sure.

From my pastoral notes:

> **Mary Ann Squires:** *Therapist. Grad, Boston Univ. Husband, Ted. No children. Very bright but says little. Reluctant about baptism.*

T onight I thought we'd have a little fun discussing church music," I said, when the Discovery Group met a week later. My opening comment was met with a concerted groan, and someone said, "Get your helmets on!" Here we were, thirty seconds into the evening, and we were already acknowledging that we were wading into what some think is arguably the most volatile issue in the church today.

Russ and John were no-shows. I knew where Russ was (a town zoning board meeting), but the fact that John was missing at the beginning unsettled me.

This would be a good time to admit that John's increasingly surly attitude at Discovery Group meetings was troubling. During the last three years, he and I had built what I thought was a good friendship. We'd done a lot of other things together, and they were not just church things. John was always the first person I called when something at our house needed fixing. We'd also hiked and kayaked together. And there had been the time when John drove with me to New York City to see one of our church members who was undergoing special treatment at the Sloan-Kettering Cancer Center. We included a New York Rangers hockey game in that trip.

But now something wasn't feeling right, and I sensed that John was distancing himself from me. I've seen this happen between Christian friends before. There are certain disagreements—about theology, politics, or church policy, for example—that can deep-freeze what you considered to be a durable friendship—and do it almost overnight. Someone needs to ask what it is about a doctrinally defined movement that makes it so easy for some people to dissolve personal relationships without warning or explanation.

John did arrive twenty minutes after we began. He offered no explanation or apology for his tardiness, and he sat through most of the evening without saying a word. During refreshments, he went off by himself and talked on his cell phone. And later, when I thought about his behavior, I realized that he never made eye contact with me.

But back to the evening.

It started with a prayer from Stan. He began the minute I nodded in his direction.

"O Lord, make us a united people, Lord. Particularly tonight if we're going to talk about music. You know my own heart about this subject, Lord. We believe that you are coming soon to take us to heaven. And, Lord, we search the Scriptures to understand when it will happen. We pray that you will come quickly, Lord! Tonight, help this meeting to be a good one. Lord, we only want what your will is. We don't want to get in the way of your plans for the church . . . so help us. In Jesus' name. Amen."

Stan's prayer reflected at least three things. First, Stan loves to use the word *Lord* as he prays. It's kind of a "spacer," I think, so that he has an extra millisecond to think of what he's going to say next. But second, you see in his prayer Stan's interest in the so-called "last days" when Jesus is supposed to come back to earth. More than once he'd told me that he wished there would be more preaching on prophecy. For Stan prophecy meant sermons from Revelation or Daniel and how they identify events that will precede Jesus' return to earth.

And the third thing about his prayer was the reference to his own feelings about music in our church. "You know my own heart," he'd prayed. I could only interpret that comment as his way of saying, "I think music in our church stinks."

Stan's prayer finished, I prepared to introduce the subject of music. I'd thought a lot about how I wanted to go about this, and there was so much I wanted to say. Fresh in my mind was a caution Gail had given me as I'd left the house—to guard my tongue and not say anything I'd later regret.

In my own childhood music had been the great unifying element of church life. I can remember our Sunday school "opening exercises," when everyone from one to ninety-nine years old met in the assembly room and sang Christian songs with gusto. Each Sunday we sang for visitors, "There's a welcome here—there's a Christian welcome here." Then we sang to everyone who had celebrated birthdays during the past week: "Happy birthday to you / only one will not do / born-again means salvation / how many have you?"

There followed a bevy of short little songs called choruses—"Climb, climb up sunshine mountain" (with hand motions, of course), "Rolled away, rolled away . . . every burden of my heart rolled away." Of course, there were always one or two hymns from the hymnbook that helped us to learn how to read the notes of the musical scale and sing harmonies—soprano, alto, tenor, and bass. After the music time we all scattered to our Sunday school classes led by faithful teachers who stayed with their classes for the entire year.

Somewhere along the line, perhaps as churches grew bigger, those inter-generational gatherings were scuttled. Churches abandoned their family culture and became "malls" of age-specific programs where the generations began to lose contact with each other. At least one side effect was that we all began to sing different styles of music.

Today music no longer seems to unify the generations the way it once did; now it seems to have the opposite effect—to divide us. And that has given rise to what are sometimes euphemistically called the "worship wars." *The worship wars!* What a fascinating term to contemplate.

I don't think I fully appreciated the power of music to unite or divide until, a few years ago, Gail and I took a driving vacation through Nova Scotia. After Stan's prayer I began the Discovery Group meeting with that story.

I recounted how Gail and I had taken the overnight boat from Portland, Maine, to the southern tip of Nova Scotia and had driven to Halifax. While there we found a huge store that sold used CDs and tapes (even eight-track tapes). Wandering the aisles, we found a section dedicated to the music of our teen years. Prominent among the artists were names like Doris Day, Perry Como, and Rosemary Clooney. And then we found Frank Sinatra and Nat King Cole, and we purchased four CDs of their greatest hits.

For the next three days, we drove the perimeter of Nova Scotia and Cape Breton Island playing those CDs over and over again. Sinatra and Cole had been on the top-ten charts throughout our youth, and now in our sixties, their songs came back to us with a rush. We were amazed how they aroused intensely emotional memories of our earlier years. Between the two of us, we could recall the words of every song.

But it was not just the songs themselves that came back to life. It was the long-forgotten stories that each song revived—of romances, sadnesses, and adventures. We filled those vacation hours disclosing parts of our earlier lives to each other—stories that had never been shared before. Some of our stories caused laughter; some, tears.

It would be no exaggeration to say that the recollections and the storytelling prompted by listening to those old CDs made that Nova Scotia vacation one of the best of our lives. And it all happened through the power of music.

Music has a way of going to the core of our souls, far below the rational level of consciousness. The rhythm, harmony, and melodic pathway seem to connect with a part of us that is so deep that we are helpless to describe or measure what is happening to us. As Gail and I learned in Nova Scotia, a piece of music can summon tears of sadness or feelings of incredible joy and well-being.

Every culture (perhaps each generation) appears to have developed its own unique musical forms and expressions—the bundling together of sounds and their harmonic combinations that create a sensation of beauty or nostalgia or vision. To those sounds we often add words. And once the melody and the words are laced together and sung, we are likely never to forget them or the circumstances in which we learned them.

In ancient times people used music to support their oral history. It was in music that they "rapped" their way through the stories of battles and tragedies, of victories and celebrations. They rehearsed their family genealogies in song. Then there were the songs that centered on the mysteries of God and his great acts. So what has changed?

We use music to reflect on our aspirations to love and be loved. We sing songs of protest or lament. There are patriotic songs, school and campfire songs, and ethnic songs that can evoke great emotion in us.

As a boy I loved Rossini's "William Tell Overture" because, three times a week on the radio, it was used to introduce the stories of my fictional hero, the

Lone Ranger, of whom it was said: "Nowhere in the pages of yesteryear can one find a greater champion of justice!"

"There is Broadway music, jazz, country and western, and rock 'n' roll. In more recent days those of us in my age bracket have struggled to accustom ourselves to hip-hop, heavy metal, and . . . well, I've run out of categories."

As I named each of these categories, various people in the group chimed in with their favorite songs and memories about singing groups and bands. As the minutes flew by, we all enjoyed a trip down memory lane. Now and then someone would break into a familiar piece of music, and we would join in until we were laughing too hard or we simply forgot the next lines. The only person at the table who seemed detached from this (you guessed it!) was John.

As the evening progressed, I kept thinking about a program on Public Television in which recording artists of the 1950s had presented a concert of their old hits. When the camera swept across the audience, people my age were crying, swaying to the beat, and mouthing the words in perfect synchrony with the artists. And in a sense, I guess, we were reliving some of those same memories around the table in the Commons.

When everyone who wanted to had offered his or her favorite musical memory, I picked up my presentation again.

"A few years ago I gave some talks at a men's conference," I said. "Instead of the typical religious music usually sung at such conferences, the band led us in singing Beatles songs. I was astonished when I realized that the hundreds of men knew every word to every song and, with no inhibitions, sang loudly and enthusiastically. I thought about the fact that many of these same men barely move their lips in most Sunday church services. What was the message in this?

"Perhaps there are experts or scholars," I said to the group, "who can tell us why certain melodies and words become indelibly engraved in our hearts and can be recalled instantly, even if we have not heard or sung them for fifty years. All I know is that they are there and can usually be retrieved in unexpected moments.

"Of course there is the enormous body of Christian music, both ancient and modern, which begins with the songs of the Old Testament, often called the Psalms. There were the chants of the Middle Ages, the great prayer and worship hymns of the last several hundred years, the gospel songs of the nineteenth century, and the highly diverse kinds of contemporary songs that have risen up in the last thirty years or so."

All of this talk about music filled the first ninety minutes of our evening.

After we took a break for some refreshments, I took the group back to Bible times. We looked at some Old Testament stories where people sang. What did it sound like when Moses and his sister led the Israelites in songs of thanksgiving after they had walked through the Red Sea? Then we wondered what it would have been like to hear Jesus and his disciples sing a hymn before they went from the Last Supper to the Garden of Gethsemane.

The group read the story in Acts 16 where Paul and Silas were arrested in Philippi and beaten and imprisoned.

When we finished the reading, I said: "So here they were—bruised and battered, probably unfed. No one, certainly not their families, knew where they were, and there was no indication of what would happen to them the next day. And in this predicament what did they do?"

"Sang duets," Winn said.

"Apparently. And the text says they sang late into the night while the prisoners listened. Why would they do that?"

Connie said, "I bet they found courage and assurance in singing. I know I do. I imagine that it helped them to cope with their situation."

"Maybe singing got their minds off the ugliness of the moment and on to something good," Ken said.

That reminded me, I said, of the familiar words that Julie Andrews sang to the frightened children of the king of Siam: "Whenever I feel afraid, I whistle a happy tune." She was simply teaching what Paul and Silas did, and what many of us do when we are troubled or feel alone or rudderless. It is the genius of many songs that their melodies and words return us to the center of hope and bravery.

Arlene asked, "Don't you suppose that they were singing to remind themselves that God is present even in prison?"

Others offered their perceptions of why Paul and Silas sang, and when they were finished, I said, "Let's talk about why we sing as Christians."

Again, someone repeated the words spoken earlier: "Get your helmets on."

"Let me tell you some of the things I hear from you when the subject of music comes up." And I read from a list I'd written out that afternoon:

- There's no choir; you're missing that, and some of you miss singing in it.

- We sing too few familiar hymns—at least what are considered to be hymns. No one sings in harmony anymore.

- When we sing, it's too loud; when the volume is turned up, our ears hurt, especially those with hearing aids.

- We repeat too many last lines over and over again.

- Some think that few of the new songs contain any "doctrine" or truth.

- Some of us literally feel physical pain from standing too long.

- Many folks are not into clapping.

The group seemed surprised that I'd written all of this down. And I think they were a bit embarrassed because so much of it sounded like nothing more than complaining. It was possible that they'd never heard their objections stacked up together in one place.

"So let's talk about this," I said, "and see if we can understand what's behind all of these comments. It may take us a meeting or two." In truth, I had no idea just how long it was going to take.

"Anyone know anything about Isaac Watts?" I asked.

Yvonne spoke: "Wasn't he a hymn writer? I think he wrote 'When I Survey the Wondrous Cross.'"

"Yep, he did. Know any of his other songs?"

"I think he wrote one of the Christmas carols," Ted, probably the most outspoken advocate of old hymns, said.

"Not sure which one?" I began humming the first line of "Joy to the World."

"Yes, 'Joy to the World.' Almost said 'Silent Night.'"

"'Silent Night' is German," I said. "Watts was English. So does anyone know anything more about him? Know when he lived?"

No one knew.

"Well, he was born in 1674; his father was a pastor. One day, the biographers say, he was walking home from church with his father, and he started complaining about the music they'd sung that morning. Sound familiar? He was bored, he told his father, with the *psalmody* that marked every worship service.

"*Psalmody* refers to the singing of the psalms. Christian people had been singing the psalms for centuries in one form or another. And John Calvin had insisted that the psalms be the exclusive hymnody of the church. If there was good news to this, it was that the highest biblical thoughts of worship were being sung regularly. But it also meant that no one ever sang anything that raised praise to Jesus.

"When people sang the psalms, they sang in a more-or-less monotone form with no instrumental accompaniment, because instruments in a church were considered worldly. So in Watts's time a man called the church clerk, or *precentor*, simply sang out a note and everyone began to sing. What I've read suggests that the noise was awful.

"So here was Isaac Watts complaining about church music to his father. And the old man must have been very wise, because rather than arguing with his son, he listened. I think you have to give him a lot of credit for not being defensive when others might have just told the young man to keep his opinions to himself and accept the status quo.

"Isaac's father's reaction may be the most important thing we think about this evening." That got everyone's attention.

"In fact," I said, "I think the way Isaac's father responded to his son is one of the most significant things that happened in the Christian movement in that entire century. And I really wish you'd think about this very carefully. What we have in this little story is an example of the way an older generation needs to respond to the younger when it's time for a change.

"Here was Isaac complaining about the music, and his father said—" I hesitated for a second to build the suspense. And then I continued, "His father asked, 'Son, why don't you mend the matter?' Meaning—write some music of your own.

"And Isaac did just that. I have no idea how many songs he wrote. Lots! I do know that if you scan a hymnbook, you'll see that Isaac Watts became one of our most prolific Christian hymn writers. There's probably a dozen or more of his hymns that have stood the test of time for three hundred years."

Ted said, "Shame we're not singing them any longer; these new ones they're singing—"

"Ted,"—I made a time-out sign with my hands—"we need to be very careful here. If Isaac's father had said what you just started to say, we might not have any Isaac Watts hymns at all. Isaac might have taken his artistic gifts out of the church and offered them to another kind of audience. Allow me to speculate. I am going to guess that, if Isaac Watts were alive today, he'd be among the very first to say, 'My songs have had a good long shelf life, but now it's time for some new writers and new music.' I don't think he'd see things the way some of us see them.'"

"I don't believe that," Ted said. "Those hymns are forever."

"Ted, Watts's hymns and many of the others are great pieces of music. We were raised with them. But they do indeed have a statute of limitations. You cannot force them down the throats of younger generations of people who are embracing totally different forms of music."

I could tell that I'd irritated Ted with my comment, and I could sense that others in the group were a bit restive. But I pushed ahead.

"It wasn't long before Isaac Watts's songs were brought across the Atlantic to New England. Let's say they got here around 1740 or so. They arrived just as one of America's greatest preachers, Jonathan Edwards, of Northhampton, Massachusetts, was in the middle of leading a spiritual revival that was spreading all across the Northeast. And Isaac Watts's music caught on as part of the spirit of the revival. People began to sing Watts's songs. Here are some of the titles: 'O God, Our Help in Ages Past,' 'When I Survey the Wondrous Cross,' 'Jesus Shall Reign,' and 'I Sing the Mighty Power of God.'"

"I sang every one of those songs when I was a child," Ernie whispered. "We sang them all the time. When my voice changed, I switched from singing alto to singing bass. I probably could sing most of them by heart right now . . . first verses anyway."

Others began to comment.

"'When I Survey' was Teresa's favorite hymn," Clayton said. "It was sung at her funeral."

GORDON MACDONALD

Winn spoke up. "I didn't know he wrote 'Joy to the World.' There's no greater Christmas carol than that one. I have an incredible video with the Mormon Tabernacle Choir and their orchestra, and that's their opening song. Every time we put it on, I have to stand up and sing along. It's spectacular! If no one's around, I pretend that I'm the conductor . . . but don't ever tell anyone I said that."

I worked hard to suppress a smile as I visualized Winn waving his arms in front of the TV screen.

Yvonne, also widowed, asked me, "Did you say he wrote 'Jesus Shall Reign'? Paul and I met at the Urbana Missionary Conference and we always remembered how the students—thousands of them—sang that song: 'Jesus shall reign where'er the sun / Does his successive journeys run / His kingdom spread from shore to shore / Till moons shall wax and wane no more.' We always thought of that hymn as ours, and every time we sang it, we thought of Urbana and our first days together."

There was a brief silence, and then Mary Ann asked, "May I say something?" Her face was wet with tears. When she opened her mouth again, no words came, and she broke down and began to sob. Kenneth put his arm around her and pulled her close. We froze. The men, of course, were immediately uncomfortable and didn't know whether to look at Mary Ann or look away. The women seemed not to be bothered at all. They understood to wait quietly until Mary Ann was ready to speak. Arlene reached for her purse, found some tissues, and passed them to Mary Ann.

Finally Mary Ann regained her composure and started again: "I'm sorry—"
Everyone assured her it was OK.

"Kenneth and I have never been able to have children. Years before we came to this church, I had two pregnancies. Each ended in a miscarriage after about three months. The doctors told us that I had a physical condition that probably would prevent me from ever carrying a child to full term. So we tried the adoption route, and, well, that's a story for another time maybe."

No one in the group was moving now. As Mary Ann spoke we were aware that Kenneth—ordinarily quiet, composed Kenneth—was on the verge of tears himself. And some of us were not far behind.

She continued: "Kenneth and I were crushed. We both wanted a baby . . . so badly. We weren't sure how to deal with this. And the people around us had almost

98

nothing to offer except platitudes and things like 'You just have to accept this as God's will. He'll have something better for you.' But we didn't want something better. We wanted a child! And then one night we were in church, and the congregation began to sing the words to the hymn 'O God Our Help.' Somehow those words hit both of us in a way that we'll never be able to explain. 'O God, our help in ages past / Our hope for years to come / Our shelter from the stormy blast / And our eternal home.'"

Now tissues were coming out of several purses as Mary Ann went on to another verse. "Under the shadow of Thy throne / Thy saints have dwelt secure / Sufficient is Thine arm alone / And our defense is sure."

Then she said, "You will never . . . ever . . . know what that hymn came to mean to us. When you said, Yvonne, that you and Paul had your favorite hymn, I realized that's what Kenneth and I have. And ours is an Isaac Watts hymn too."

Something like a holy moment was beginning to form among us. I'd not anticipated anything like this when the evening began.

"Every time," Mary Ann continued, "Kenneth or I feel our hearts breaking all over again, we return to this hymn. We hum the melody, or if no one is listening"—she smiled through her tears here—"we sing it. We know all the verses . . . don't we honey?" Kenneth nodded. "So, Gordon, when I hear you tell the story of Isaac Watts getting encouragement from his father to write these songs, I ask myself, *What if his father had said something different, something discouraging, and Isaac had never written that hymn?* If he wrote that song for no one else, he wrote it for Kenneth and me."

Mary Ann had spoken very little during the weeks that our Discovery Group had been meeting. In fact, I'd wondered from time to time if she was glad to be there. I'd wondered if Kenneth was dragging her to our gatherings. I'd had almost no indication that the meetings were a useful experience for her. But now this remarkable moment of self-disclosure made me realize that she was in deep with us.

Our Discovery Group was never the same after Mary Ann's moment of vulnerability. She led the way in our growing ability to speak honestly about the subject of music and what our true feelings were.

"Mary Ann . . . Kenneth," Ted said. "You may or may not know that Nancy and I lost a daughter to leukemia . . . changed our lives. It's been eight years now, but we've never . . . never stopped grieving. When we're at our lowest, Nancy goes to the piano and begins to play 'He Giveth More Grace.' And we're like you. If no one's listening, we start singing, 'He giveth more grace when the burden grows greater / He sendeth more strength when the labors increase.'" Now Ted was the one with tears and the struggle to speak. Finally, he finished the words of the song: "'To added affliction He addeth His mercy / To multiplied trials, His multiplied peace.'

"Now that's a more modern song, I believe," Ted said when he'd dried his eyes with a tissue offered by Arlene. "But I, too, know what a hymn can do for you in your worst moments."

I'd never heard Ted tell that story, and I'd never appreciated this deep bubble of grief that lay in his and Nancy's heart. But where in the life of our church would there have been an occasion for him to tell such a personal story? And would he ever have told it if it hadn't been for Mary Ann's transparency?

It became difficult to want to move forward. I had a lot of things I wanted to say before the meeting ended, but it seemed as if God had mysteriously taken the agenda out of my hands. Here we were talking about music. We weren't even singing the songs, just talking about them. But something, something *precious—priceless* maybe—had happened to us. We were not a group any longer; we were becoming more like a family. There was some deeper connecting going on, and that couldn't be ignored.

I couldn't begin to recount for you everything that was said in the following thirty or forty minutes after Mary Ann and Ted opened their hearts to us. But there were several others who told us of hymns and gospel songs that had played a significant role in their lives. I wish I had a recording of the things said. I'd play it for young people who much too often sweep aside the older Christian music with a cavalier wave of the hand. They do not have an understanding of the deep musical furrows plowed into the souls of the older generations of Christians who have loved or been rescued by these old melodies and poems.

Finally, I interrupted the conversation and said, "You know it's really late, we need to end this and pick it all back up again next week. I'd like to pray, but before I do, I have one final Isaac Watts story.

"When Isaac's music began to spread around New England, many so-called Christians utterly rejected it. In fact, there were churches that split down the middle over Isaac Watts hymns. There have been four times in American church life when people split over music and forms of worship. This was the first of the four."

"There were people dividing over Isaac Watts hymns?" Lillian exclaimed. "I can't imagine anyone—"

"Lillian, we are not the first generation to struggle over music in the church. There was a lot of bitterness back then, just like there's some bitterness now. In those days more than a few people simply would not sing any Watts songs. They stood silently, or they walked out of church. Knowing that, you can appreciate the lines of one of his hymns, 'We're Marching to Zion.' Recognize it?"

Lillian began to hum the first line, and a couple of others began to sing the words: "Beautiful, beautiful Zion / We're marching upward to Zion—"

Then I pressed ahead. "Remember I said that a lot of people hated the new music, and they weren't afraid to show their hostility by not singing. Now listen to the words of the second verse: *'Let those refuse to sing / Who never knew our God* / But children of the heavenly King / But children of the heavenly King / May speak their joys abroad / May speak their joys abroad.'

"I think Watts was slipping a sucker punch into his song. He was saying if you won't sing these words of praise, you may not be a child of the King." I ended the story right there.

Then I began to pray. "Lord," I said, "this evening has been amazing. None of us had any idea that we would say some of these things when we came tonight. But some of us have felt free to trust the group with our feelings and the deep hurt inside of us. Thank you for giving strength in particular to Mary Ann and Kenneth. Thank you that they're a part of our fellowship. And thank you for Ted. Now I know why music is so important to him. Thank you for Isaac Watts and for whoever wrote 'He Giveth More Grace.' Thanks that those words and those melodies have endured so that they could touch us today. And thank you, finally, for Isaac Watts's father. Maybe you could use some of us to do the same thing for young musicians and artists today who are trying to honor Jesus with their gifts. Amen."

It was difficult for people to get up from the table. Perhaps the time had been so highly charged that no one wanted to break the spell. But when we did move, several people went toward Kenneth and Mary Ann and offered warm embraces.

A couple of the women could do nothing but simply weep. The men were awkward at this, of course, but they got their message of admiration through to Kenneth.

John was the first person out the door that night. I watched him go. He slipped away without a word to anyone. It seemed to me that he was the only one of us who was out of alignment with what had happened in the last hour. Perhaps I should have followed him and asked him what he was thinking. But I suppose the truth is that I really didn't want to know. Deep in my heart a suspicion lingered that an encounter with John at that moment would spoil my mood. So I reasoned that staying and helping with the cleanup was the more important thing. Then I headed home, eager to tell Gail about everything that had happened.

> *Ted Patton:* *Married to Nancy. Accountant. Undergrad degree in business. Converted in his late 20s when daughter died of leukemia. Loves Bill Gaither's music. But also is into Mozart, C. S. Lewis, Geo. MacDonald, and Chesterton. Distinguished Eagle Scout. Hyper about sticking to church bylaws.*

A rlene called this afternoon," Gail said when I met her for dinner two nights later. "The Discovery Group wants to know if it would be OK if everyone came an hour early next week and ate dinner together. They already have a plan as to who will bring what. They just want your OK. She was very excited about it . . . wanted to know if I could come."

Arlene's call to Gail stayed on my mind through the evening. *They actually want to eat together,* I thought. What a contrast to the collection of somewhat irritable people who'd gathered weeks ago at my invitation and had come on that stormy Sunday night to express their disappointment in the way I was leading their church. These had been the people who, at an earlier business meeting, had voted no to an initiative that would have upgraded our sanctuary. Their signal had been clear: *we've had enough!*

But now they wanted to eat with Gail and me. What was happening?

For one thing the group was taking on a life of its own. You could see caring, curiosity, mutual respect, leadership, even fun growing among them. And, best of all, what we were doing wasn't really a program. It was just a very natural joining of people who were discovering that they shared similar stories and questions. And another thing: they were beginning—just beginning—to see the possibility that there might be other ways to do church and that they needed to open their minds just a bit.

When the next Tuesday night rolled around, everyone was there. The group welcomed Gail as the honored guest, and I was delighted that she got to see how the group had jelled. The word that came to me again as I watched both men and women scurrying about getting all the food set out was *family.* And this after only a few weeks. Could this kind of camaraderie last?

Arlene's gift of organizing people was obvious from beginning to end. She had Russ provide all the eating paraphernalia from his fast-food restaurant. That meant no dish washing. She'd assigned others to bring salads, meat dishes, and bread. And Kenneth and Mary Ann had been detailed to bring a decadent dessert.

An hour later the table was cleared and wiped off, and Bibles and notebooks were in place for the evening's discussion to begin. Since we'd already prayed at the beginning of dinner, we launched right into conversation.

"What are the most significant recollections you have of last week's meeting?" I asked. There was the usual moment or two of silence, and I broke it by saying, "Connie, I know you're bursting to say something."

"Isaac Watts's father's encouragement to his son," she said.

Ted picked it up from there: "Let those refuse to sing . . . I love to sing so much, and I can't imagine anyone rejecting one of those songs. But then I think I love everything musical."

There was one of those collective "umms" around the table as various people signaled their understanding of what Ted had said.

"I'm still hearing what Mary Ann said last week," Stan offered. "I'd never known the two of you," Stan turned to look down the table to where the Squireses sat, "until we started these meetings. And even then, you were really, well . . . strangers . . . until you told your story, Mary Ann. I just have to thank you." Both Mary Ann and Kenneth nodded in response.

Clayton spoke up: "I'm like Ted. I still can't believe that there were people who refused to sing. I mean, how could anyone find something wrong with 'When I Survey the Wondrous Cross'? Here we are begging to sing this song at least once a year, and you tell us that there were people who wouldn't have anything to do with it."

"Clayton," I said, "there were people, lots of people, back then who not only refused to sing but who wouldn't dream of having an organ in their churches. And there are still people who feel strongly about any kind of an instrument in the sanctuary. If the New Testament didn't mention instruments, they reason, then there's no place for them. Here's this irony again: the thing that probably is the most powerful unifying element among people can be the most powerful divider. Anyone else with thoughts about last week?"

Arlene spoke: "I thought the things we heard people say about various hymns and what they had meant to them pointed out exactly what you said in the beginning. That there's something about music that is very deep within us. You talked about songs back in the fifties and how that brought back so many memories for the two of you. Then those men singing Beatles songs from the sixties. Now our grandchildren are interested in totally different kinds of music. I don't understand it; I don't even like it. Seems devilish to me."

Arlene's words gave me the launching pad for the things I wanted to cover during the evening.

"Here's the most important thing I'd like for us to consider tonight. Virtually every generation produces some kind of music that reflects its own view of reality. Both the notes and the words of their music will tell you how they see life and what's most important to them. And this is true in the Christian movement.

"Go back five hundred years to Martin Luther. Here's a man who, in his time, was really out on the edge. You could say that there was a contract out on his life because of the things he was saying in his critiques of the Roman Catholic Church. So every day was a day filled with fear . . . unless he could gain a sense of serenity from God's assurances. One day he opened his Bible and read from Psalm 46: 'God is our refuge and strength, an ever-present help in trouble. . . . Therefore we will not fear.' He went on to read that even if the whole world were to disintegrate, he shouldn't be numbed by fear.

"Then, based on Psalm 46, he wrote the words to the hymn 'A Mighty Fortress Is Our God.' He put his words to a simple melody. One legend says that he and his friends sang it on their way to the city of Worms in 1521 where Luther was to defend himself against charges that he was a heretic.

> *A mighty fortress is our God,*
> *A bulwark never failing;*
> *Our helper He, amid the flood*
> *Of mortal ills prevailing.*

"A bulwark is a shield or a protective wall. And he found such a protection in an unfailing God. And when he wrote, he didn't have one problem in mind but a 'flood' of ills that seemed overwhelming.

"When you think of the enormous force of institutional religion that was stacked against him, you can appreciate what it meant to sing, 'And tho this world, with devils filled / Should threaten to undo us'—listen to these words—'*We will not fear,* for God hath willed / His truth to triumph through us.' I mean, you read those verses and you imagine what he was going through and how much courage he needed. And this song points to the strength Luther needed to keep going.

"Now that's something we need to keep remembering. There is music created by the great artists—Bach comes to mind—to be sung and played by other exceptional artists, and that's magnificent stuff. But then there is a genre of music—we often call it popular music—that comes right out of a life of suffering. And that's what strikes me about Luther's 'Mighty Fortress.' It's written in the heat of spiritual battle.

"The other day Gail gave me this quote from a book about the writing of hymns. Here's Martin Luther on the subject of music:

> Music is a gift and grace of God, not an invention of men. Thus, it drives out the devil and makes people cheerful. Then one forgets all wrath, impurity, and other devices. . . . The Devil, the originator of sorrowful anxieties and restless troubles, flees before the sound of music almost as much as before the Word of God. . . . I wish to compose sacred hymns so that the Word of God may dwell among the people also by means of songs. . . . I would allow no man to preach or teach God's people without a proper knowledge of the use and power of sacred song.[1]

"Now, if Luther's right—and I think he is—you can see that Christian music is going to throw light on everything we are and believe. It's going to tell you exactly what people are going through at the moment, what questions they're asking, what fears they have, what hopes they derive from walking with God.

"And when you listen to the music of the younger generation today, don't forget that a lot of it comes out of their perceptions of contemporary struggles. Many of them feel fatherless; they feel overwhelmed by the moral and spiritual challenges of the times. They feel impotent. And their songs often reflect these themes. They haven't grown up in the relative stability of the times we have all experienced.

"Last week we talked about the revolution in music that came during Isaac Watts's time. And it took a couple of decades for his kind of music—which was more popular—to gain acceptance in most churches. And you have to ask your-selves—I'm going to remind you of this several times—*Would you have embraced Watts's music when you first heard it, or would you have resisted it?*"

There was a bit of speculative conversation about this. Some in the group were frank to admit that they probably would have been among those opposing it. Others were sure they would have instantly loved it.

Minutes later I continued: "Not long after Isaac Watts, came the hymns of Charles Wesley, John Wesley's brother. What he wrote came in the latter half of the 1700s. His hymns were not unlike those of Watts. They generally followed great theological themes. I jotted some of his titles down before I came tonight. You'll recognize most of them. 'O For a Thousand Tongues to Sing,' 'Love Divine, All Loves Excelling,' and 'Jesus, Lover of My Soul.' Did you know that he also wrote Christmas music? 'Hark the Herald Angels Sing.' And Easter music? 'Christ the Lord Is Risen Today.' "

As I read these titles, I tried to sing some of the first lines. And each time most of the group would immediately join in. We'd sing a line or two and then, one by one, drop out as our memories of successive lines began to fade. But there was no question about it—we all knew and loved these songs.

"Charles Wesley's greatest hymn, in my opinion, was

> *And can it be that I should gain*
> *An interest in the Savior's blood?*
> *Died He for me, who caused His pain?*
> *For me who Him to death pursued?*
> *Amazing love! How can it be*
> *That Thou, my God, shouldst die for me?*

"And Charles continued writing: 'Long my imprisoned spirit lay / Fast bound in sin and nature's night.' He goes on to tell his own story:

I woke—the dungeon flamed with light!
My chains fell off, my heart was free,
I rose, went forth, and followed Thee.

. . . and concluded,

No condemnation now I dread:
Jesus, and all in Him is mine!
Alive in Him, my living Head,
And clothed in righteousness divine.
Bold I approach th'eternal throne,
And claim the crown through Christ my own.

"He ended each verse with the exclamation: 'Amazing love! How can it be / That Thou, my God, shouldst die for me?'"

"These were the themes that Charles's brother, John, was preaching in the streets of English cities. Great themes of personal salvation to people who had never heard them in a lifetime in most churches. Seeing prisoners in chains was a regular occurrence in those days. People were well aware of dungeons. This poetry is somewhat imaginative to us, but to people in Wesley's day, it was real. They'd seen these sights.

"And about the same time, along came John Newton, the converted slave trader, and he gave us 'Amazing grace, how sweet the sound / That saved a wretch like me.' Newton was well acquainted with the evils of slavery, and he wrote the song with that in mind. He had been a wretch of a man, and he knew it. That's why grace to him was so amazing.

"All these hymns reflect a magnificent, saving God and, at the same time, pictures of real life as people were experiencing it right then and there. Some of the melodies were borrowed off the street as music familiar to that generation. Here and there melodies were specifically written to fit the poem, but even those tunes matched the music of the common people of that time."

"So is what you're saying," Connie asked, "that when everyone heard 'Amazing Grace,' they were able to sing it because they already knew the music?"

"Exactly. The original melody was either an Irish or Scottish folk tune and is often associated with the playing of bagpipes." Aware that time was moving fast, I continued.

"Remember last week when I said there were four times in American church life when people went to war over music? Let me take you to the second of those.

"It came about during the time of the Civil War (and immediately after) here in America. It's hard to give it a specific date, but we're talking about a time that was a century or so after Watts and Wesley and Newton. One year does stand out—1859. The country went through a devastating economic downturn, really a depression of sorts, and countless people were roaming the streets of cities in desperate poverty. Churches began opening their doors for people to come in and pray. And there was an enormous spiritual revival in America and England. They call that period of time the 'Open Door Revival.'

"With the revival came an eruption of a new kind of music. This time it was music that was, in terms of subject matter, more personal, more testimonial, more about one's personal experience with Christ. There was a greater and greater emphasis upon the individual and his or her connection with God. Jesus is more of a friend than anything in this new kind of music. If the music has a fault, it's that it tempts you to get too chummy with Jesus. And I'm not sure we really want to presume on Jesus that way.

"But those were the days when the songs of people like Fanny Crosby emerged. Fanny Crosby's music reflected the individual conversion experience that happens when people come to Jesus. This was a time when people were more and more conscious of making what we call 'personal decisions for Christ.'

"Fanny Crosby was just one of many, many people who wrote gospel songs during this time. But she may have been the most prolific. It's been estimated that she wrote about eight thousand different pieces of music under at least two hundred pen names. Look in the hymnbook and see if anyone has written more songs than Fanny."

"What's a hymnbook?" Ted asked with a broad grin. He was reflecting the angst some people feel, because in our church we no longer use the hymnbook.

Ted's comment took us off track for a moment while people talked about missing hymnbooks. One of the women said she could probably name fifty songs in the old church hymnal and even tell you the page numbers. It was clear that everyone felt nostalgic about hymnbooks, although Winn admitted that the words on the screens were easier to see and that you could look up while you sang. But Ted countered with the regret that without a hymnbook we had forfeited the ability to sing all four parts to a song. All we had now were words but no notes.

And Yvonne said, "Well, you can't sing parts to the new stuff anyway. Try doing it . . . you can't. The people with the instruments make the harmony. All we sing is the melody." And then with obvious regret in her voice, she said, "I really do miss the days when we used to sing all four parts without the instruments. We could be a great choir."

"OK," I said. "Back to Fanny Crosby. She was blind, you know. And it's interesting to see how many times she referred to sightedness as her great anticipation when she got to heaven. 'And I shall *see* him face to face,' she wrote in one of her hymns."

"Didn't she write 'Blessed Assurance'?" Mary Ann asked.

"Yes, it's probably her best-known hymn. And it reflects her most important theme: *Jesus is mine*. See the emphasis on relationship to Jesus? 'This is *my* story / This is *my* song.' Wesley tended to write about his relationship to God, but Crosby talked more about her walk with Jesus. 'Tell Me the Stories of Jesus,' or 'Pass Me Not, O Gentle Savior,' 'Near the Cross I'll Watch and Wait.' Many of these songs were written at the request of Ira Sankey and D. L. Moody who were holding enormous evangelistic campaigns and wanted songs that would call people to Christ. 'Rescue the Perishing' would be a good example.

"Once again, this is my point. The music—both melody and content—reflected what was going on at the time. There was a growing emphasis on calling people to a personal conversion to Jesus, and many of these songs written in this second wave of Christian music speak right to that. Again, the words and melodies rose out of the language and tunes of popular culture.

"I brought a book with me tonight that I really value. It's titled *Sankey's Story of the Gospel Hymns*. It was written about a hundred years ago by Ira Sankey himself. He was one of the very first people to appreciate what music could do in a large meeting where people were being called to surrender to Jesus.

"Sankey wrote about an evangelistic meeting in Scotland: 'We now faced the problem of "singing the gospel—"'" What an interesting term, which Sankey seemed to think was a brand-new idea—to sing songs that tell the story of salvation. Remember Fanny Crosby's 'Tell Me the Stories of Jesus'?

"So what did he sing? He sang titles like 'Jesus of Nazareth Passeth By' and 'Hold the Fort, for I Am Coming.' His most famous song—which Moody was always asking him to sing—was 'The Ninety and Nine.'

"Sankey had read a poem, written by a twenty-one-year-old woman, in a newspaper. He saved the words, and one night, *in the middle of an evangelistic service while Moody was preaching*, he pulled them from his pocket and decided to sing them when the sermon was finished. He accompanied himself on a little pump organ and made up the melody as he went along. Listen to the words:

> *There were ninety and nine that safely lay*
> *In the shelter of the fold*
> *But one was out on the hills far away,*
> *Far off from the gates of gold—*
> *Away on the mountains wild and bare,*
> *Away from the tender Shepherd's care.*

"The song describes the Shepherd's passionate search for the lost sheep. And then, in the last verse, the sheep was found. And Sankey sang:

> *But all thro' the mountains, thunder-driven,*
> *And up from the rocky steep,*
> *There arose a glad cry to the gate of heaven*
> *'Rejoice! I have found my sheep!'*
> *And the Angels echoed around the throne,*
> *'Rejoice! For the Lord brings back his own.'*

"This song, I'm guessing, probably attracted as many people to Jesus in those days as Moody's preaching. And the song is centered on the theme of rescue . . . being lost and then being found. That resonated with the many people who felt themselves lost and bewildered by all the changes in the world.

"But there's a sadness to all of this. There were other people, once again, who totally rejected this music or its content. And they rejected the use of a pump organ to accompany the singing of the crowd or the soloist. They derisively called the new music 'human hymns.'

"Here's a paragraph from Sankey's book that got my attention. He wrote about Moody's first visit to England:

> The first meeting was attended by less than fifty persons, who took seats as far away from the pulpit as possible. I sang several solos before Mr. Moody's address, and that was my first service of song in England. It was with some difficulty that I could get the people to sing, as they had not been accustomed to the kind of songs that I was using.[2]

"Nothing seems to have changed, has it? Nevertheless, as the nights went by, the crowds grew to a very substantial size. Soon they were singing and preaching to twenty thousand people. But everywhere Sankey and Moody went, some Christians gave them a terrible time about the music that Sankey chose. They were shocked that he sang solos. Sankey wrote about a meeting in Scotland:

> On another occasion . . . while I was singing a solo a woman's shrill voice was heard in the gallery, as she made her way toward the door crying: "Let me oot! Let me oot! What would John Knox [the great Scots reformer] think of the likes of you?" At the conclusion of the solo I went across the street to sing at an overflow meeting in the famous Tollbooth Church. I had just begun to sing, when the same voice was again heard, "Let me oot! Let me oot! What would John Knox think of the likes of you?"[3]

"Over and over people would walk out in the midst of the music crying out what must have been something of a cliché: 'You're singing human hymns . . . human hymns.'"

"What did they want?" Kenneth asked.

"Most of them were Calvinists who insisted that the only legitimate songs worth singing were psalms . . . or Isaac Watts songs."

"But why couldn't they accept the new with the old? What did they have against something that was up-to-date and that would put the gospel in language everyone could understand?" Evelyn asked.

All I could say was, "Evelyn, think about what you just said the next time our worship leader says, 'I want to introduce you to a brand-new song.'" Again, there was one of those contemplative, quiet moments as the group around the table reflected on this.

"So as you can see, the music wars are nothing new. And the question—not an easy one to answer at all—arises: how does each generation open the door for the next generation to sing the gospel in its own fresh way? Think of it: the music that many of us at this table love the most—the music of Wesley, Newton, Crosby, and those that came after—was fought bitterly by many people when it was first introduced. What if"—I paused here for emphasis—"what if those people had been successful in their opposition? It's not unlike the question you reacted to last week. What if Isaac Watts's father hadn't encouraged his son's musical creativity?"

"I don't know the answer to your question," Winn said. "And maybe we need to find out if there is an answer."

"Does all the music we love have to be thrown out the window just because the young people want something different?" Lillian asked. "Isn't there anyplace for the music we grew up loving?"

"Well, maybe there is. I know that there's a small movement among younger artists to bring back the old hymnody with different melodies and maybe some upbeat arrangements," I said. "Maybe we can talk about that later on. Let me continue with my musical-history lesson. There was a third music war that emerged in the 1920s and lasted for about twenty years, give or take. America was in the roaring twenties; it was the beginning of the jazz era. And a new generation wanted to sing the gospel—to use that phrase again—in an up-to-date way.

"A man by the name of Paul Rader, who was a pastor and evangelist in Chicago, started encouraging young musicians to write choruses instead of the standard gospel songs with their four or five verses and repeated endings. Rader wanted short, bouncy melodies that could be sung over the radio and picked up by listeners after they'd heard the song only once or twice. I guess he wanted tunes that could be sung and hummed all through the week. And, frankly, I think he was on to something.

"Today they might call this a sonic logo. A quick, perky tune that drives one basic theme or idea deep into the heart. Little advertising songs where you identify a particular product with a jingle of a song. Or like the famous NBC radio chime—N . . . B . . . C," I sang.

"So these young men in Chicago began writing the simple gospel choruses Rader wanted. Here's a sample:

My sins are blotted out, I know,
My sins are blotted out, I know.
They are buried in the depths of the deepest sea,
My sins are blotted out, I know.

"I remember singing that as a boy," Ernie said. Two or three others also said they remembered it.

"There were other choruses that spread far and wide. 'Rolled away, rolled away, rolled away . . . Every burden of my heart rolled away. Every sin had to go, 'neath the crimson flow, hallelujah . . .' And there were simple children's songs: 'Zacchaeus was a wee little man, a wee little man was he—'"

The minute I began to sing the Zacchaeus song, almost everyone at the table started singing it with me. And they sang it with the hand motions we'd all learned as children. We were laughing again because none of us had sung the Zacchaeus song for fifty years, but here we were singing it as if we'd sung it just yesterday.

"These choruses were added to a bevy of newer gospel hymns with words like 'When we all get to heaven / What a day of rejoicing that will be' and 'When the roll is called up yonder, I'll be there.' They came out in the early years of the twentieth century, and they were set to upbeat tunes that you could march to or even roller-skate to. Almost all of them were rhythmic and extremely singable. They got into your heart, and once there they never left.

"There was another version of this new twentieth-century music emerging in the Deep South. Its roots were, for the most part, in the spirituals that rose out of the African slave culture. A scholar might have much better words to describe it, but my sense is that it was a very soulful kind of music that bordered on a wailing produced by suffering. And it was a music that spoke of a future hope. People who sang it seemed to feel a momentary reprieve from the ugliness of real-world life.

"And from these roots came gospel music sung by quartets and choirs. It picked up a jazz flavor from New Orleans. Most of the music was emotional, very stirring to the heart. Of course, just as we've seen before, most established church leaders rejected gospel music at first. Here's a comment from one of the most famous African-American song-writers, Tommy Dorsey who wrote some of the very best gospel songs, such as 'Precious Lord Take my Hand,' in the mid-twentieth century. He said,

> Gospel music was new and most people didn't understand. Some of the preachers used to call gospel music 'sin' music. They related it to what they called worldly things—like jazz and blues and show business. Gospel music was different from approved hymns and spirituals. It had a beat.[4]

"Gospel quartet music became the rage throughout the South. It was a catchy, rhythmic kind of music that put the story of the gospel in graphic word pictures that common people could relate to. At first it was sung in storefront churches and in tiny places where people who were often dirt-poor could escape their miseries and find a bit of joy. But as it grew popular, the new music became widespread in Saturday night 'sings' in theaters and auditoriums. Finally, it made its way into the churches as part of praise and worship.

"But, as I said before, there were critics. They compared these songs to jazz and popular music and said the new music was sensual and worldly. But there you are. These are the origins of the songs that you and I grew up on. And an older generation—the more respectable people—didn't like the stuff at all."

As I talked about these early twentieth-century forms of music, I could tell that no one in the group had thought about where the music they loved had come from. It hadn't occurred to them that it came from earlier generations eager to touch the souls of people both inside and outside the Christian movement. They just assumed that it had always been there.

We discussed favorite gospel hymns that grew out of this time a hundred years ago. Some songs sounded as if they came off the Broadway stage; others from the militant rhythms of band music. "Open My Eyes That I May See," "We've a Story to Tell to the Nations," "Jesus Is Coming Again." We named song after song, and every once in a while someone would start singing, and we would all join in.

I looked at my watch and realized that we were getting toward our closing time. And I hoped I could say one more thing about the evolution that Christian music had gone through.

"There's a fourth music war, and I guess you'd have to say it's happening right now. It's been going on for about thirty years or so. We're still in it, and it's going to be a little while before we can fully appreciate or understand what's going on. Have you noticed, by the way, that these so-called wars are becoming more and more frequent?"

"So you're willing to admit that we're in a war?" Ted asked in a sarcastic tone.

"The new music comes from various sources. Once again it comes from popular sources—jazz, country and western, soul music, and the passionate expressions of, frankly, rock 'n' roll and all the styles that have followed. I'm not smart enough to figure it all out. But you know it when you hear it. Some people say that contemporary gospel music goes back to 1969 and the overwhelming popularity of one song 'O Happy Day.'

"If the music of the early 1900s employed the piano as its most important instrument, this new genre of music made use of the guitar. It's an instrument that's portable, much more so than Ira Sankey's original pump organ. The guitar can be played on street corners and around campfires as well as in church. Not like an expensive pipe or electric organ, which is, more or less, restricted to the church building. Guitars can be played by almost anyone who can carry a tune, and that's why you find yourself listening one day to someone who's really, really good and on another day to someone who can barely strum three chords, but dreams that he's the next Bono. You can play and sing the new music anywhere—in prison, in school, at home. Anywhere . . . just as Paul and Silas did.

"The most recent form of music emphasizes great passion and feeling. It's not the controlled, stylized music that we learned when we were young. It sometimes flaunts the musical rules. A musician can reconstruct the music any way he or she wants. The important thing is that it fits the times. But feeling the music is the important thing."

"What's so great about feeling the music?" someone asked.

"Because the younger generation thinks that personal experience is everything. *Genuineness* and *authenticity* are their big words. They don't need perfection or slickness. They don't want to sing the notes the same way every time. They want to reflect the moment and its ethos. So they are drawn to raspy voices that sing about pain and brokenness, about loneliness and anger. They want to let it all hang out, and they're somewhat suspicious of all of us who worked so hard to create an image that everything is perfect, that our Christian lives have no flaws."

And then Ernie said, "When Gretchen and I were in Latin America last year, we were amazed at the singing. There were men dancing with their children in their arms. Young people were waving big banners. Everybody was into it: clapping, dancing, swaying. And we got caught up in it. After a while I wanted to be a part of their joy. And if you promise not to tell anyone, I did some dancing myself."

We all looked at Ernie with no little astonishment. None of us could imagine it. Then we all laughed and applauded him. I decided it was a great end to a rather intense evening, told everyone we'd pick up on this next week, and said a prayer. Then we all went home.

Jason Calder: Has applied to Gordon College for next year. A born leader, excellent on guitar. Father and mother not overly active but always present when Jason's band is leading in worship service. Committed to Christ at summer camp.

On Saturday, just before noon, I stopped by Panera Bread to pick up some dinner rolls for Gail. At a table in a corner, I saw six or eight teenagers from our church, and after buying my rolls I went over to say hi.

We have some great young people at our church. Most of them have grown up together, and their friendships are solid. They have been very open to me in spite of the fact that I am old enough to be a grandfather to any of them. It has not been unusual for some of them to encourage me about a sermon now and then. As I approached the table where they were seated, they invited me to join them. No pastor with a brain would ever refuse such an invitation.

"Let me grab some coffee," I said. When I had my flavored decaf, I returned to the table, sat down, and asked, "So what are you guys talking about?"

"Worship," Cheryl Ferguson, a high school junior, said. "Next week is the fifth Sunday of the month, and our band is leading the morning services. We're planning the order of the songs and the prayers and the video."

Next week—the fifth Sunday! Immediately I understood.

Let me tell you the story behind fifth Sundays and why these kids were at the table talking about worship leadership. With some background, you'll understand some of the comments made by members of the Discovery Group.

During the last several years (beginning before I'd come to the church) our music and worship leaders had been slowly changing the way our church worshipped. As you know already, we no longer had a choir. And soloists sang fewer and fewer songs. In the process the congregation was being introduced to so-called contemporary songs, most of which had no resemblance whatsoever to traditional Christian hymnody.

When the church's organist, Ted Steele, had to retire because of poor health, the worship people decided to lock up the organ and introduce the people to music accompanied by guitar, drums, and other electronic instruments. Most people accepted the change at first, thinking it was temporary until another organist was found. Then as time passed, they realized that there would be no new organist . . . and no organ. (Actually, we still turn on the organ for funerals and some weddings, but we have to hire an outsider to come in and play it.)

With the new instrumental accompaniment in worship, occasional attempts were made to get the people clapping to rhythmic songs, and I could tell when I got to the church that there was a lot of self-consciousness about this. Sometimes I joked about having clapping and nonclapping sections in the sanctuary, and people laughed. But their laughter simply masked the fact that there were some strong feelings among some of the people as to where these changes in worship were taking us.

The restiveness over ways of worshipping grew even more energetic when some folks—usually newcomers—raised their hands when they sang. For some New Englanders that was the last straw. Raise your hands at ball games when the Sox were winning—fine! But raise 'em in worship? Not in "our" church.

A personal confession. I found myself *wanting* to raise my hands on certain occasions, but I didn't yet have enough courage to get my hands above my shoulders. It's obvious that Gail shares my feelings, but I can tell that she is reluctant to raise her hands any higher than I'm willing to go.

Somewhere along the line, as we added more and more contemporary songs to our singing menu, we stopped using the hymnbooks and began projecting the words—traditional or contemporary—on a screen in the front of the sanctuary.

All of this created a palpable sense of uneasiness throughout the congregation. On one hand were those who were thoroughly resistant to these alterations in worship. On the other hand were those who felt that we were not changing our forms of worship and music fast enough. And everyone else with an opinion was somewhere in between. There were times when I wearied of this bickering over worship. No one seemed to be totally happy, and as with other kinds of church changes, we had a few who headed for other churches as a result.

Then early last fall our youth pastor approached me and asked if the youth worship band could lead a Sunday morning service. He told me that Jason Calder had organized a super team of young musicians and singers and that they could do a great job. After getting the agreement of our elders and our regular worship people, I agreed to give it a try when there was a fifth Sunday in a month. A week from tomorrow would be the third time for Jason, Cheryl, and the others. So far the experiment had worked extremely well in spite of criticisms from a few that the drums were too loud and that the music was unsingable.

As I drank my coffee, I learned that Jason's group had been practicing at the church for the past two hours, and now they were here working out the final details of the worship order. I listened for a few minutes as they concluded their planning. The discussion I'd had a few nights before with the Discovery Group came to mind. I wondered what Ted and Connie and the others would have thought if they could have been bugs on the wall listening to this conversation and the intensity with which it was conducted.

When the group finished I asked what songs they'd chosen. They went through them one by one. The first was a Brian Doerksen song, "Now Is the Time to Worship," (a good choice), the second by Chris Tomlin, "How Great Is Our God". Then there were songs written by Larry Norman, Darlene Zschech and Matt Redman. Each of these writers has been part of a remarkable shift in how people have worshipped in many churches during the past fifteen years.

The group also planned to finish their "set" with "Fairest Lord Jesus" sung to a new melody that moves a lot faster than the old traditional one.

Just for the fun of it, I asked if they might consider "Come Thou Fount of

Every Blessing." My question really wasn't a serious one, but it did get everyone's attention. There was silence, and then someone said, "I've never heard of it." No one else in the circle (no one!) knew it either. I pretended to be appalled. No one knew "Come Thou Fount of Every Blessing"? "You can't be serious!" I said. "It's been around for 250 years, and you don't know it? An English guy, Robert Robinson, wrote it."

I think the group was beginning to wonder if inviting me to the table had been a good idea.

"Here's how the first verse goes:

> *Come Thou Fount of every blessing / Tune my heart to sing Thy grace;*
> *Streams of mercy never ceasing / Call for songs of loudest praise.*
> *Teach me some melodious sonnet / Sung by flaming tongues above;*
> *Praise His name—I'm fixed upon it— / Name of God's redeeming love.*

They listened politely. But I could tell that it was a reach for them to understand the meaning of the words. *Sonnet* is not an everyday word, and we don't talk much about streams of mercy today, although perhaps we should. Then I made the mistake of going on to the second verse: "'Here I raise mine Ebenezer—'"

"Raise what?" Kevin Schendler, one of the guys, asked. "Ebenezer—? Like in Scrooge? We had him in English lit the other day."

"No," I said. "Just plain Ebenezer. It's a word that comes from a story in the Old Testament where Israel fought the Philistines and creamed them. And the prophet Samuel built something like a memorial near where the battle had happened and called it Ebenezer. It means, 'the Lord has helped us up to this point.'"

"Why sing a song if no one knows what the words mean?" Bethany O'Rourke asked.

"Well, I admit that the word *Ebenezer* and the Bible story where it comes from are a bit obscure—"

"I don't think I ever heard of it," she replied.

Then Jason, the group's leader, said, "You know . . . a lot of those hymns—they're just not our songs. They don't sound like anything we listen to during the week. And they use words we just don't understand . . . like Eb . . . eben—"

"Ebenezer," I said.

"Yeah, Ebenezer. There doesn't seem to be any life or energy in those songs. You can't really get into it."

"Funny, you'd say that. I guess my age is showing. I was in a meeting the other day when someone simply starting singing 'Come Thou Fount of Every Blessing,' and I found that I could hardly finish the song because it conjured up some past emotion I didn't know I had. I guess if I put it in the words you just spoke, *I really got into it.*"

I could tell that no one at the table knew how to react to what I'd just said.

Then Jason said, "I don't know if this makes sense, but I bet there are songs you love that I can't even sing. The music is so different from our music that it sounds as if it came from some foreign country. I just want to run from it."

Now it was my turn to be flustered for a moment. If his comment described where a lot of young people were in the Christian world, then we really had a bigger problem than I'd realized. He was suggesting that we have generations who not only don't understand each other's words, but they don't even have an ear for each other's music.

In that moment the memory of a program on National Public Radio popped into my mind. The host of the show had interviewed a music therapist who said, "Sound touches us just like a hand might touch us affectionately in a caress or aggressively like in a slap."

The therapist described how sound—musical sounds or spoken sounds— enters the ear and through an intricate process reaches an entry point in the brain where an instant decision is made as to whether it is friendly or unfriendly, understandable or not understandable, alarming or welcoming. Loud, sudden sounds—like a harsh warning buzzer—can be startling or unsettling, and the brain reacts and tells the body to respond in a defensive way. Unfamiliar sounds can do the same thing to the brain. They can cause confusion or anger. I remember the therapist saying it was not unlike how we might recoil when we put something that is bitter tasting in our mouths. Again, a clashing sound to which we are unaccustomed can have the effect of a bad smell or a horrifying sight. There are messages of negativity that spread through the brain and scream, *Get away, get away!*

When Jason said there were songs he could not relate to and that he wanted to run from, I wondered if the music therapist would understand what he was saying. Was Jason speaking for a lot of young people and telling me that his brain was not wired to accept the music that I loved so much? And if that were true, was it equally possible that my brain and the brains of the members of the Discovery Group, for example, were not wired to easily receive or appreciate the music that Jason and his people wanted us to sing? The idea that this could partly explain the worship wars we'd discussed the other night stunned me.

We talked for at least fifteen minutes more about the kind of music that was important to us. And as we named various songs that each of us considered to be favorites, it became even clearer that there was a significant gulf between what spoke to my heart and what spoke to theirs. These kids loved rock, rap, and country and western—all sounds their brains received (and enjoyed) with enthusiasm. I liked jazz, classics, and big band. Could we ever get together?

I had a brainstorm—*a truly great idea*. And I threw it out to the young people at the table without giving myself a chance to do any second-guessing. "I've got a thought for you, and I want you to consider it seriously." Everyone was listening.

"Next Tuesday night there will be a small group of people about my age who will be meeting to talk about music in the church."

"Are they meeting to complain about us being up in front on Sunday morning?" Jason asked.

"Good grief, no!" I said. "Where would you get an idea like that?"

"Well," he said, "my folks don't particularly like the music we do. My father is always asking me to turn down the volume on our speakers. They think we sound too much like a rock band. He told me that a lot of the older folks just don't like our music at all. They don't like standing; they don't want to clap; they don't like it if we repeat certain lines too many times. It doesn't sound as if they like much of anything we do."

Jason's comments took me back to Isaac Watts's father and how different he was from Jason's.

"OK. I understand, but this is not what that's about. I want you to come and talk about music with these older people . . . like me. You talk about why you like the music you do, and let them ask you questions. And maybe they could talk about the kind of music they love, and what it has meant to them. We'll eat some food and have a good time. Don't worry, I'll protect you."

There was some nervous laughter, and then Jason asked the others, "How about it?" Various ones shrugged or nodded or muttered, "Cool!" And they were committed.

A few minutes later I said good-bye and let them know how thankful I was that they had invited me to join them. I said we'd be getting together in the Commons at seven on Tuesday night. And they said they'd be there.

The second-guessing began as soon as I got into my car. *What had I done? How in the world was I going to make Tuesday night work?*

WHEN I SAW JASON AT CHURCH THE NEXT DAY, I asked if he'd e-mail me the words to the songs the group was going to use in next week's worship. I told him that on Tuesday night I wanted everyone at the table to have a copy. Jason is a dependable young man, and on Monday morning, the words were on my computer in an e-mail attachment.

As I read through them, I was struck once again with how musical themes in the church have evolved throughout the last hundred years. Next Sunday Jason and his group would lead us in singing:

> *One day every tongue will confess you are God*
> *One day every knee will bow*
> *Still the greatest treasure remains for those*
> *Who gladly choose You now.*[1]

It was straight out of Philippians 2. The next song went,

> *I'm coming back to the heart of worship*
> *And it's all about You, Jesus.*[2]

When I read the words of this second song—one of my favorites—I thought of something I'd read by its composer, Matt Redman, in his book *The Unquenchable Worshipper*. He and his pastor had become disturbed about the substandard worship in their church. As a result they stopped all the music for a time until everyone could examine his or her heart and come to a fresh understanding of what it was like to call upon the living God of the Bible, the Father of Jesus Christ.[3]

Indeed, when I read through the words of each song, I realized that the youth worship team saw worship a lot differently than my generation. For these kids worship was a very serious matter. It was, as Redman had written, "all about you, Jesus."

I thought of a church leader in my first church who used to pray without fail each Sunday morning in my office, "Lord, bless the pastor as he enters the sacred desk, and bless the *preliminaries*." The preliminaries! That was one man's view of worship: three songs, announcements and offering, a solo, and the sermon. For him—and many others—the songs were merely a warm-up to what they hoped would be a good sermon.

But these young people planned to use songs, Bible readings, and prayers with specific themes to bring us—they hoped—into the presence of God where we might be humbled, reassured, challenged, and given courage for the days that would follow. Having listened to them over coffee, I had the sense that they felt that the worship they would be leading was equal in value to my sermon. No, I'll go a step further. If they had to choose between the two, I think they would have valued the worship over the sermon. *A scary thought*, I said to myself. But a thought, nonetheless, that represented a dramatic shift that has taken place in the church during the past fifteen years.

Next Sunday morning the pulpit area would be jammed with thousands of dollars of electronic devices to make a huge musical sound in worship. A far cry from the simple song leader and piano player of fifty years ago. How had we gotten from there to here? What had triggered this fourth music-and-worship war?

Some day musical historians will provide us the scholarly answers. All I know is that somewhere in the sixties, a whole new kind of young man or woman began to enter certain churches. I say *certain* because they were not welcomed in many places with their long hair and peasant dresses. They were called *Jesus people*.

A Christian movement that had always insisted that it worshipped a God who looks not on the outer appearance but on the heart seemed to forget its theology and, in too many places, closed its doors to this new generation. As writer Stuart Briscoe asked in the title of one of his books, *Where Was the Church When the Youth Exploded?*

The result was an outbreak of newly planted churches where a younger generation could create its own communities of worship and mutual support. It was a time when many churches, the ones that made an issue out of long hair and secondhand clothing, began their slow death.

The songs in these new churches no longer followed the typical four verses and a chorus. They were ballads, folk songs, and rock tunes that seemed to wander all over the chart, breaking (or perhaps rebuilding) all the acceptable rules of songwriting. They were accompanied by drama, dance, banners and flags, and media presentations.

And as this new generation sang to God, they expressed themselves with passion, their entire beings caught up in the music and its words. They clapped, swayed, even danced to the new music. Soloists and groups sang with rough, untrained, even undisciplined voices. They were less interested in being impressive and more interested in being real, or—a favorite word—*authentic*.

The people in our Discovery Group found much of this to be an offense to their generational culture when the changes came to our church. They found it almost impossible to make the turns in the road. The result? Our church was likely headed for a life-and-death struggle for its very existence. It would not be too long before these young people would be reasoning among themselves that there were more hospitable places to receive them. Soon their parents would be wondering why their sons and daughters had chosen other places—if indeed, they remained inside any kind of church.

The truth is that we have difficult days ahead if these generations can't find a way to talk with each other and find common ground. I couldn't imagine what might happen on Tuesday night.

> ***Cheryl Ferguson:*** *Junior in HS. Father, an elder; mother on*
> *regular worship team. Can't remember when she wasn't a*
> *Christian. Very athletic: soccer, lacrosse. Would like to be a pastor.*

On Tuesday evening I got to the church early. Gail joined me; she was as curious as I was to see how the evening might unfold.

Before we left for church, we had a light supper and talked about ways to encourage people from both groups—the younger and the older—to mingle with each other. We decided that if everyone had assigned places at the table, we could fix it so that every young person was seated between two older ones, and every older person was . . . well, you get the picture.

On the drive to church, Gail made place cards with the names of everyone we knew who was coming. When we arrived, we set up the tables and chairs and put the place cards out.

Arlene walked in a few minutes later and, when she saw what we were doing, signaled a slight annoyance. I think our seating plan had encroached on her organizing responsibilities, and she was feeling a threat to her control. After Gail explained our little scheme, she seemed to adjust. But not before she grumbled, "Lillian and I *always* sit together."

"Think *change*, Arlene," I said. "Think change. You'll get a star in your crown for the sacrifice."

So that no one in the Discovery Group would be surprised that we were having guests, I had e-mailed everyone on Saturday night:

I've invited Jason Calder and his worship band to be our guests Tuesday night. I am hoping that two generations of people can talk out of their hearts to one another on the subjects of music and worship. Here's your chance to ask any question you like and, on the other hand, to explain some of the feelings you have about life in a changing church. Of course you may get some questions too.

Everyone in the group was there at least ten minutes early, even John who seemed to be in the habit of arriving later and later each week. Perhaps it was my imagination, but I thought I sensed both anticipation and anxiety as they stood around the table. Now that I think of it, I wonder if, in the life of our church, there had ever been a gathering quite like this.

Ted was the coffee man, and Russ was the designated food provider for the evening. I expected a box of individually wrapped pies from Russ's fast-food store. But he and his wife, Debbie, had made some huge homemade chocolate éclairs. He was also smart to bring along bottles of juice and soft drinks for those among the worship team who might not be coffee drinkers.

A minute before the hour, Jason and his worship team arrived. When they entered the Commons, they were walking—all eight of them—about as close to each other as possible. Clearly they were sticking close to sustain courage. It hadn't occurred to me that this might be a daunting moment for them.

I wonder how frequently young people feel that way in the average church. In their day-to-day world, they tend to run with people their own age; they speak a youthful dialect, a type of subcultural language. And then they come to a church—many of them coerced by parents—where the culture is laden with adult perspectives and practices.

Do they nurse the suspicion that older generational people don't like them, don't care about their opinions, don't think they have anything to offer?

In fairness they may have a right to such suspicions. What they may not understand, however, is that older people may not be dealing with *like* or *not-like* categories; the truth is that older men and women can be fearful of younger people. People my age and older see young people clustered together at a shopping mall or on a street corner, or even in church, and our first instinct is to avoid them, to walk in another direction.

Why? Because we're sometimes mystified by their choices of clothing and accessories that often seem to convey a message of anger and hostility. They walk about with earbuds listening to music that is often strange, maybe hostile, to our ears. They seem to be forever talking on cell phones or tapping text messages on tiny keyboards.

The stories that older people hear about young people seem to center on drugs and drinking to excess. We do not work hard enough to listen to the good stuff that, if we did, might make us realize that the larger body of young people today may be accomplishing more, learning more, doing more than any generation in the past.

When the worship team entered the room, Kenneth and Mary Ann were the first to step forward and warmly greet them. They introduced themselves and expressed great enthusiasm that we were going to have the evening together. Their approach to the youth worship team apparently broke the tension, and before long all the others in the Discovery Group were introducing themselves to those they didn't know and giving hugs to those they did.

Then, soon after, we were all seated at our designated places eating Russ and Debbie's éclairs. Here and there some awkwardness was evident. There was the sense that people from both groups really didn't know how to talk to each other, and occasionally, there were spots of silence when it was easier to eat or drink than find something to say.

I kept procrastinating calling the meeting to order, because, frankly, I had very little idea how to get things started. The fact is that I had no agenda. I just wanted people to talk with the hope that something bright and wonderful might happen. But now I was on the edge of self-doubt. What had I done in that impulsive moment on Saturday morning when I set this all in motion? *How would this evening end?*

I probably would have waited even longer to start except that Gail, seated across the table from me, kept pointing to her watch. Detail person that she is, Gail is often reminding me to be more mindful of the clock, and tonight was no exception.

So I sucked in my breath and called our little meeting to order. Even though the place cards indicated everyone's name, I introduced everyone anyway. And then I called on Clayton to offer our prayer.

Sensitive to Clayton's reluctance to pray in public, I'd asked him on Sunday to do this, and he'd agreed, asking if he could prepare his prayer as he'd done the last time. I'd told him I was as happy for him to do it this time as I was when he'd led us in prayer before.

"Heavenly Father," he read. "Thank you for my friends. And thank you for these Tuesday evening get-togethers and for the pastor's interest in us. Help us to be humble as we listen to each other and learn where we need to change—"

Clayton paused at this point, and there was an awkward silence. And then he seemed to abandon his written prayer and began speaking spontaneously. "And thank you for these wonderful young people . . . I just can't remember the last time I sat at a table with boys and girls this much younger than me." Clayton paused again, and we were aware that he was having difficulty continuing. Was it emotion? Or was it that Clayton was in over his head, giving in to his fear of praying out loud?

You may remember that I spoke earlier about Clayton's problem with his young adult son. I still wasn't sure I fully understood why father and son weren't speaking to each other, and Clayton hadn't invited conversation on the subject. But at this moment it seemed as if all of Clayton's loneliness—the result of his wife's death, his daughter's choice to live so far away in California, and the fact that his son, though living nearby, had rejected him—seemed to be provoked as he struggled to get through his prayer. It took him ten or fifteen (interminable) seconds to resume speaking. And we just waited. I had no idea what Jason's group was thinking.

Then Clayton started again: "Lord, I pray that we'll get to know each other tonight and that each of us will learn something we've never known before. Thank you . . . thank you that these kids are willing to spend time with us. . . . Amen." *Amazing! A small but noticeable step in Clayton's Christian growth,* I thought. He had abandoned his card and prayed out of the heart. And he'd let us know just a bit more of who he was.

I dived in. "Clayton, thank you . . . and Jason, thanks so much to you and your team for being with us tonight. Next Sunday morning you will be leading us in our worship. So let me ask you: when you think about worshipping God and leading all of us in that service, what's on your mind?"

Jason took a deep breath and said: "If I can take a few minutes to give you some background, I think it will help. I don't think worship meant much to me or to any of the rest of us here until last summer. Most of us have grown up in this church . . . everyone—he pointed to Rod—"except Rod. He's a new Christian."

"Welcome to the family, Rod," Winn, who was sitting right next to him, said. Several others clapped for a few seconds.

"So, Jason, what happened last summer?" I asked.

"We all went on a missions trip to the Dominican Republic, to paint some buildings at a Christian camp. On the two Sundays we were there, we attended a church near the camp and sat for almost three hours in a Spanish worship service. Most of the songs they sang we'd never heard. So we just listened. They probably sang for an hour?" Jason spoke his sentence as if it were a question and turned to others in his group as if seeking their agreement to what he was saying. They nodded their heads.

"When they prayed . . . in Spanish . . . there was something so authentic about the way they talked to God, so awesome. All over the room people began to pray. There were times when everyone was praying at the same time . . . out loud. It was wild. No one would ever do that here. But the praying was so real . . . it was really, really . . . real.

"Then they took up the offering. And it was different from here. Everyone lined up, walked to the front, and dropped their money into baskets. Some didn't bring money. They brought food they had grown at home and stacked it up near the baskets.

"The sermon was long—at least an hour—and in Spanish, so we didn't understand much.

"But we saw what worshipping God is really all about. They were the poorest people we'd ever seen; yet in worship they were, well . . . excited. There was a real happiness among those people that we had never seen before.

"I guess what I haven't said was how they let it all hang out when they sang. They clapped, they danced, and they looked up at heaven while they did this. It was so real. It was almost like a rock concert, but this time it was all about Jesus . . . and we told each other that we wanted to worship like that.

"When we got back to the camp that afternoon, we talked about everything that had happened at that church, and we kept wondering why we couldn't do it like that at our church. Why are people here so serious? And why are they always arguing about how we worship so that they never really get any worshipping done?" Turning to the others, Jason said, "Any of you guys want to add something?"

Cheryl immediately said: "I know that was the morning I learned what worship was all about. I was seated where I could watch a woman who was crying all during the first part of the service. I didn't know why she was crying, but it was pretty obvious that something awful was going on in her life. As we sang, the women on either side of her put their arms around her and both of them prayed prayers into her ear . . . I think it was praying anyhow. And then you could tell that the songs began to get to her, and before long she was singing with everyone else. I felt . . . like whatever her problem was, God had done something for her through her friends' prayers and through the music. She seemed to change, and, as Jason said, she began to show joy on her face. *You know,* I said to myself, *those people know a lot more about how to care for each other than we do."*

I looked around the table at various people in the Discovery Group. No one was restless. Everyone was riveted to these descriptions of a worship experience in another culture. Did I detect a sense of unbelief in them that young people could have these sensitivities? Or were they wondering how long it had been since they'd had similar feelings about worship?

"At first I was turned off by the preacher," Colin Gummere, the drummer, said. "I mean, he was walking all over the place, and he was shouting . . . and, man, was he ever wild! And the people were talking right back at him—sort of like black churches you see here. I didn't know anything he was saying, it was all in Spanish, but I realized that even though there was all this shouting, everyone was into everything he said. Man, he was like a father to everyone. I don't think you'd ever get bored with a sermon like that if you could understand what he was saying."

Now I was beginning to get uncomfortable. I always try hard not to get overly emotional about anything when I preach, but Colin was saying that this was the very thing that captured his attention.

Then Jason spoke again: "So as I said before, all of us returned to the camp after the meeting was over and talked about worship and what it really means. And we realized that, as Christians, we needed that same kind of experience. I mean, we're in school, and—it's a great school—but it's tough if you want to be in our school and be a Christian. We need worship to keep us going just like those people needed it. You need to go someplace where you can be encouraged and tell

God you're sorry for your sins and get some encouragement about what it means to be a Christian. And we wondered why—sorry, Pastor Mac—we didn't feel that way about our church.

"I mean there's no excitement in our singing. And we don't understand most of the songs anyway . . . like we talked about on Saturday morning."

Several of the kids gave a nervous laugh and looked in my direction. I told the rest of the group something about our Saturday morning conversation and about Ebenezers.

And then Jason went on: "Most of the songs we sing here are not the songs or the music we sing all week long. And . . . we don't normally listen to the sermons. They don't seem to make a difference to people our age.

"So we wondered if we could change things a little bit. And that's when, after we got home, we formed a band and began to play at certain youth events. Now they've asked us to lead worship in the church sanctuary every once in a while."

I said, "Jason, tell us what you want to make happen next Sunday."

"We'd just like to see people start singing as if Jesus was in the room and get real excited about it. I mean, I've seen my folks really excited about football. But I've never seen them come close to that here at church when we're singing to God. So we'd like to see that. And we'd like to see people become more real about the things that are bothering them and pray and ask God to touch them and heal them. And—Cheryl brought this up last Saturday—we'd like to see some people become Christians because of what we did."

"So what songs are you going to make us sing?" The way I phrased the question—*make* us sing—elicited some laughter around the table. Stan, who used to sing in the choir, said, "I bet the first song will be 'A Mighty Fortress Is Our God.'"

" 'Fraid not," Jason said. "Colin, got the list?"

Colin read the names of the songs the band had practiced.

"So why did you pick 'Now Is the Time to Worship'?" I asked.

"Because we all need to be reminded that there is a time to open ourselves to God. When we were praying about the songs we'd sing, Karen said that it's easy to come to church with all the things you have on your mind and never realize that you're here to do one thing only—to reconnect with God. So we decided to put this song in first: *now . . . now . . . is the time to worship.* Maybe we'll get somebody's attention."

I tried to look about the table without making it obvious. I would have given anything to know what was going on in the minds of the Discovery Group people. What did they make of this? Was it youthful idealism to them? Was it foreign to their understanding of church? Or was it registering in their minds that these kids weren't that shallow?

We lost our train of thought about next Sunday's songs when Evelyn broke the silence: "Jason, you and your friends simply amaze me. I've got something to learn from you. Could I ask a silly question?"

Jason assured her that she could.

"I've wanted to ask somebody why young people want to stand all the time when we sing. I mean, standing that long is painful for me. My knees and my hips really begin to hurt. I need to sit down so badly. But I don't want to because other people will think I'm being uncooperative . . . but then I find myself getting very irritable, so I guess I'm not worshipping, am I?"

Cheryl said, "I don't think we ever thought of that . . . Evelyn . . . is it OK if I call you by your first name?" Evelyn said she was happy for that, and Cheryl continued, "We never thought that some people might find it difficult to stand. We just assumed everyone would like to do that. It's kind of like dancing to us. You can't sit down and dance. But I hear what you're saying."

Turning to Jason, Cheryl asked, "Couldn't we tell people that they could sit during certain songs . . . or sit whenever they wanted?"

Jason said he saw nothing wrong with that at all.

Then Evelyn spoke directly to Cheryl: "Well, let me mention a couple of other things. The noise is sometimes unbearable to my ears. Do you have any idea what it is like to wear a hearing aid and what that does when the music is loud?"

"Turn it off, Evelyn," John said with feigned gruffness. There was a great moment of laughter that even enveloped Evelyn, and she said, "That's what I do, John. Especially when you begin talking—" More laughter.

Jason spoke: "I'm sorry that we've made it painful for you. We'll talk about that. But you see, we don't only want to sing the music; we want to *feel* it. We want it to crowd out all the other noises of the world when we sing. I guess it is what making a joyful noise means to us. And, as Cheryl said, we kind of think of it like dancing."

Winn spoke up, "Do you young people ever sing the hymns that were in our hymnbook? If you kids take over the worship every Sunday, will we get to a point when we never sing the hymns again?"

I wondered how Jason was going to handle that one. I hadn't expected the conversation to become this candid so quickly. But Jason seemed to know exactly what to say.

"We don't understand the hymns. We were talking with Pastor Mac about this the other day. When we got home from the Dominican last summer, Olivia found a book about worship written for our generation. And we learned that most hymns were sung with the same tunes that people sang on the other days of the week. Someone said that many of the oldest hymns are sung with music that was sung in bars during the week. So we want to sing songs that fit the times in which we live."

"Do you think it would be possible to sing one old hymn on those Sundays when you lead?"

Bethany, a member of the worship team who had been silent thus far spoke up: "I like to sing hymns when I know who wrote them and why they were written. A few weeks ago we were in church and sang a song I'd never heard before. What was its name . . . you know"—she turned to Cheryl—"we talked about it later."

"'It Is Well with My Soul'?" Cheryl asked.

"Yes . . . 'It's Well with My Soul.' Well, I didn't like the song until Jason told us the story about how it was written. He said that the writer's wife and daughters were on a ship that sank. Only one of them was saved."

"The wife," Jason said.

"Yes, the wife. Well, anyway, God comforted the husband, and he wrote that song about his experience. The minute I heard that story, I reread the hymn, and I understood what was going on. I'd like to sing that song again, because now I know why it's there."

Winn said to Bethany, "That makes perfect sense to me. It never occurred to me that we all ought to know something about the stories of these songs." Turning to me, Winn said, "She's right. Where could we find the stories behind some of these hymns?"

I said, "There are all kinds of books. Gail has a pretty big collection of hymn stories. She'll help you out." Everyone looked at Gail, who promised the group that she'd give them a list of books by Sunday.

Yvonne spoke up: "The thing that sometimes bothers me about your music is that we can't sing it. And I look around and see that a lot of other people aren't singing either. It's too hard. It's just my opinion, but I feel as if the old songs are very simple. We used to sing all the parts: bass, tenor, alto, and soprano. Remember, Ted, when the song leader would tell the instruments to be quiet and we would all sing the parts like a big choir? I loved those moments."

Suddenly, Ted began to sing,

> *Crown Him with many crowns,*
> *The Lamb upon His throne;*

And all the older people around the table began to sing in parts while the kids sat silent, listening. Ted began to wave his arms in the style of a music conductor or choir leader.

> *Hark! how the heav'nly anthem drowns*
> *All music but its own!*
> *Awake, my soul, and sing*
> *Of Him who died for thee,*
> *And hail Him as thy matchless King*
> *Thru all eternity.*

When everyone finished, the young people clapped, not politely but enthusiastically. For all of us it was a warming experience. I imagined a barrier or two that seem to separate the generations beginning to crack.

Winn said to Jason, "What bothers me about the new music is that it doesn't really seem to teach Christian doctrine. Many of us learned our Christian truth not from sermons—sorry, Gordon—but from the songs. Remember these lines?" Winn looked around the table.

> *Living he loved me; dying he saved me*
> *Buried he carried my sins far away.*
> *Rising he justified, freely forever.*
> *One day he's coming; O glorious day.*

"See, the whole story of Christian salvation is in that song."

"Wow," Cheryl said. "That's neat. Come to think of it, one of the songs we love to sing does the same thing. You know: 'Lord We Lift Your Name on High.'"

> *You came from heaven to earth*
> *To show the way*
> *From the earth to the cross*
> *My debt to pay*
> *From the cross to the grave*
> *From the grave to the sky*
> *Lord, I lift your name on high.*

Jason looked very thoughtful for a moment. And then he said to Winn, "You've given me something to think about. And we'll have to make sure that the songs we choose have some of that in them. But I know this. We are a generation that needs to be called to action and to joy. We've got a lot of friends telling us that the only fun there is comes from drinking parties or getting high on drugs. I don't know what it was like when you were in school, but if you want to be a Christian today in our school, you really need all the help you can get. So we need songs in our lives that remind us every day to fight these things off. So our songs are loud and sometimes pretty wild. But we are living in a wild culture, and they bring us back to Jesus' way. We download them into our iPods, and we sing and play them whenever the band gets together."

The conversation continued for another hour until I finally said that we all needed to be on our way. Lillian volunteered to give the concluding prayer:

O Lord, thank you for these delightful young people, these new friends of ours. I can't imagine what they face each day that I never had to face when I was young. I pray a covering on each of them, Lord. Don't let their joy be ruined; don't let the devil influence them. And if I have to give up my songs and sing theirs so that they will be strong in you, I'm willing to do that. Amen.

What happened next was something I will never forget. Cheryl rushed over to Lillian and hugged her. Stan shook hands with Jason and then began to hug him.

And all around the table the same thing began to happen—the older and the younger each extending their arms. I've only told you a small part of the evening's story. But perhaps it's enough to give you an idea that something remarkable was happening in the lives of two generations. They were beginning to hear each other, to respect each other, and, most important, to care for each other. Perhaps the stolen church was being returned.

*I was walking down Main Street last Monday and suddenly had
an idea. I decided to ask strangers if they could give me directions
to our church. I bet I approached 15 people. Not one of them . . .
not one of them! . . . had ever heard of our church.* And we were
less than 2 blocks away from here. *One guy asked me, "Why
would you be looking for a place like that?"*

A few weeks after that memorable evening when the Discovery Group met with Jason Calder and his worship band, another matter that had been simmering for a couple of years in the life of our church—a pretty big one in fact—came to a boil. Church leaders refer to it as *the great name change* issue.

I think I own the dubious honor of being the father of the name change issue, because one Sunday morning, a year after I'd come to the church, I raised the question of our church's identity in the city where we are located. In my sermon I described a series of random conversations I'd pursued on Main Street a few days earlier. What I discovered in these encounters was that no one I approached knew of our church or where it was located. One man made it clear that he held all churches in contempt. Another mumbled about churches and property taxes.

I admitted to the congregation that the sign out in front of the sanctuary with our church name and our supposed distinctives was an embarrassment to me. "What does our name mean to anyone who has no church background?" I asked. "And what do words like *premillennial, Bible-believing,* and *evangelistic* say to someone who has had little or no exposure to Christian theology?" I could imagine, I said, someone looking at our sign and saying to himself, *Beware! Beware! These religious people are weird!*

I pushed the envelope a little bit by wondering out loud if there was one person in fifty in our church that could offer a definition of the word *premillennial.* Yet, I said, it was one of a trio of words selected to identify our essential life together. I suggested—jokingly, of course—that I was going to interrupt the sermon and pick some people in the service to define *premillennial* for us since it had such a prominent place on our sign. A nervous wave of laughter swept across the sanctuary.

For a few people who heard me that morning, twenty to thirty maybe, my comments about the church's name were like red meat tossed to hungry dogs. Within twenty-four hours I was the recipient of e-mails and notes, some urging a name change (and a new sign) and others expressing frustration that I had been so cavalier in "trashing" a name that had been on our front door for more than one hundred and fifty years. These strong expressions were evenly divided—about ten of each. Samples:

We have had our name for one hundred and fifty or more years. We love it. Leave it alone. You're changing too many things too fast.

About changing the church's name. What took so long?

As you might discern: not a lot of deep thinking in those two e-mails. But then again, they seem to indicate that name change could be a volatile matter. You could also sense that the question of the church's name, while important, might be symbolic of other things in church life that were bothering some people. For a moment I regretted what I'd done and worried that I might have forfeited the confidence people had shown in me since I'd come to the church.

But, as they say, the genie was out of the bottle. The number of folk with opinions about the name of our church grew in number as the months went by. When the elders and members of our church council discussed the topic—and they would eventually accumulate two years of discussion—they referred to one group as the *name changers* and the other as the *name keepers.*

Now, sandwiched between the two groups, was a large majority of our church people who could be called the *undecideds.* They'd not given much thought to what's in an organizational name, and they wished the subject would go away. In fact, their response to this and other similar matters tended to be summed up by: Why can't we all just get along?

I am of two minds about this. As a pastor I tend to appreciate people who don't make waves, who like to get along. But then again, I want people to care about the place of the church in their lives and how it is regarded in the larger community where the church is supposed to be known as a servant organization. I guess I came to believe that caring people are going to give thought to issues like their church's name. And, human being that I am, I guess I'd like them to see it my way.

Here's part of a letter that one church member sent to me:

My company spent lots of time and dollars over two years seeking a new name. Their branding team claimed that people form first impressions of a company and its products in just a matter of seconds. They also found that, when that first impression is formed by a potential customer, it hardly ever changes. I would be amazed if any person under thirty-five in our community has a good first impression of our church if all they know is its name.

Another person wrote:

I'm for a church name that identifies us as a group of people that are congenial and receptive. I wish we had a name that suggested that we've found something that charges life up and gives it purpose.

Not long after my notorious "name-change" sermon the church council (our elders and our program leaders) met, and the topic was raised immediately. I braced for polarization among the leaders but was surprised when I discovered that most people around the table were actually in favor of name change. Only one or two had reservations, and they seemed "persuadable."

For the next six months we kicked the name change idea around at each council meeting. It became a fascinating series of discussions. I often encouraged leaders to circulate in the congregation and, whenever possible, raise the subject and gain a sense of peoples' reactions, and they did.

One evening we tried to summarize what we'd learned through our information-gathering efforts. Here are some of my notes as council members played back what they'd heard:

- The Donaldsons originally came to us because of our church name.

- Name reflects an organization that is old and worn out.

- Friends call our church religious extremists—would never visit.

- Name is equated with TV evangelists who are emotional and seeking money.

- Name identifies a historic tradition; visitors know what they're getting.

- Churches with names like ours are the butt of jokes in workplaces.

- Several people said: our name connotes people who are angry and judgmental.

- We don't always have to fit the convenience of the world.

- Keep the name. The Lord warned of persecution.

Persecution? I guess it was hard for me to imagine being persecuted for a church name. Ridiculed? Possibly. Ignored? Probably. Perceived as irrelevant? Predictable. But persecuted?

That same night one of our elders, Rob Magee, spoke in support of the name change. But he reminded us that our church's name spoke of a rich tradition that we should be careful never to repudiate. It was a needed reminder for those (me?) who tend to get excited and stampede to some conclusion without counting the cost.

"There are two or three things that I always take pride in when I think of churches in our historic line," Rob said. "Our kind of church and the way it is governed is similar to instant coffee. You can brew one up like ours in no time. And that's why congregations like ours were among the first to appear on the scene whenever there was a new town or village formed as Americans moved westward. All you needed was a small group of Christians who had a desire to meet and worship and be faithful to the Scriptures. Poof! You had a church in the making. You didn't need some long, drawn-out accreditation process from some denominational headquarters hundreds of miles away.

"And I have always loved our congregational form of governance. We're not a top-down people with bureaucratic officials telling us what we can and can't do. Every member has some say in our decisions. We seek the Lord together and make our choices. We believe that every person stands on level ground before God. And, by the way, I like the idea that although we want our pastors to have a seminary education, we place a higher value on their spiritual qualifications—godliness, Christian maturity, is one of them—than on their professional qualifications. And so, I'm for changing our name. But I'd be among the vocal opposition if it meant we were abandoning our structure of congregational life."

I appreciated Rob's words. But as we walked out the door at the meeting's end, I mentioned to him that our tradition seemed to be losing its way. As churches like ours grow larger, the very congregational participation that he loves so much seems to diminish. It is too often sacrificed, I told him, to the charisma of very powerful leader-types who love to build church empires and parlay these into positions of national reputation and influence.

As the months passed the name change discussions progressed and the leaders saw that the decision to seek a new name forced us to ask questions about the direction of our church and the people beyond us that we really wanted to reach.

Again my notes from one council meeting show us as all over the place with our thinking.

George Huntoon: "Are we an outward-bound church or an inwardly focused church?"

Lisa Benedict: "Do we want to be a people whose real work for Christ is done in the places where we live and generate income, or do we just want to create a safe little society that pretends (or tries to) that the real world doesn't exist?"

Sondra Willard (several times): "Remember—it's not about us."

Rich Fisher: "You can't pretend to think that this is a place with a warm welcome to outsiders, with a name like ours."

Sara Bunyan: "I'm ashamed to admit it, but if anyone asks me where I go to church, I try to cough as I say our church's name."

Tom Davis: "You are who you are regardless of the name."

The discussion was slowed for a moment when George Huntoon read a letter he had received from one of our older members: "I've been a member of this church for forty-two years, and the idea of changing its name would be highly offensive to people like me. My grandparents went to this church, and my parents brought me up here. Change the name, and I'm gone!"

My first reaction: sooner or later there is always someone who puts the "leaving" card on the table. For a moment the letter George read left us stunned. Then someone said, "Sorry to say it, but let 'em go." It sounded so cold, and Sondra Willard reacted with, "Forty-two years is a long time, and I want to think carefully before I'm ready to let anyone like that go."

And so we kept on talking. When we had exhausted ourselves of more to say, we all agreed that a name change would not guarantee that we were suddenly an up-to-date church reaching out to our community. But it would, on the other hand, signal an intention that we wanted to become something different, something better.

Looking back on those conversations—now that the name-change decision has been made—I realize we learned more than a few things as a group of leaders.

One evening, at my invitation, Lisa Benedict opened a council meeting with some devotional thoughts. She incorporated our thoughts about name change with some biblical insights.

Lisa began by reading the paragraph in Genesis 32, where God changed Jacob's name to Israel: "Your name will no longer be Jacob, but Israel, because you have struggled with God and with men and have overcome" (v. 28).

Lisa continued, "There were several name changes in the Bible that signified a change in a person's character or commitment. Jesus changed the name of Simon Peter, the disciple. The early church appears to have renamed a man named Joseph as Barnabas ("son of encouragement") because he was such a source of personal inspiration. And Saul of Tarsus became Paul the minute he began to do missionary work in the Greek world. Perhaps it was Paul's way of refitting himself name-wise to each cultural situation so that he could better connect with people."

As I hinted at the beginning of this story, there came a crunch-time leadership meeting when everyone became fully convinced that a name-change initiative was a worthy one. The council and the elders urged me to mention the possibility to the congregation whenever possible. Their thought was for the people to be familiar with the idea so that when decision-making time came, it would not come as a shock.

And that's exactly what I did. Whenever it was appropriate, I would add *name change* to a list of things people should think and pray about. At first there was no reaction from anyone, and I wondered if changing the church's name was an issue at all. Which shows how naïve I can be.

We were eighteen months into the name-change conversations when, one evening, the leadership met, and someone said, "It's time to fish or cut bait. Are we going to do it or not?" Someone else said, "I'm ready." And with that, everyone came to agreement. Within a few minutes we set a target date to get the congregation's approval. So which name would we choose? More discussion.

A month later Rich Fisher (Rich was a history teacher at the high school) asked if he could make a presentation to the council on the history of church names, and he did a fabulous job.

"Church names that include words like *First* or *Second* or even *Tenth* were very important in the 1800s," Rich said. "They indicated those churches in a community that had been there the longest time and were, supposedly, the stablest and most solid.

"Then there were churches that chose geographical locations for the purpose of identification. Smithtown Baptist Church, First Presbyterian of Centerville, and 19th Street Methodist would be good examples."

Rich mentioned denominational names that had been very popular until recently. Names like Methodist, Baptist, Congregational, Presbyterian, and Episcopal are familiar to us all, and their significance was great in a time when there were marked differences in church structure and doctrine. Most people knew the difference each name signified.

Rich talked about church traditions that have used the names of great Christian figures or place names as a way of memorializing people or events in history: St. James, St. John, St. Paul, for example. Or Aldersgate or Galilee or Knox Church.

Then he talked about the evolution of church identities in the twentieth century. "There was a flurry of new names that used biblical words like *Grace*, *Faith*, *Redeemer*, or *Trinity*. Many churches liked adding the word *Bible* to emphasize the importance of Scripture to their church life. Grace Bible Church and the Gainsville Bible Church are good illustrations."

In the last decades of the 1900s, Rich told us, churches began to choose totally different kinds of names. He noted the name *Vineyard*, which represents a network of churches around the world. Some congregations, he went on, began to refer to themselves as *Christian centers* rather than churches, because they thought that the word *church* was out of date or even pejorative in the minds of outsiders. Names using words like *chapel* or *community church* became increasingly popular, and Rich wondered if these new names might reflect the desire of Christians to adapt to the realities of a secular society that knows little about Christian church life.

And then Rich took his history lesson one final step. "In the early years of the twenty-first century," he said, "we are seeing a new batch of names I would never have imagined. Poetic and metaphorical names like *Liquid* or *River* or *DreamCenter* are being used. Names like *Mars Hill* seem to suggest a church that wants to be known as a thoughtful fellowship."

Rich then asked, "What do you hear when a church calls itself *The Community Church of Joy*? Or how about *NewSong* for a church name? And here's one that will blow your mind. Ever heard of *The Scum of the Earth*? You'll find it on the World Wide Web, and it's located in Denver."

"Where did they get a name like that?" someone wanted to know.

"From 1 Corinthians 4. Remember verse 13: 'We have become the scum of the earth—'? If you're a totally broken person, if you feel like a failure, if you're convinced that you have made more mistakes than a lifetime can resolve, doesn't The Scum of the Earth sound like a place where you might find a welcome?"

I asked Rich if he had reached any conclusions from his studies.

"Well, I see churches trying to send a message with their names, but this time the message is toward the unchurched public rather the 'churched.' If you want to attract Baptist people, then call yourself a Baptist church, I guess. But if you want to extend a hand to anyone who is not in the Christian faith, then you pick a name that speaks to his or her curiosity. Scum of the Earth is the best example of that."

"So let me make sure I hear what you're saying," Sondra Willard said. "You think a church's name ought to be designed primarily for people who are not professing Christians, not even part of our church right now?"

"I do, and I'll go you one further," Rich replied. "I've come to the conclusion that a church should consider changing its name about every ten years or so. The meaning of words change, and you want to be sure you're right on the edge if you want to connect with the newest generation."

There was an audible groan when Rich said that. But when that meeting was over, we were a far more thoughtful group of church leaders.

What would our new name be? I wondered over the next many days. I had lots of brainstorms, but the minute I "test marketed" any of them with various leaders, I could tell that they failed to ring anyone's bell. I guess I'm really not that creative.

Then one evening our elders and council met, and someone (I can't remember who) threw out a name. There was a brief silence, the kind that happens when you're taste-testing food you've never eaten before. Then almost spontaneously everyone started saying yes! The proposed name sounded great; it said what we wanted to say to our community about ourselves; and it seemed to compress into just one word what we believed about Jesus the Savior.

I'm not over the top when I say that we—all of us—instantly embraced the new name. Someone said, "With a name like that, I could be proud to tell people what church I'm a part of." Someone else said, "That name gives you a sense of a group of people going somewhere and doing something that has significance to it." Everyone seemed to agree, and I asked myself, *Have we all been that embarrassed by our old name and lacked the courage to admit it to anyone?* Was the truth now coming out in our exuberance?

In that moment of excitement, none of us could have known that we had just been through the easy part of the name-change process. Despite the fact that we knew there were name keepers out there, I guess we just assumed that when we presented this new name, everyone would share our excitement and march with us.

But in a more clear-headed moment, I should have known that we would be in for a bumpy ride. Here in New England issues like a name change get a thorough going over because we are a people who think that everyone has the right to an independent opinion. Even when the best of us agrees with leadership, there is something in us that loves to raise the alternative just so that we can feel that we had an opportunity to be part of the process.

Our leadership meeting ended that night with a round of prayer that was accented with thanksgiving and anticipation. As each person left the building, they urged me to get the proposed name out into the congregation as soon as possible.

I introduced the proposed name to the church the next Sunday morning and expressed the excitement of the elders and council. A graphic artist in our congregation had spent his Saturday producing several possible versions of what the new name might look like. And as I spoke we were able to put each of his renditions on the screen so that everyone had a visual perspective on what the name might look like on our sign, our worship bulletin, and our stationery.

To my surprise both of our morning congregations showed almost no reaction at all to the name or the design, and that was disconcerting. I guess I'd expected a burst of applause. I had pictured people falling all over themselves to voice their support. I even imagined someone rising from the pews and asking: "What are we waiting for? Let's vote right now!" Maybe in California—but not in New England.

I told both congregations that we would vote on the name change in two months and that the elders (they had met on Saturday morning) had decided that approval of the new name would require an 80 percent majority. They'd made an arbitrary decision to do this because they believed the matter required an unusually large majority of the people. A split decision—let's say 52 percent to 48 percent—would be too divisive.

On Monday our church attorney registered our proposed new name with the secretary of state's office so that we would not be embarrassed by voting on a name that was already spoken for by some other organization in our state. Not long afterward she notified us that we had our new name on record and we could begin using it when the church voted its approval. So far, so good.

The eight weeks went by quickly. The number of name changers grew, and they cheered on the leadership.

But I couldn't ignore the fact that, unfortunately, there was also an increasing group of name keepers. You saw them gathered in the corners before or after church gatherings, and you knew what they were talking about. Every one of them was a good person, earnest and convinced that retaining the old name was the right thing to do. I couldn't think of them as enemies by any means.

Then came the business meeting where the name-change question was on the agenda. The meeting started at 6:00 p.m. with a prayer and a song. There followed about ninety minutes of other business before the proposal to change our name was introduced. We hadn't anticipated that these other things ("nits" I called them) would take so long, and you could tell that with the passage of time people were getting restless. Some young couples slipped out to get their children home for bed. A few older people left, concerned about driving home in the dark. If we had known that other items were going to absorb ninety minutes of valuable time, we'd have put the name-change matter up at the front.

Finally, the moment of decision arrived. And—why was I surprised?—there were more questions about why we wanted to change the name. There were a few stirring speeches about why it would be the wrong thing to do. And, of course, there was a rebuttal or two. All this in spite of the fact that we had invited people to discussions about the name change long before this decision night. In some cases it sounded as if people had never even heard of the name change idea before this moment.

Again, I asked myself, *Why didn't more people get up and speak in favor of the motion? Why was it that in these church business meetings we only heard from the naysayers?* Well, that was my perception anyway.

Please understand—I haven't given you all the details of this saga. In the eight weeks between my announcement and the church business meeting, our leaders met again and again with many different groups of people so that every question could be answered, every doubt addressed. I think it's fair to say that the leaders did their homework, and I felt I'd done my part in the pulpit, explaining the virtues of the decision.

Yes, we were aware that the name keepers were at the meeting in full strength. They had encouraged everyone who had a problem with a name change to be there. We knew that a few of them were on record as being prepared to leave our church if the name was changed. But the overall mood of the meeting seemed positive, so we were surprised that there were even thirty minutes of discussion before someone said, "Call the question."

The vote was by secret ballot, and it seemed an eternity while the counters tabulated the vote. Then came the announcement of the result. The name-change proposal had fallen short by six votes. Six teeny-weeny votes! The leadership (including me) was devastated. Perhaps demoralized is more accurate. We had gone on record as being unanimous in recommending something to the congregation, and our influence hadn't carried the moment.

I was left to close the business meeting with a prayer, and I remember struggling to find appropriate words to thank God for what was truly (to me anyway) a disappointing evening. I was told a few days later that a few of the name-keepers gathered in the parking lot after the meeting ended and shared "high fives" over their "win."

A few days later the church leaders gathered to assess the situation. Had we set the bar (80 percent) too high, they asked? No. We agreed that we hadn't. Had we failed to realize how serious changing a church name might be? We didn't think so. Had we been unwise to even make such an attempt? Some on the council admitted they were tempted to think that was so.

In the days that followed, there were people who spoke to our leaders and apologized for not coming to the meeting. "We were out of town," a few said. "We didn't think our vote would be needed," others claimed. And there were those who said that "the meeting was too long; we had to leave before voting time came."

Interestingly enough, the subject of a name change refused to die. It was clear that a majority—a large majority, in fact—of people had really desired a new name for their church. The result was an increasing pressure to call a second business meeting where the name-change question could be reconsidered.

So two or three months later the elders and council met again in a special session to consider another "go" at the matter. And there was unanimity. In the not-too-distant future, the name change should be brought back to the congregation for a second vote.

You had to know the entire story to appreciate what happened at our next Discovery Group meeting.

> **Stanley Baker:** *Married to Grace. Former CFO, long-time church treasurer—knows finance matters inside and out. Former choir member. Sensitive on music issues. Has a harsh, sarcastic sense of humor. A pastoral side to him also.*

Gail and I met for dinner at Friendly's Restaurant (great crispy-chicken salads), and then we headed for the church to meet with the Discovery Group at seven. It had been a few weeks since our memorable evening with Jason and his worship team, and subsequent nights had been taken up with further discussions on worship and music. Then we wearied of the subject, and I knew we should move on to something else.

To my delight Gail had started coming with me to more and more of the Discovery Group meetings. I found her presence a great advantage because she often provided me with insight into who might be disturbed by our conversations and who was responding positively. A week or two back, for example, Gail commented that she'd been watching John closely and that she was alarmed over his increasing unhappiness with the direction the group was going.

That word of caution came instantly to my mind when John called me on my cell phone earlier in the day and asked if the group could talk about the name-change issue that night.

We were just two weeks away from the second vote, and I knew that John had strong reservations not only about the name change but the fact that the leadership was reintroducing the matter to the congregation.

Even though I had planned a different direction for the evening meeting, I agreed to John's request, thinking that it would be one

more chance to review the reasons why changing the church's name was so beneficial for all of us. At that moment I felt confident that I could persuade any lin-
gering name keepers who were at the table. After all, hadn't the last few
Discovery Group meetings been real trust-builders for all of us?

Yvonne had brought the evening's refreshments; Ernie and Stan had set up
tables and chairs; Connie was designated to pray. Everyone seemed convivial as
we got started, but I must admit that there was a growing check in my spirit
prompting me to wonder if this meeting would end well. I couldn't put my finger on it, but something just wasn't right. Later Gail told me that she had the
same impression the minute she entered the room.

Arlene spoke immediately after Connie finished praying and confirmed our
anxieties. "Some of us," she said, "decided to ask you why we have to face this
name-change thing again. Didn't the church say no last spring? Is this going to be
brought up again and again each time the membership says no?"

I was stunned by the strength in Arlene's voice. Usually she is a remarkably composed woman who supports the leaders of our church and does it with great enthusiasm. But I knew instantly that this was a different occasion.

I guess my first reaction was to feel ambushed. There are certain people in a
church from whom you expect such a frontal attack. In fact, I had anticipated
something from John judging from the sound of his voice on the phone earlier,
and I'd come to the Discovery Group prepared to deal with him. But I hadn't
anticipated facing Arlene, our weekly organizer! As I looked around the table, I
realized that she was speaking for some of the others. This opening comment in
our meeting seemed to have been planned.

I spoke slowly so I could regain my equilibrium. "Well, Arlene, the answer
to your second question is, no, the leadership isn't going to bring this issue up
again and again. If the name change proposal tanks this time, the matter won't
come up for a few years, until there's a new set of leaders in place. And they'll
have to make up their own minds.

"Now let me answer your first question about why it's coming back up. We
had a vote last spring that was just a few votes short of 80 percent. Can I ask you
to think about that? 80 percent! That means that a significant, not a small but a
significant, majority of the church membership really wanted to do this. And

there were many others who didn't make the meeting who asked the leadership to reconsider the matter.

"There's nothing unusual about a reconsidered vote here in New England. Selectmen in our town meetings bring up issues such as buying a new fire engine or floating a school bond initiative, again and again and again until the town gets the message that they're really necessary. People run for the state legislature, get defeated and run again. I know there are reasonable limits, but I don't think it's unusual to reconsider something that is favored by so many folks. If the matter dies a second time, it dies, for as long as I'm around anyway."

Winn, whom I've come to realize has more vision in his little finger than any other ten people in our church, spoke up: "I'm thrilled we're getting a second shot at this issue. I've been waiting for years for people to get smart. When we first started talking about this, I went on the Internet and studied church names. Know what? The top several hundred churches in size in this country almost all have names that reflect reality in the twenty-first century. A few exceptions, of course, but they're mainly in the South where there is a more Christianized culture. But one of the reasons most churches are growing is that they carefully selected a name that tells the community what they're about."

"But we voted no," Arlene said. "I don't care what other churches think or do. I'm not ashamed of our name, and if there's anyone that is ashamed, then let them go somewhere else."

"Arlene, dear," Winn said (he should not have said "dear," because it came across as patronizing, and you don't do that with Arlene), "I'm not your enemy. But you're wrong. You're living out of your generation and trying to impose it on the future. You just can't do that and expect this church to survive. I've heard Pastor Mac say many times, 'We're not going to be here in fifteen years.' We've got to let this church move into the hands of others who know what's best for their time. After all, our parents did it for us."

Winn had made some good points, but he'd lost Arlene by the way he spoke to her. I cringed a little bit, took a millisecond glance at Gail, and could see that she was thinking the same thing I was.

"Our parents didn't give up without a fight," Yvonne said. "That's what's bothering me about all of this. Does every generation go through this? I remember back when Reverend Tally wanted to change the pews in the church because the old ones were so uncomfortable. My parents fought him tooth and nail. In truth they hated those uncomfortable pews, but they weren't going to give them up because he said so. He kept saying that no one would come back to our church a second time after having to sit in those straight-backed pews for an hour or more.

"But our parents—you know this, Connie, you were there—fought him for the longest time. And we young upstarts were frustrated with them. We kept asking why the older people didn't let the younger generation make some decisions, for heaven's sake. And when they finally bought new pews, my father stomped out and stayed away for a year. He only came back after Reverend Tally left. But the truth was that he couldn't find a better church in the area. He'd have come back sooner if it hadn't been for his pride."

Kenneth, who hadn't said much during the last couple of Discovery Group meetings, raised his hand, and for some reason everyone paused and gave him their attention. "Mary Ann and I left a so-called mainline denominational church to come here. The church we left was just plain dead, going through the motions. We came here on a Christmas eve with friends, and we were so impressed with the spirit of the people. Over the next months we kept coming back until we decided that we wanted to be a part of this place.

"One of the things we liked about this church was its can-do spirit. We loved watching people work together and make things happen. And we felt that we were welcomed and included almost immediately.

"But I'll tell you the truth. The hardest thing for us to overcome was the church's name. We didn't want to be labeled with this name. And there have been times when Mary Ann and I have invited people to come with us for something here, and more often than not, we have sensed their reluctance when they found out what church we were going to. As far as we can see, it had a lot to do with the name. The name just doesn't tell the truth about what's going on here . . . who we really are.

"Now some of you have been a part of things here for . . . well, centuries." His small stab at humor caused some laughter and broke the iciness of the moment. And then Kenneth continued: "You don't think anything about the name any more than you notice that the right, front chandelier in the sanctuary isn't working."

"Hasn't worked for several years," Ted said.

"Point made," Kenneth responded. "But those of us who walked into the sanctuary for our first time noticed almost immediately that the light wasn't working. You've grown used to it, Ted. And it's the same thing with the church's name. Means nothing to you; you're accustomed to it. Know what? The name's not for you anyway. It's for people who know nothing about the church and need something to call it. They think about the meaning, or lack of meaning, in the name immediately."

As Kenneth spoke, I caught a glimpse of John's face out of the corner of my eye. I didn't need Gail to tell me that he was seething. Everything about him—his reddening face, his body language, his heavy breathing—signaled "Watch out!" And when Kenneth finished, John blew. And when he blew I knew that he hadn't really heard a word Kenneth had said.

John slapped his open hand down on the table, and several people were visibly startled. "I'm sorry," he said, his voice shaking, "but I'm getting angrier and angrier about this. This church has had the same name for more than one hundred and fifty years. It's been good enough for every generation that has come along until now. Suddenly we have younger people who think we should all just turn the church over to them and let them change anything they want. Does anyone care anymore what people like me think? Pretty soon there's going to be no reason left for me to be a part of this church any longer. And changing the name is the last straw. We voted on this once, and I would think that the vote of the congregation was God's way of saying that the name should stay the same."

I started to speak even though I wasn't sure of what I was going to say, but Winn put up his hand as if to say, "Let me speak first."

"John, you and I have known each other for years. I've heard you say those same things just about every time we've ever wanted to do something new here. With respect, John, I've wanted to say this to you for years. You're always going to be against anything different because it takes you out of your comfort zone. We haven't made that many changes around here. The fact is that you just don't like change of any kind."

"I'm sick of talking about change," John came back at Winn. "Every place I turn someone wants to change something. Nothing ever stays the same anymore, here at this church or in the city or any other place. What's wrong with keeping a few things the way they are? Three generations of my family have gone to churches with this same name. It's been a good name, and now you want to kill it."

"I don't want to kill our name, John," Arlene said. "That's why I put the subject on the table."

"Well, most of you do," he said. A couple more around the table, Yvonne and Stan, I think, said they didn't want to change the name either.

But Winn wasn't backing down. He spoke again to John: "You say that the congregation voted no. Well, it really didn't, John. Only one-fifth of the people at that meeting voted no. Four-fifths of the people voted yes. I'm glad the subject is coming up a second time. If we reject this name-change issue that the leaders—all of the leaders, John—recommend, then we're taking a step back into yesterday."

I was trembling. This meeting was getting hot. How were we going to bring the evening to any kind of a gracious conclusion? How were we going to salvage this group that had been building up to such a fine spirit of unity?

Suddenly, John pushed back his chair. He stood up and looked at Winn and then around the circle and said, "I'm not getting anywhere here. Best for me to leave. Being part of this group was a big mistake." Looking at me, he said, "You're leading this church into a disaster. You're making a big mistake; don't say I didn't warn you." And then looking around the table, he said firmly, "You probably won't see me around here again." With that he left the room. A minute later we could hear the clatter of his diesel-engine pickup truck as it exited the parking lot.

I was incredulous. John had been a part of this church for more than twenty-five years. He had led several building-renovation projects. He was signed up every time the men took an outdoors trip. John would have been included on any list of people who made up the core of this church. And now with almost no warning he told us he was probably going to leave the church.

How can a man do that? How can he say—even in a moment of temper—that he's going to trash twenty-five years of relationships? Was John that kind of a man? Or is there a moment when someone can stand the tidal wave of change no longer and simply runs away?

After a moment as we all sat quietly trying to make sense out of what had just happened, Arlene spoke right to me: "Pastor Mac, John was wrong. But he reflects the feelings of some people in our church. They won't be as blunt with you as he was. But they agree with him. And more of them will leave this church too, if the name is changed."

When I answered Arlene I tried to make my voice as quiet as Mr. Rogers's voice used to be. "You know, Arlene, I think you're right. There are probably some who are going to leave. I have no idea who they are other than the possibility that we're going to lose John and Whitney. But it's predictable that as many as 10 percent of the people may leave if we go through with this. Everything I've ever read tells me that if any kind of organization—school, church, business, or club—tries to make significant changes in its direction, it loses 10 to 12 percent of the people.

"Jesus lost a lot more than that when he spoke to the crowds. The minute he raised the issue of change, people walked. I wish I knew whether or not it hurt him, because it sure hurts me. Frankly, there have been times when I soft-peddled changes I knew were really necessary because I didn't want to lose anybody. And the long-term consequences were always bad. So I've had to accept the fact that people I really like—and I guess John is among them—will drop out when they don't get things their way.

"But do you know what bothers me just as much? I'm bothered by how many people may leave the church if we don't make this change. And I'm bothered about the many who will go unnamed or unidentified, who won't ever come toward us if we don't make this change. I know some of you will struggle with my reasoning, but I couldn't be more serious when I say this."

There were some other comments about name change that evening, but you could tell that we were all a bit disheartened by John's outburst. We were facing the likelihood that John would probably not be a part of our Discovery Group ever again, probably not a part of our church. John had always been a stubborn man, and it was unlikely that he would yield this time. But that didn't mean that we didn't have affection for John. I tell you, it was so sad.

For forty-five minutes we talked. But you know, we really didn't say much. Regardless of how we felt about the name-change matter, we all were deeply hurt by what had happened. If everyone was like me, we all wanted to get out of there, but on the other hand, we were afraid to leave. Perhaps if we stuck around, someone would say something redemptive and would get us back to the moments in previous weeks when we had been so open and endearing to one another. But it didn't happen. The redemptive words did not come from anyone—not even from me.

Finally, I asked Ernie to end the evening with a prayer, something I usually did myself. But my heart wasn't into praying at the moment. "Dear God," Ernie prayed, "please be near to our friend John tonight . . . He's really angry, and we . . . don't . . . fully understand why he would get so upset . . . I wonder if . . . there are some other things in his life that are bothering him. Let him know that . . . we really do care for him. And give the church patience as it votes . . . in a couple of weeks. And give us wisdom, Lord, because we old codgers really . . . well, struggle with this stuff. Amen."

Since I had a trip to make during the next several days, I suggested that the Discovery Group take a week off. We'd meet again after the church voted on the name-change issue. I think everyone was relieved at my suggestion.

After Ernie's prayer, Arlene came over to where I was sitting. "Maybe I was too harsh," she said. "I didn't mean for the meeting to go that way. But I had to say what I felt. I think you're making a big mistake."

"So if the church decides to change the name, will you be one of those who leave?" I asked Arlene.

"Of course not. Who do you think I am? I believe in this congregational process of ours. Everyone has a voice; everyone has a vote. And if my position is voted down, I live with it. Perhaps it's God's will after all. At least it's the will of the people. When that happens, you accept it! And you get on to other things. But I'd never leave just because I didn't get things my way."

This was typical Arlene, I decided. I'd seen two perspectives this evening. John's, which was *lose, therefore leave.* And Arlene's, *Make your point as strongly as you can and then live with the result.*

We cleaned up and slipped out the door one by one without saying much to each other. The momentum of good feelings developed during the last few weeks seemed to be gone. It was almost as if we were back at square one in this search for understanding about how a church changes and faces its future.

As Gail and I drove home in separate cars, I struggled with deep feelings of failure. *How do other pastors do it?* I kept asking myself. *Some churches seem to slide through these difficult moments so easily. People in other places seem to cheer, even to boast in their ability to make changes. But here in our church? It seems to be another story.*

I SLEPT VERY LITTLE THAT NIGHT. I kept recalling every one of my words to John and to Arlene. Had I needlessly offended them? Could I have handled things better? Would there be any way to approach John and talk this thing through to a resolution? I oscillated from one position to another.

One minute I would imagine a conversation with John when we settled the issue that stood between us and he came back to the group full of apologies. Then the next minute I found my heart hardening and saying, "We're better off without him." But you know something? That second option has never been my way. I didn't go into the pastoral ministry ready to bail on anyone.

The next morning when I checked my e-mail, there was one from John. It read, "Pastor MacDonald: God didn't send you here to destroy this church, but you're apparently going to help make that happen. I want no part of it. Please withdraw my name and my wife's name from the membership list."

E-mail was John's chosen form for communication. For the moment I accepted it although Gail urged me to try to get a meeting with him. I wrote: "John, at this moment I am heartbroken. Perhaps we both need a few days to quiet our hearts and then say what needs to be said to each other." I clicked on reply, and my message was sent.

TWELVE DAYS LATER THE CHURCH MET in another business meeting. The first item on the agenda that evening was the most important one: the name-change issue. Again, there were about thirty minutes of discussion. But there was something different about this meeting, and it was obvious from the very beginning.

The name changers were on their feet this time. One after the other they spoke of their enthusiasm for the proposed name, their belief that the name would be a rallying point for other initiatives and, best of all, that it would appeal to people who noticed us and wanted to be a part of a church that presented itself in that fashion.

Arlene was also present, making her feelings about the name change known. But she did it with dignity, and one had to show respect for her opinion and the way she expressed it. John, regrettably, was not present.

I should mention that someone in the Discovery Group had run into John and his wife at a soccer game a few days before the business meeting, and he refused to discuss either the name-change issue or whether he might come back to us. He just dismissed the subject with a wave of the hand. "No comment," was all he said.

When the question was called, the ballots were distributed, marked, collected, and put into the hands of the counters. Fifteen minutes later the church clerk was back in the meeting to announce the result.

Before he spoke, the moderator of the meeting wisely requested that no one cheer or clap when the results were announced. A matter of respect, he said, and he was right. I'm not sure that I would have been as smart as he was if I had been in his shoes.

Then there was dead silence as the clerk came to the microphone. Our dear church clerk, for whom we all had much affection, clearly enjoyed these moments when he possessed information that no one else had. He liked to draw out the suspense with his Yankee dignity. And then he gave us the numbers. The name-change issue had passed by 83 percent!

We were a church with a new name. By Wednesday morning there was a new sign at the entrance to our building. The people at the telephone began answering calls with a hyphenated arrangement of the old name and the new one. The local newspaper was alerted with a press release; the church bulletin was redesigned; and I suggested that we penalize ourselves a quarter every time we used the old name by mistake.

But in the midst of all this good stuff was another reality. Our Discovery Group had lost someone, and the confidence of a few others was probably shaken.

From my pastoral notes:

I should have been more aware of how some people were feeling about the name-change issue. What about forming an "Information Team," whose job it would be to constantly find ways to listen to what people are thinking and asking? Such a team could plan a year of information gathering by sitting with leaders and asking what they need to know to make good decisions and offer sound leadership. Then they could play back to leadership what they hear people saying about these issues.

In the days after we had voted to change the church's name, I began to pick up rumors about people who were going to leave the church. News of that sort spreads like the flu in a congregation. It doesn't take long until the impression grows—at least in a pastor's mind—that dozens and dozens of people are rushing for the door. So if you're like me—someone with a vigorous imagination—it can be a testy time.

When I am thinking objectively, I am quite aware that bold changes of any kind in an organization result in dropouts. John and his wife, Whitney, were likely to be only the first on the casualty list. I knew it, but I didn't like it.

A church is not helped by those who move about the building saying with lowered voices, "We've really got to pray. There are a lot of upset people around here." Or "Some people are saying that this is the last straw, that they can't take all these changes." Or "I hear that a group got together the other night, and the word is that they—"

We heard in a direct way from only two of those rumored to be leaving. The first was Tony Moore, one of our church ushers who asked to meet with me and said that the name change was a signal to him and his wife that the church was headed in a direction with which they were uncomfortable. He regretted the "dumping" of the church's old name, he said, because he felt it identified a doctrinal (I think he meant ecclesiastical) persuasion about which no one should be ashamed. He wished me well and thanked me for the times I'd been there for him.

I felt badly, of course, but I had to admit that Tony had handled things in what I thought was a Christian way. We would be able to run into each other on the street in days to come and not be embarrassed.

Not so the other person (whose name need not be mentioned) who called and in a mean-spirited way expressed herself to Kelly Martin, our church receptionist. I heard about it later. Over the phone she accused the leadership of being unethical and dictatorial and accused me of wanting to build an empire. She'd seen my type before, she told Kelly, because she'd watched some of the megachurch preachers on television and believed that I was positioning the church for a run in the same direction. The name change, she opined, was a public relations gimmick pointing toward the day we'd go on TV.

I laughed (but probably shouldn't have) when Kelly told me about her call. How could someone so totally misread me? You'll have to look long and hard to find any pastor who has a greater aversion to religious television than I have.

Looking back after the dust settled, I think we lost about fifteen people when we changed the name. A few were core members of our church, and they left big holes in a couple of our ministry programs. Filling their shoes would be difficult. Most of the fifteen (three families and three singles) went to a church with a traditional name where they sang the traditional hymnody and boasted a fidelity to the King James translation of the Bible.

Are there any words that a pastor dreads more than "leaving the church"? There must be, but I can't think of them right now. *Leaving!* I tend to associate the word with defeat or failure—mine. OK, there's probably a sense of hurt pride too. Add to that the second-guessing and the self-doubt that goes on. What could have been done differently or better?

Some are going to ask, Why the fuss over fifteen people?

The truth is, speaking as a pastor, you give your heart to the people of a congregation if this work is indeed a calling. You invest in them, think about them constantly, try to find ways to build *Christ* into their lives. You exalt in their spiritual development. You share their difficult moments. And you rejoice when good things happen to them.

I think Paul was trying to say this when he wrote to the Philippians: "I thank my God every time I remember you. . . . It is right for me to feel this way about all of you, since I have you in my heart" (1:3, 7).

If you really do give away your heart, then when people leave, they take a piece of it with them. I have known more than a few pastors who have given their hearts away piece by piece until one day there was nothing more left to give. It's not unusual for some pastors to reach a point where they can no longer manage the disappointments of people leaving or just hanging around and making trouble. Something dies within them, and they either quit or begin to treat their work as a regular job in which a person counts the days until retirement.

To be honest, sometimes there are people who leave the church and you feel relieved. They demand a disproportionate amount of attention, or they generate a chronic kind of complaining. You finally come to the conclusion that this is not a happy experience for them or for you. They have to be released to find a place where they'll find a better fit.

But to be fair, the fifteen or so who left us after we changed our name were very good people. And that's why I took every one of their "leavings" personally. I loved them, and I felt that I'd tried to give them my best again and again. I'd been a part of some of their lives in an intimate way. I'd dedicated their children; I'd prayed with some of them in tough moments; I'd even helped one couple resolve a marital separation. Now they'd exited from my life.

But among those who left, none affected me more deeply than John Sanders with his angry outburst that night at Discovery Group. Losing him troubled me most. In a moment—in the twinkling of an eye, as they say—he had lost his cool and dumped on me and everyone else at the table. And the Discovery Group people—church-wise anyway—seemed to have been among his best friends. Over and over I asked myself (and Gail) how a man could slough off years-long ties that quickly, that easily. In the days that followed, I replayed the fatal Discovery Group evening over and over again in my mind wondering what could have been done or said differently.

The night after the business meeting when the name change was voted through, George Huntoon stopped by John's house. George had told me ahead of time what he was going to do and that he thought he could talk sense into John. But he couldn't. John was immovable. "Talk to me about golf, the stock market, or house paint," John said to George. "I just don't want to hear about the church anymore. I'm through with it."

When George asked him where he might go to worship, he said, "Nowhere.

I'm through with church. I really am. There's more than enough preaching on TV to keep me occupied. Whitney and I are going to join TV church."

I was in disbelief when George told me this. *Through with church?* It was so out of keeping with everything I thought I knew about John. Was he succumbing, as some older people do, to a bitterness and anger that had been deep within him over the years? Was he unable to cope with a feeling that his world was out of his control? Had John simply grown cold spiritually?

I imagined walking up to John and saying, "John, what kind of a man are you? You and me—we're followers of the Lord. And that means you don't walk out when you don't get your way!" I could hear John saying, "Gosh, Gordon, you're right. I don't know what got into me. I'm so sorry for the way I've acted. See you at the next Discovery Group meeting."

But I never did go to see John. George's account of his conversation with John convinced me that a personal encounter with him might do more harm than good.

So I resorted to writing a letter to John, which I mailed a day or two later.

Dear John,

This is not some official letter coming out of our church offices. It's from me, your friend, a guy who has not been just your pastor but who has enjoyed a lot of good times with you. I have memories (mostly good ones) of times we have sat together and talked over the challenges and blessings of church life. But my most important memories, John, are of the times when you and I did stuff together. You taught me how to put a new washer in a faucet, how to caulk windows, and how to tune up a snowblower engine. You were the person with whom I first walked the forest in snowshoes. You were the man who went with me to New York City when I visited Kyle Sodorstrom at the Sloan-Kettering Cancer Center. And you were the friend with whom I hustled tickets from a scalper at Madison Square Garden so that we could see the Rangers play the Bruins.

John, it's hard for me to believe that all those good experiences could so easily be tossed aside over a disagreement in one area of church life.

So I'm writing to tell you that I'm grieving over our parting of the ways.

And I want you to know that I would be overjoyed if we could get past this moment and that you would retake your place in the "family" and among my friends. And I'm also anxious to say, one more time, that I will always think of the things you've done for me and be grateful every time. John, please don't drop out of our (my) lives.

Gordon

John never responded.

About ten days later John's wife, Whitney, acknowledged my letter with a Christian greeting card. On the front it said, "Thank you, Pastor." It wasn't hard to discern that she was choosing her words very carefully, and I sensed that she was writing out of a broken, and maybe embarrassed, heart. She was writing because he couldn't or wouldn't. She was trying to cover for his bad manners.

Pastor Mac,

Thank you for writing to John. I believe he misses you too. This is all too hard for him to bear, and I don't think he knows how to respond. I'm sure that you and the people at the church have done what you think is best. Pray for us.

Whitney

John just disappeared out of our lives—out of my life. A twenty-five-year relationship with his church screeched to a halt. We all saw John about town occasionally, but the encounters were never more than a wave and a "Good to see you. . ."

But John is not gone from my thoughts—as you can see. Sometimes in an unguarded moment, I have feelings of anger toward him for leaving, and for leaving in such a hostile way. His final words had been a personal attack. In effect he had said that "all the times we've spent together do not contain enough goodwill to overcome this one clash of minds."

One night when our elders were meeting, John's name came up, and someone wondered aloud how he could just drop out of church altogether. And Kurt Yetter said, "You guys need to know that John and Whitney are not the only dropouts who have checked out of church. I could name you at least five older couples that used to be very active here, and one day they just decided that they'd put in their time, that no one really cared about them any longer, and it just wasn't worth the effort to get dressed and push through bad weather for a place that didn't seem like 'home' anymore."

I'm not the youngest pastor, but neither have I reached an age where I could feel like that. But even as Kurt spoke, I began to think of the number of older people who were no longer seen around this church and the others I'd pastored. And Yvonne's words from the very first Discovery Group meeting came back to me: "What I want to know is, who stole my church?"

In all those seminars on church change that I'd attended during the years, no one had offered a workshop on how not to steal a church from a generation that had done the work, paid the bills, and maintained lifelong loyalties.

A month or so later, Gail ran into Whitney Sanders in the produce section at Shaws Supermarket. She told me that Whitney immediately began to cry as Gail offered her a friendly embrace.

When Whitney had gained a bit of control over her emotions, she simply said, "Oh, Gail, I miss you all so much!"

"Then why can't you come back? We miss you too."

"You just don't know John, Gail. He can be a terribly resentful man. I know your husband tried to reach out to him, but—until this name-change thing—Gordon's never seen John when he gets his back up. He's stubborn, and when he doesn't get his way, he can get fierce. I've spent our whole married life tiptoeing around him. He's never hit me, but there have been times—"

Then Whitney began to weep again. And suddenly she said, "I can't talk about it anymore—please forgive me." With that she grabbed her purse from the shopping cart and rushed for the door.

When Gail told me what had happened, I began to wonder again how I'd missed this side of John. Of course I'd seen it that night at Discovery Group, but I'd taken it as a one-time event—something out of John's character. But Whitney seemed to be telling Gail that there was another side to John that most church people had never seen.

Later, after dinner and after we'd cleaned up the kitchen, Gail and I talked about what all of this meant. "Where has God been in John's life?" I asked, not really expecting any answer. Had Jesus ever been on the inside of John's life or simply on the outside? Could a truly converted man maintain a double life like the one Whitney seemed to be describing?

The next morning at the church office I went through the membership files until I found John's church membership application. It had been filled out about twenty-five years ago. On the first page were the usual spaces for name, address, phone number, and birth date. Then on the second page were several questions, the first of which was "When did you become a Christian and what were the circumstances?"

John had written, "1956. High school retreat. Prayed with the speaker to receive Christ."

John had been baptized several years later, and as I pieced the dates together, it looked as though he had joined the church about the time he and Whitney had been married. Thus the baptism, because our church required it of all church members. Did these small details suggest that John's church life was driven by his desire to please or win Whitney and satisfy any questions she had about the wisdom of their getting married?

The elder who had interviewed John for church membership had a brief notation on the back of the application. "I like John. I'm not sure that John *fully*" —he'd underlined this word—"understands what it means to be a Christian. He says all the right words, but I don't know if they truly come from the heart or if he's simply trying to pass the test."

There was a further notation, with the signature of the pastor at that time, that John was baptized on Easter evening.

I put the membership application back into the file folder and went to my desk. I wondered if there was a connection between the elder's suspicions and what I had seen in John's conduct thirty years later.

So now you may understand why these last few weeks had been less than happy ones. In spite of the fact that we'd had a wonderful victory in the matter of the name change, we'd lost some good people. And even though the books said that this was predictable, my heart had something different to say about it.

> **Arlene Lewis:** *Became committed Christian at Billy Graham
> meeting when teenager. Divorced. HS grad. Loves to organize
> things. Red Sox fanatic. Mother, four adult children. Leads small
> group of young mothers. Rather outspoken.*

Forgive me. I may have spent too much time on this matter of changing our church's name. In doing so I've neglected some other significant events in the life of our church that need to surface.

I think it was the Wednesday after the name-change business meeting that I came into the church office and found a note in my box saying that Arlene had called. "Call her ASAP," Kelly Martin, our receptionist, had written.

Gail had been pushing me to call Arlene for the past three days. She'd said, "Arlene has been a pretty loyal supporter of yours, and she's probably hurting and wondering how you're feeling about the fact that she opposed you and the leadership. She needs to hear the sound of your voice and know that you're not mad at her."

"But maybe I am mad at her," I'd muttered in response to Gail's suggestion. I meant the comment to be humorous, but I suppose that, deep down inside, I was irritated by Arlene's opposition to the leadership on the matter of the name change.

On Monday morning as I was leaving the house, Gail said once again, "Don't forget to call Arlene," and, although I said I would, I kept on procrastinating—all that day and the next.

But now it was Wednesday, and Arlene had called *me*. The message seemed to indicate a sense of urgency, but Kelly had gone to the office supply store and I couldn't ask if she had more information.

As I sat down at my desk and began punching in Arlene's phone number, I thought of how many times I have told younger leaders, "Never allow any distance to grow between you and those who disagree with you, especially if they have a track record of being on your team." I was guilty of violating my own principle.

When Arlene answered, I knew she'd recognize my voice, and so I simply asked, "Are we still friends?"

"Pastor Mac? That you? What on earth do you mean—still friends? You provoked at me for some reason?"

That was the way our conversation began, and all my anxiety immediately dissipated. Arlene, ever the master of her emotions and always mindful of keeping things in perspective, was letting me know that the name-change issue was not going to jeopardize our relationship. I immediately thought, *Why couldn't John Sanders be like Arlene Lewis?*

"Well, Arlene, I suspect that the other night was tough for you, and I feel badly."

"It's over. We all said our piece, voted, and heard the decision. So I'm aboard. Let's get past it. I need to know if you want the group to meet again—or are you sick of us?"

All this in one nonstop statement. Should the group meet again? Arlene wouldn't call it the Discovery Group. That was window dressing for her. Call it what it was; and for Arlene it was just *the group*.

"Arlene, are you always like this?"

"Not always. If I ever find you rooting for any ball team except the Red Sox, I'll get violent. But changing the name of the church? I'm OK with that. So what about the group? We meeting again?"

"Everybody good for next Tuesday night?"

"Yeah. They're all asking what's happening. So is Gail coming with you?"

"I haven't asked her, Arlene, but I'll see if she's free."

"Well, everyone likes it when she's there. You know that we love her, don't you? We only *like* you."

This banter was Arlene's version of affection. It's a kind of off-key, dry humor that you have to be alert for, and it's what makes me love New Englanders—most of the time.

I hung up the phone feeling almost an adrenaline high. I realized just how frightened I had been that I might lose Arlene's friendship and encouragement. The fear was gone now and replaced with a sense of well-being. I guess that's why I had avoided calling her. I was too worried that I might have another "John Sanders" on my hands. Of the two of us, Arlene was the much bigger person.

That night after the evening news on TV, I began to think about the Discovery Group meeting. We needed to step back a bit from the confrontational mood of the previous meeting and find something amiable that we could talk and learn about together. I went to my bookshelf and scanned book titles for some ideas. After a few minutes my eyes fell upon a thick book with a black cover. Its title: *The Diffusion of Innovations* by Everett Rogers.[1] I had read it (no, skimmed it) a few years back.

Everett Rogers's book is not exactly recreational reading. But there's a point or two in his book that could become the basis for a good discussion on Tuesday night. And so while Gail addressed a month's worth of birthday cards to friends, I spent an hour or so reacquainting myself with Rogers and his erudite book.

WHEN TUESDAY EVENING CAME, Gail and I ate some cereal at home and headed for the church.

As we entered the Commons, we could hear the vigorous chatter of a group of people who sounded as if they were very glad to be together. Everyone was there except Clayton. He'd called me that morning to say that he was going out on a real date—dinner and a Bruins hockey game—with his special friend, Sara Hughes. I'd chided Clayton about his lack of commitment to the group, and just as he began to think I was serious, I laughed, wished him a good evening, and told him I expected a detailed report about everything that happened.

Just before he hung up, I asked, "Clayton, any chance you're falling in love?" All he said in return was, "I'll talk to you later."

Of course, there was another person missing from the Commons: John Sanders.

Arlene went out of her way to get this evening off to a good start. She'd asked Russ to provide flavored coffee from his fast-food place, and she'd selected a couple of chocolate cakes for refreshments. If we got nothing out of these meetings on Tuesday night, we were going to get calories. It's not hard to engender an elevated group mood with all that chocolate. Soon we were one very happy collection of people.

While everyone was loosening up, I approached Mary Ann Squires and said, "Mary Ann, I don't think I've ever asked you to pray at the beginning of one of these sessions. Would you be—"

"Oh, Gordon," she said. "I couldn't. I don't know what I'd do if you asked me without warning. I've just never prayed out loud in a group before."

"Hey, no problem," I said. "Would you be up to it next time if you had some warning?"

Mary Ann paused and then said, "If you don't mind me praying from notes like Clayton did a few weeks ago. It takes everything I've got not to panic when I know everyone is listening to me. That's why I don't talk much in the group though I love being here. But I think I could work on praying next time, if you want."

"Deal," I said.

Then I asked Ernie, and he quickly said yes. And then I remembered how slowly Ernie prays. "Ernie," I said, "I need a *brief* prayer." He gave me an odd look and then grinned.

But Ernie didn't get my hint, and his prayer took several minutes, or so it seemed. But it was a heartfelt prayer. He recalled the name-change meeting in his prayer and asked God to bring us all together. When he said that, there were several "umms" in the room, and it gave me the sense that everyone was mindful that we needed to work to get back on the same page. Although I tried to concentrate on what Ernie was saying, I couldn't help but feel warmed by the efforts (Arlene's preparations, Ernie's prayer, Mary Ann's desire to pray next time after some preparation) that the group was making to heal any wounds that had been opened in recent days.

When my mind returned to Ernie's prayer, I heard him say: "Father, you've been convicting me that I'm out of touch with people outside of this church. I wonder if it's too late. Am I too old to be of use in helping people find Jesus? If changing the church's name is going to help us get better acquainted with people around here, perhaps you can change something about me?"

It was a curious comment that Ernie made in his prayer. But I could sense his sincerity. He was not speaking empty words. You could tell he meant what he was saying. Little did I realize that in the not-too-distant future, this prayer would be answered in a way that none of us ever could have expected.

When Ernie was through, I looked around the table and said, "I've missed you the last few weeks. You're very special to Gail and me. I know that we've just gone through a tough moment where we didn't all agree about something. And I feel terrible about the loss of a friend at this table—"

"Has anyone tried to get to John?" Evelyn asked.

"George Huntoon has," I said, "and I've written John. But George was unable to convince John that he shouldn't leave us. Why do you think that people can talk about the importance of a church with a congregational system where everyone has a vote—like a democracy—but then walk out the minute the vote doesn't go their way?"

No one immediately answered, and so I continued, hoping to stir up discussion.

"I've been a pastor almost all my adult life. I'm usually the one on the 'selling' end when it comes to programs and budgets and changes. I've never really had the luxury of disagreeing with church leadership. I'm part of it. So I don't really know what it's like to be part of a congregation and develop strong feelings against something. But if I was a church member, I'd like to feel that, after I'd said my piece, I'd go with the majority opinion unless the issue was something totally alien to my faith. I can't imagine walking away from friendships I've developed over a long time."

"Maybe you're making a wrong assumption," Winn said. "Maybe you're assuming that all the people in the church are good friends with each other. But many of us—maybe too many—come here to church and then go back to our families and a few friends in other places. There are a lot of people in this church—and John is one of them—that I hardly know at all. And I've been around for years."

"If you're referring to John, Pastor, very few of us knew him that well," Stan added. "We worked with him on various projects, and we clowned around with him a lot. But I'm not sure that we ever knew John's heart. Or that he knew ours."

"I think Stan's got something there, Gordon," Ernie said. "John has always been a hard worker. He drives himself in his business, and he drives everyone else around him. And his life here at church has always been about work. You could always get John to do something at church if it was related to the building. Give him something to build, and it got done. But the truth is that we never got close to him. And what happened here the other night was not a surprise to me. I've never seen John get that angry, but I always felt that it was a possibility if he didn't agree with you."

"John is a stubborn man," said Lillian. "And I've never seen him do very well at changing his mind. He loves our church in his own way. But his love was a controlling love. And he wanted you to love the church in the way he loved it. That meant keeping it the way it always was. The name change was the last straw. If it hadn't been that, it would have been something else."

Gail suggested that we stop for a moment and pray for John and Whitney. Everyone thought it was a great idea, and so we returned to prayer, with two or three folks talking to God about John on our behalf.

With the last amen spoken, I reached into the knapsack at my feet and I pulled out the Everett Rogers book. "Anyone ever see this book?" I asked. No, no one had ever seen it, and I wasn't surprised.

"This book was written about forty years ago, give or take, and attempts to deal with the whole question of change and innovation. How do you get people to change? Why do some people embrace change while others instinctively resist it?"

"Sounds like a book we all need to read," Ted said.

"Not if it has that many pages," Connie commented.

"There are about five hundred fifty pages in this edition," I said. Connie rolled her eyes in reaction.

"It's not a book that any of us will ever read thoroughly. But there are some fascinating stories and quotes here and there. For example, Rogers tells the story of the Toshiba Corporation that produced the first laptop computer back in the 1980s. How many of you have laptops?"

I think at least ten people raised their hands. I was surprised because our average age was a bit up there. Yet most of us had laptop computers.

"Rogers says that the top leaders at Toshiba were vehement in their opposition to producing laptops. They could not be convinced in the usual way that this was a worthy project."

"And they were crazy, of course," Kenneth said. "Now everyone uses them. Every other person on an airplane has a laptop open the minute you reach altitude."

"Sure, you're right," I said. "But there was a day when some smart company leaders said 'no way.' And the only reason Toshiba manufactured laptops was one man. He really believed in the future of laptops and took a few engineers off to a secret location and built some. If he'd been caught, he would have been fired."

"So how did he convince the leaders to change?" I think Yvonne asked the question. And before I could answer, Kenneth spoke up. He obviously knew the story, perhaps better than I did; this was his business.

"He took those laptops to Europe and convinced some of Toshiba's best customers to try them out. Pretty soon they were moving like hotcakes. And the results convinced Toshiba's leaders that they had a winner. Toshiba never looked back after that. For years they were the number one producer of laptop computers."

"Well, anyway," I said, "that's one of Rogers's stories. And he is illustrating the fact that change never, ever goes down easily with most people. There's a very powerful idea in this book that I'd like us to think about. Rogers has studied the way people respond to changes."

I turned to page 281 in my copy of *The Diffusion of Innovations*, and I showed the group a diagram. It was a simple curved line that rose steeply from the left side of the page to a peak and then fell off just as steeply to the original level on the right side.

"Anyone recognize this?" I asked.

"Sure," Stan said, "it's a bell curve."

"Remember studying bell curves in school?" Almost everyone nodded.

"Well, Rogers's research showed that when people face the question of change, their different ways of reacting can be charted on a bell curve."

Before we'd started I'd set up a whiteboard on an easel just behind my seat. I stood up, pushed my chair out of the way, and traced a bell curve with a black dry-erase marker.

"Let's pretend that the curve represents a congregation like ours. And this congregation is being asked to make a major change in the way it does church.

"Rogers suggests that there will be about 2.5 percent of the people—just a real small group—on the right side of the curve, and he calls them *innovators*. Innovators are people who *love, absolutely love,* change. He calls them 'venturesome.' And he says that you can characterize them as daring and risky. They all welcome risk, and they don't mind failing or being defeated occasionally. They have their eyes on a breakthrough success that is going to happen somewhere along the line.

"Innovators can live with ambiguity or uncertainty. They believe that you should always begin reaching out for things that will improve whatever you're doing or changing what you're doing if it will get greater results.

"I've often wondered if Barnabas in the book of Acts wasn't an innovator. What impresses me about him is that he was always the first to take a chance on some idea or some person. He was a generous giver; he was the first to reach out to the newly converted Saul of Tarsus; he visited a brand-new gathering of Christ followers doing crazy things in Antioch and came back applauding it as a new kind of church. And he was the one to set Saul up in a teaching and missionary ministry. He seemed to love making new things happen."

After we clarified a few other characteristics of *innovators,* I walked back to the whiteboard.

"Now next on the bell curve, just as the line begins to climb, is another group of people who are a bit larger in number. In fact, Rogers's research suggests that in any typical group of people, like our congregation, about 13.5 percent will be these guys. He calls them *early adopters.*

"Early adopters are key people throughout the congregation whom others are likely to trust. And they're trusted because they do not jump quite as fast into change as the innovators, but they do know a good thing when they see it. So when there's a decision to make, everyone looks to the adopters to see how they're feeling about things. And if the adopters point their thumbs up, a lot of other people will begin to march.

"So put these two groups, the innovators and the early adopters together, and Everett Rogers suggests that they will make up about 15 to16 percent of any organization. If there are going to be great changes made in an organization, these two groups have to be in alignment. Their influence will bring the rest of the people along. Can any of you think of places in the Bible where this theory might be demonstrated?"

There was a moment or two while people thought.

Then Winn: "Were Joshua and Caleb part of that first group when they challenged the Hebrews to cross over into the Promised Land?"

I agreed with that possibility.

"How about Jesus' disciples? Were they innovators or adopters?" asked Stan.

"The disciples?" I thought for a moment. "Well, some of them had to be up among the front runners—Simon Peter, perhaps—he was a risky, impulsive, foot-in-the-mouth guy. Yes, I'd call him an innovator or an early adopter. But then you have Thomas, who seemed to be at the back of the bell curve. So he was probably something close to a laggard. But he was a laggard who could be convinced when the end of the story came.

"My favorite candidates would be the small band of soldiers that Gideon recruited to be the vanguard of the mighty army that finally routed the enemies of Israel. You can do a lot more with a small group, at first, than with a large crowd. It seems to me that throughout the Bible you find that the people who had a great, great faith qualify as innovators and adopters. Stephen, the first Christian martyr, comes to mind."

We talked for a while about people in our church who would fit this 15 percent. I kept challenging people to tell me why they would mention this person or that. And always we came back to men and women who believed deeply in the faithfulness of God, who were highly motivated to connect with unchurched people, and who possessed an infectious optimism about everything.

Then I took the group back to Everett Rogers. "In the book the bell curve climbs upward and over the top and then descends to represent the middle 68 percent of the people in an organization. This group, which is the largest, Rogers divides into two groups (34 percent each). The first group he calls the *early majority*, and the second he calls the *late majority*.

"The word he uses for the early majority group is *deliberate*. These folks, Rogers says, like to think, evaluate, watch, talk a bit. He quotes Alexander Pope, the philosopher: 'Be not the first by whom the new is tried, nor the last to lay the old aside.'"

"I'm like that, I guess," Russ said. "It's been my struggle in business. The franchise people come at me with all sorts of new ideas, and I find myself resisting. I want to think for a while, and I want to watch and see if something works in other places. I guess I'm that way at home and here at church, come to think of it. Hey, I'm in the early majority. Unless you guys think I'm in the late group."

Russ took some kidding for that last comment. Lillian told him that he was hopelessly off the back end of the bell curve, and Ted wryly compared him to the knocker inside the bell.

When things were back in control, I continued: "Rogers said that the late majority is made up of skeptics. They approach everything with caution. They've got to see some results—not just a few results, lots of results. They want to be safe, and heavy risk is not in their game plan."

"That's Ted," Connie said with laughter.

But Ted wasn't laughing. "No, the truth is, Connie, you're probably right. Maybe that's why I'm an accountant. I want to make sure all the numbers are working out before I jump. I'm looking at this thing," Ted said as he pointed to the bell curve, "and I'm not sure I like where I am. I don't want to have them say at my funeral some day, 'Good old Ted! He was always in the later majority' . . . sounds awful."

The conversation at the table became more and more fascinating as various people tried to place themselves in one of the sections of the bell curve. More than a few of them revealed things about themselves and their attitudes that might not have come out in any other circumstance. A few told stories about times in their pasts that they thought illustrated why they might be numbered among the early adopters or, on the other hand, among the late majority. One minute we were laughing, and the next moment we were compelled to great seriousness.

I began to watch the clock because I wanted to finish this conversation about Rogers's bell curve before we would have to leave and head for our homes.

"Let me mention one more group on Rogers's bell curve. Sixteen percent of any community or organization, he says, are what he calls *laggards*. They are essentially bound by tradition. They're the last to change . . . if they ever change. If the innovators have their eyes fixed on the future, the laggards have their eyes glued to the past.

"Don't always think that laggards are clueless or even bad people. They can embrace change, but it takes them a long, long time to feel happy or secure. Laggards may be people who have been terribly burned in the past by some terrible failure. That's one of the reasons that people who lived through the Great Depression tend to be against change. They were shaped in a time when people were terrified to risk anything. What you have you hold on to was their perspective."

"Is that a reason why so many of our oldest people fight change?" Connie asked. "I've been sitting here not saying much because I've thought a lot about my parents and how oppositional they were to every possible change there was

. . . everywhere—in town, at the church, even in our home. And they were dirt poor during the Depression. Is that what explains them?"

"I'd say it's worth thinking about, Connie," I said. "I always assume that anyone in their seventies is likely to have the effects of the Depression and the Second World War written on their hearts. There are exceptions, of course. But most people in that era didn't have time to develop their emotions or their sense of risk. They were too worried about where the next meal was going to come from. And I've learned the hard way not to be defensive or impatient toward that generation. They have lots of reasons to appear to be laggards. They know what it is like to lose everything."

The Rogers bell curve turned out to be a wonderful success that night. Before the evening ended, I invited the members of the group around the table to go to the whiteboard and put their initials at a point where they felt they were at this moment and then a second set where they would like to be. Everyone acknowledged a desire to be nearer to the front of the curve.

Two or three stood at the board in silence as they struggled to understand themselves. Some were even emotional. And when we had finished the exercise, we were a collection of people who felt more affection for one another than ever before. It seemed as if we had recouped the losses of an earlier meeting when I wondered if we'd ever meet again. When the evening was over, I thanked Arlene for taking the initiative. "You're an incredible leader," I told her. "You have a wonderful way of bringing people together under tough circumstances."

Arlene was embarrassed by my efforts to affirm her. But I could see in her eyes that she heard me and that the words were a precious gift to her.

Gail and I almost had to push people out the door that evening. And as everyone left, it was clear that they were thinking rather seriously about their places on the bell curve. For some it had been a powerful moment of self-revelation. And for others it was a moment for some hard questions.

Connie Peterson: *Widow, grew up in church, parents were church leaders in the 60s. Husband, Lars, died in hunting accident several years ago. Great reader. Loves all Republicans. Lives modestly although she is more than financially secure. Loves being secretly generous.*

The morning after the bell curve conversation, Connie Peterson called and asked for fifteen minutes of my time. She had a question, she said, about someone who was in trouble. We agreed to meet at the church that afternoon at three.

Connie was universally appreciated in our congregation. She and her brother, Carl—whom I'd never met and who now lived in Virginia—had grown up in the church, their parents (Verne and Dorothy Jacobs) being the kind who were always there if the doors of the building were unlocked.

Other than two years of college in Pennsylvania, Connie has always lived in this area. At the end of that second college year, she came home for summer vacation, met a young man, Lars Peterson, at an interchurch singles retreat, fell quickly in love, and married a few months later. As a result Connie never finished college, and that was regrettable because she is an unusually intelligent woman. I had learned during my three years at the church that if I needed something done (and done well) I should call Connie Peterson.

Married for thirty-five years, Connie and Lars never had children. A couple of years before I came to the church, Lars was killed in a hunting accident up in the Connecticut lakes region of northern New Hampshire. Then in the year following his death, both of Connie's aged parents died of cancer. The church, I'm told, was treated to a display of great courage as Connie dealt with this compounded sadness. Simply put, separated from her brother who lived hundreds of miles away, Connie had to build a life without a supportive family.

In contrast to many in our church who were of modest means, Connie was a wealthy woman. She and Lars had built a successful, statewide, sand-and-gravel company that she sold the year after he died. But even though she was now in possession of a massive sum of money, Connie's lifestyle remained unchanged. She lived in a modest home, drove a midsized car, and clipped coupons from the Sunday paper.

Connie was neither miserly nor greedy about her money. Quite the contrary. She became an intentionally generous woman. She funded a private foundation and spent significant amounts of time vetting organizations where substantial financial gifts could make a difference. Her decisions were never based on emotion or sentiment, nor were they influenced by the sometimes slick and disingenuous approaches made by professional fund-raisers. Connie did her research; she prayed; and then she wrote her checks. More than once she said that money wisely given blesses, but money foolishly given often destroys.

I might add that, more than once, I had been the "broker" when Connie wanted to give anonymously to someone in our church who was in financial difficulty. Under such circumstances the gift came from her personal funds rather than from the foundation.

I tell you this so that you will understand my surprise when Connie arrived that afternoon and told me that it was not money that she wanted to discuss but a person. A person whom I would later believe was sent to us by God.

Connie began by telling about a phone call she had received the day before from her brother, Carl Jacobs, in Virginia. Carl wanted to talk with Connie about his son, Ben, age twenty-eight, who apparently was in the middle of a life meltdown. He had been involved in a disastrous relationship with a woman; he'd gone through a job failure; he was fooling with drugs; and (why was I not surprised?) he was showing signs of depression.

What did Connie's brother want? Just this. Would Connie consider having Ben come to New England and live with her for a few months? Perhaps a change in Ben's living situation would be helpful. Since he had always admired his aunt Connie, Carl's brainstorm was that she might be a turn-around influence for him.

After Connie had told me all this, she asked, "What do you think?"

The truth? My first instinct was to suggest Connie pack her bags and take a slow cruise around the world. I couldn't see much merit in her brother's idea, and my suspicious mind assumed that he might be taking advantage of Connie's generous ways. I think Connie picked up on my resistance to the idea, because she began to offer all kinds of reasons why she thought she ought to do it. Soon I realized that Connie wasn't really asking for my opinion. She was seeking affirmation—and assurance of pastoral support, whatever that might look like. In short it was not mine to frustrate her but to cheer her on in another kind of generosity—giving herself instead of money.

We traded a few stories of people we'd known in the past who mirrored Ben's life patterns. I suggested some ground rules that Connie might want to establish if Ben did come to live with her. We tried to think of people in our church who might have something to offer a broken person like Ben. And the truth was that we really couldn't name anyone—which bothered me. The kinds of people whom our congregation might absorb was rather narrow, I concluded. Ben—should he ever show up at our church—would test our ability to welcome and embrace broken human beings.

Connie and I talked about this for a long while. What would it take for our church to be a place where Ben types could feel as if they belonged? Could such people find God's love among us? Could they find Christ and his power to redeem? Could they come under the influence of God's Spirit who seeks to make us into new kinds of people? Would they meet Christian people caring and supportive enough to give someone the opportunity for a fresh start? We hoped so, we said, but we weren't honestly that sure.

Finally, our conversation concluded, I said a prayer in which I interceded for Ben and for the chance he would come our way. As Connie left I told her that I admired her intentions. I really did.

THE NEXT SUNDAY—FIVE DAYS LATER—I entered the sanctuary about twenty minutes before the first worship service was to begin. The worship band was finishing its sound checks, and the ushers were beginning to greet early arrivals who like to claim certain seats (the same seats every week) before anyone else gets there.

I was there for about thirty seconds when one of the ushers, Nate Emerson, came to my side and said quietly, "Wait till you see what's over there." Nate directed my attention across the room with a nod of his head. And I saw the *what* that Nate was trying to discreetly point out.

Sitting "over there" was a rather large young adult male. The first thing I noticed was his hair. Long—but long hair is no big deal. But what did get your attention was that it was styled in dreadlocks, a—well, how do you say this?—style that conveys the impression to those not in the "know" that the hair hasn't been washed in several weeks.

Moving in that direction, I could see that our visitor wore black pants and a black shirt. There was a string of beads around his neck and a small ring through one eyebrow. Getting nearer, I was impressed by his expressionless face and the deadness of his eyes. To be frank, he seemed totally out of place in the sanctuary that was beginning to fill with people, many of whom were wearing upscale clothing—business casual it's now called.

When I reached him, I said, "I'm Gordon," sticking out my hand.

He didn't stand. But he did respond to my offer of a handshake with a weak, almost lifeless grasp.

"Ben," he said in a voice so quiet I strained to pick it up over the sounds of the instruments up front.

Ben! Instantly I realized I was talking to Connie's nephew. I hadn't realized that what we had discussed on Wednesday would happen so quickly. Connie must have sprung into motion soon after our conversation and invited Ben to New England.

"Aren't you related to Connie?" I asked.

"Yeah, my aunt," was the only answer I got from someone who wouldn't even pay me the courtesy of a look in the eye.

"Connie mentioned to me the other day that there was a possibility her nephew might be coming for a visit."

"Yeah . . . maybe for a little while."

There was not a shred of vitality in this young man. If I'd been in need of a masculine-ego boost, I would gladly have challenged him to a three-mile race. Even with my forty additional years, I would have beaten him soundly.

Suddenly Connie appeared and said brightly, "Hi, Gordon, I see you've met

Ben. He got here yesterday afternoon. I met him at the train in Boston." We talked about Ben's arrival from Virginia, while he continued to sit, looking straight ahead, seemingly disinterested.

Later I learned that one of the ground rules that Connie had set was that her nephew would have to accompany her to church on Sunday. But if Ben had any desire to meet me or anyone else, he hid it well. Finally, I made one more attempt to tell Ben I was glad to meet him—even if I was struggling to be glad—and excused myself because worship was about to get started.

I stole a glance in Ben and Connie's direction a couple of times during the worship hour. When we all stood to sing, Ben remained seated. When our congregational prayer time came and I invited people to greet each other, Ben showed by his body language that he was unapproachable, which is why the people in that part of the sanctuary just ignored him. When I preached, Ben never looked up. He must have been lost in space somewhere.

In the Commons after the service, people milled around drinking coffee and eating doughnuts. I watched from across the room as Ben followed Connie through the coffee line. She tried, in her most enthusiastic way, to introduce him to as many people as she could, but Ben didn't respond to them any better than he had to me.

If you watched closely, you could see that most people really wanted to get away from him as quickly as they could. His appearance (the hair and the ring in the eyebrow were too much of a problem for some) and his lack of engagement were just too much for the average person to handle. And so for the rest of our coffee time, Ben sat in a corner doing nothing except waiting for Connie to indicate that it was time to leave. Just before I headed back to the sanctuary for our second service, I saw the two going out the back door to the parking lot.

I worried for Connie. What had she gotten herself into?

When the Discovery Group gathered on Tuesday night, I came equipped to pick up the discussion of Everett Rogers's bell curve. I was hoping that we'd nail those various categories of people to the wall and figure out what made them tick and whether or not we could identify such people in our congregation who were either embracing or struggling with change.

The first person I saw when I arrived was Connie. She was helping Ernie and Lillian set up the tables and chairs. Kenneth and Mary Ann were the evening vice presidents (as I like to say) for refreshments, and they were arranging things up at the coffee counter.

As I started toward Connie, I was aware that the door had opened behind me and Ernie and Ted were entering the room. I heard Ernie say to Ted (Ernie has this booming voice that can be heard everywhere): "Did you see that 'crazy' with the long stringy hair in church Sunday? He was a piece of work. All dressed in black, ring in his eye, gold chain, looked kind of homosexual. I could only imagine the smell. I mean that hair—betcha it hasn't been washed in months. You wanna be careful shaking hands with a guy like that. Who knows? Those kind can easily have some kind of disease."

Everyone in the room who heard this froze. They stopped whatever they were doing and looked at Connie. I think we were all horrified. We all—but apparently not Ernie—had heard about Ben's arrival, and we couldn't imagine how Connie was going to handle what she'd just heard Ernie say.

Five seconds of silence, maybe more, passed. And then Connie said, "Ernie, not to worry. The 'crazy,' as you put it, washed his hair Sunday morning—in my bathroom. And you can relax; he doesn't have a disease."

Ernie's face was pure confusion. He wasn't sure what Connie was saying, and she repeated herself with a bit more elaboration.

"You're talking about my nephew Ben. He's come to live with me for a while. And he washed his hair before coming to church. And he isn't homosexual either. Maybe depressed. Of course, I don't like the ring in his eyebrow either, but it comes with the rest of him."

You could tell that Ernie felt like the person in the Southwest Airlines commercial who has just embarrassed himself beyond words and hears a voice saying, "Wanna get away?"

But once again Connie showed herself to be a big person. Some people might have mishandled this delicate moment poorly and destroyed the evening for everyone. Connie didn't do that. She walked right toward Ernie, gave him a polite hug, and said, "Ernie, you couldn't have known who Ben was. It's OK. I guess he can be a kind of scary-looking person. But maybe when you meet him, you'll feel a bit better about who he is."

Ernie mumbled apologies to her and then looked at the rest of us and said, "My words were really out of line. I really screwed . . . really blew it. I'm sorry."

We all responded with words like "No problem" and "It's OK, Ernie" and "We understand."

Thanks to Connie's grace the uncomfortable moment passed rather quickly, and when others came, we gathered at the table, coffee in hand, and sat down.

Remember when I'd asked Mary Ann if she would pray sometime? Well, she had come up to me a few minutes earlier and told me that she'd worked on her written prayer. I was delighted and told her to get ready.

"Mary Ann is going to get our evening started," I said.

And she started, reading from a piece of paper. At first she read in a somewhat nervous voice, but it strengthened as she went along. "Our Father in heaven . . . we thank you for your Son, Jesus, and for the Holy Spirit who guides and teaches us. We thank you for the Bible that can help us understand the Christian life. And we thank you for the church and its mission in the world. I want to thank you for this . . . this Discovery Group that has meant so much to Kenneth and me. And thank you for our minister who is so patient with us. Please make this evening a special experience for us. Through Christ our Lord, amen."

When we looked up, Mary Ann said (and it almost seemed out of character with her tendency to be a bit formal), "That's the first time I've ever prayed out loud in my life." You could tell that this was a surprise to some around the table who'd been praying out loud forever and couldn't quite imagine that for someone else this was a pretty big deal.

Then someone started to clap, and we all did it out of affection for Mary Ann. Someone else said, "Mary Ann, that may be the greatest prayer since Martin Luther." The comment caused laugher, and you could tell that Mary Ann felt the affection of the group and was now very much at ease.

When things grew quiet, I opened my mouth to begin the session. But before I could say a word, Connie spoke.

"Gordon, something happened a few minutes ago that I think we need to talk about. But the subject is bigger than what happened between Ernie and me. And I'd like it if I could take a few minutes and tell you what I'm thinking."

I suppose that some who had been present when Ernie had spoken so offensively about Ben began to worry that Connie was about to provoke a scene. But it was soon clear that this was not her intention.

"You all know me as a pretty conservative person," she began. "Gordon talked to us last week about change and that bell curve. I went home thinking that I'm probably one of those . . . what do you call them . . . *late majorities*. I fear that I've become one of those footdraggers who always take a lot of persuading if I haven't had the idea first.

"I was against the name change; I think some of you know that I struggle with loud, repetitive music. And some of you know how I miss the organ, people dressed up in church, things like singing the doxology, and the old-time Sunday evening service. All the way through these group meetings, I've enjoyed myself immensely, but I've always held something back in my heart because I've not understood why the church has to change so much.

"Then Gordon brought Jason and his worship team into the room a few weeks back, and I was amazed at the clarity with which those young people understood what they were doing and why they were doing it. And . . . I . . . just loved them. They awakened something in me."

In saying this, Connie—good old New England-tough Connie—began to lose a bit of her composure. But she pushed ahead with what she had to say.

"I was here the night that John reacted so badly to our discussion about the church's name change. I have always liked John, known him for more years than I'd like to admit. When Lars and I had the gravel company, we did a lot of business with John. But I could not stomach the way he acted that night and the way he's acted, or not acted, since. Forgive me if I'm being judgmental, but I saw more maturity in those kids than I saw in John, a man more than three times their age. It forced me to think: *Who am I, Connie Peterson, more like these days? John Sanders or the young people?*"

There was a bit of silence, and then Connie said, "You don't want to know my answer.

"To be fair to myself, I did see a bit of myself in those young people. I'm talking about the kind of person I was when I was their age. I used to be motivated just as they are. But somewhere through the years I lost a lot of that excitement and began to settle for church-as-usual.

"But that wasn't all I saw. I also saw some of John in myself. I've reacted a lot in the same way that John reacted. I just didn't show it as he did. The same kind of anger we saw in John that night is deep within my heart, and I've had to face it and renounce it. What I really want is more of the same enthusiasm those young kids have. Honestly? I don't want what John showed us. I don't want it in any of us. And I'm afraid it's there.

"Some of you know that I support a few organizations and missionaries with occasional financial gifts." This was an understatement, of course, but it was Connie's typical self-effacing way.

"It came to me that I was contenting myself with thinking that I was a super-spiritual person because I threw a few dollars here and there to worthy projects. During the last few weeks, I've begun to feel God's rebuke. I've sensed him asking more of me than just money. One day I realized that He wanted *me* to give away *me*, not just my stuff. He had some serving for me to do . . . at my age. But I had no idea where this was leading.

"And then—in the middle of all this soul searching—I received a call last week from my brother, Carl, in Virginia. Some of you know him. Carl wanted to talk to me about his son, Ben, who, it turns out, is in trouble. His whole life seems to be falling apart. The bright, lovable nephew I remember has turned into a sullen, maybe even suicidal, twenty-eight-year-old, and his parents are desperate. So, what he was calling about was to ask if Ben could come here and live with me for a while . . . get away from things. He felt that I—and this blows my mind—might be good for Ben. I told Carl I'd call him back, and when I did, I asked if he'd put Ben on the phone. I told Ben I'd heard he'd had some disappointments and I'd like him to come and visit me.

"By Saturday Ben was here, and we've done pretty well together for the first three days. I told him right out of the box that I expected him to look for a job and that I thought Winn might put in a good word for him at Home Depot. Of course, I insisted that he come to church with me. Oh, some routine jobs around the house too . . . and no drugs or drinking and no stupid stuff with women. And he agreed to everything I said.

"So Ben was with me in church on Sunday morning. Ernie didn't know who he was. And that's OK, friend," she said turning toward Ernie.

Then looking around the table, Connie said, "Now here's the important thing. After church, when we had lunch, I asked Ben what he thought of church. And his first word was *Cool!*"

"*Cool!*" Connie repeated the word a second time for emphasis, and then she went on. "Ben thought *our* church was cool! I asked him what was cool about it.

He said he liked the songs even if he didn't know them. He liked the fact that Gordon wasn't all dressed up and pompous. He thought the video that kicked off the sermon was good. And he was fascinated that all of us church people would stand around so long afterward and just talk. He said he loved watching all the children lined up to get doughnuts. And he was impressed with how the old and young people were talking together. And then do you know what he said? He said, 'You people act as if you belong to each other . . . like a family.'

"Do you know what?" And Connie lowered her voice and spoke with deliberate slowness. "All the things Ben liked . . . *all the things Ben said he liked* . . . were things I opposed when they first happened at our church."

When Connie said this, it became so quiet in the room that you could hear each person breathing. Everyone seemed shocked by this insight.

Finally, Connie went on.

"I never realized how difficult a home life Ben had when he was a boy. My brother was an ambitious businessman on a plane every other day. Hardly ever at home. And Julie, his wife, was busy building her own career in real estate. My nephew was put in day care from the first year of his life and pretty much raised himself. As difficult as it is for me to say, I think it's clear that Ben never experienced a home where he could feel safe or deeply loved. It must have been a kind of dormitory in which everyone doted on his or her own interests. I never realized that when I visited Carl's family. So now at twenty-eight Ben is reaping the consequences.

"Now I know what God has been saying to me. He was preparing me to give myself to whatever it's going to take to help Ben find a new direction in life."

Ernie was the first to speak into the silence that followed: "Connie, it's no secret that I have a loud voice and a big mouth. And what I said when I got here tonight was totally out of line. So again, I'm really sorry."

Connie stifled some emotion and murmured a quiet "Ernie, it's really OK."

But then Ernie said, "Connie, can I tell you something that I'm ashamed to admit?"

Connie nodded her head.

"You know that Gretchen and I have a daughter who lives thousands of miles away and her whole life is wrapped up in trying to reach out to people like your nephew, Ben. I go there and see the kinds of people they meet on the streets and have in their homes. And Ben is a saint in comparison to the folks they connect with. So now, even as I speak, I'm sitting here and asking myself, why do I admire what they're doing with broken-down people and yet have a completely different attitude when a struggler walks through the doors of *my* church? When did I become like this? My daughter and her husband would have been the first in line to greet Ben and, for all I know, invite him to dinner on Sunday."

When Ernie finished, Russ spoke up. "Connie, I need for you to know that I have a grandson who sounds a lot like Ben. Maggie and I worry constantly about him. I'd give anything if he would come and live with us so that we could love him as you've done by opening your home to Ben. Ben's a lucky guy."

Stan followed. "I didn't know that, Russ. You and I have something in common. Grace and I also have a grandson who we don't talk much about. We've never felt free to say this to our Christian friends, but"—and now Stan swiped at the beginnings of a tear—"our grandson is a homosexual—his mother and father prefer that we call him gay—and we don't know what to do with the situation. All my life I guess I've despised homo . . . gay people . . . because their lifestyle seems so repugnant to me. I've listened to radio and TV preachers who condemn homosexuality. I've sent those guys money; I've bought their books. And then suddenly I discovered I have a grandson whom I've always loved . . . and he's gay. And more than a few times I've said the meanest and ugliest things about gays in his presence. I can't imagine . . . I can't imagine! . . . what he thinks of me. And you know what? My grandson is not a bad person! He's really a great kid. He doesn't fit the descriptions that those preachers have used over the years."

Kenneth raised his hand as if he wanted to make sure he got the next word. "Thank you for what you've said, Connie . . . Ernie, Russ . . . Stan. Mary Ann and I are the new kids on the block in this group. Some weeks back we told you that we grieve the loss of a couple of unborn children. But we didn't tell you the entire truth, and I apologize for that. I guess we wondered if we could really trust everyone with all that's gone on in our lives. What you don't know . . ." Kenneth turned toward Mary Ann as if to get her permission for what he was going to say next, "is that we actually lost a third child, a daughter that we adopted when she was seven. Her name is Mimi, and when she was eighteen she ran off and never told us where she was going. She's thirty now, and we have no idea where she is. Every effort we've made to find her through the years—police, the Internet, even a private investigator—has been fruitless. Hardly a day goes by that we don't wonder what it was that we did that caused Mimi to disappear. We don't know if she's on the streets somewhere doing drugs—selling herself. She could be dead, and we'd not know it. When we came to this church, we decided that this would be our secret, that we just wouldn't talk about it. The situation was just too hard to explain to people who don't know us."

Mary Ann put her hand on her husband's arm, indicating that she wanted to speak. "When you're a therapist and you're talking every day to people with family problems, you experience a newly broken heart every time you try to help people deal with issues that apparently you couldn't solve in your own home. We understand all the issues that pertain to adoption and abandonment, but . . ." Mary Ann stopped there and couldn't continue. Kenneth put his arm around her and pulled her as close to him as he could.

What in the world is happening here? I asked myself. It was as if we were at a costume party where, at the stroke of midnight, everyone had to remove their disguises. People were exposing their broken hearts and sharing the darker parts of their own private stories for the first time. Faces, usually smiling and projecting confidence, were now marked with deep pain and struggle. Burdens of worry, grief, confusion, and regret, never before mentioned, were being placed, as it were, right on the table.

No one in the room was more shaken at these disclosures than I was. I'd been preaching to these people week after week and didn't have the slightest idea that some of these things were going on in their hearts. *What in the world is church life about,* I asked myself, *if stories like these remain hidden in the hearts of people you thought you knew well?*

Two or three others in the group took their turn to speak of similar experiences going on in their lives. Lillian talked about alcoholism in her family; Winn spoke of a suicide in his. Words like *abuse, prison, gambling addiction,* and *Alzheimer's* came to the table as people recounted things going on in their extended families. And as I listened to all of these descriptions of human tragedy, I couldn't help but conclude that there must be open wounds in every pew in our church, far more than I knew about.

When there was a brief lull in the conversation, Arlene turned to Connie and took her hand.

"Connie, you started all this, and I am so grateful." And then she spoke to all of the Discovery Group. "You all know what I went through when Chip dumped me for a younger woman. So I'm like the rest of you. I love my church, but I am always aware that I have to be careful what I say and to whom I say it. I always feel as if I'm one step away from someone writing me off because I'm a loser. After all, I couldn't hold my marriage together. So my question is this: Do we all have to continue to live like this? Holding secrets from one another? Do we have to pretend each time we come to church, study the Bible, and do things like this . . . this . . . this *Discovery Group?* If this is about discovery, then why aren't we doing more to discover ourselves and one another and what God wants us to know about him?"

"Because we don't feel that we have permission," Clayton said. "I know, like some of the rest of you—Connie, Yvonne—what it's like to grieve; I'm still in the process up to my ears. But—I'm kind of changing the subject here—I've been dying to tell all of you, in spite of that, that I've met a woman I think I can love. I've been afraid that you'd criticize me because I haven't waited long enough since Teresa died. But, honestly, I don't know how to live alone. And I think God has sent someone into my life to love me. But who do you say things like that to?"

Ted said, "Clayton, I'm delighted for you. You bring that woman—is it Sara? Sara Hughes?—to church with you, and we'll all give her a big hug and tell her some things she needs to know about you." It was a good time for a laugh, and Ted provided the opportunity.

And then Ted went on.

"I think we've got homework to do here. For weeks we've been chattering about who stole our church and why we don't like loud music and a bunch of other things. And all the time we were ignoring the most important thing: how God wants to use us, in the midst of all our difficulties, to encourage each other. And if we do that, then we can get on with providing a safe place for people like Ben. Shame on us. We're talking about the wrong things. Connie, you tell me that the very things that Ben liked about us are things you've fought against. Thanks for saying that, because a lot of us could have said the same thing. So if loud music, videos, and doughnuts in this room are going to get the attention of people like Ben, I've got some attitude changing to do. We've got to make this church a place where every person we love and have been talking about could come and find the possibility of new life."

This discussion had lasted ninety minutes. We'd forgotten to take a break to get more coffee, eat food, and visit the bathroom. No one had wanted to stop. And you could tell that something had happened that would leave this Discovery Group forever changed.

Then I spoke. "Since I'm supposed to be in charge, I'm going to pray the ending prayer tonight. Some of you have felt constrained to apologize tonight. And I need to join you. I'm embarrassed that I've been so busy running programs and plotting growth plans that I've not been close enough to see how many burdens you all are carrying. You deserve better than I've been giving.

"But I want you to go home tonight and think about what you've said and heard. And remember there is a strict confidentiality about what we've shared. No one leaks. And then I want you to come back next Tuesday night and be prepared to talk about how we become a church that is hospitable to Ben and all the other broken people who need to be put back together again. I think God is saying something, and we've got to hear what it is. Fair enough?"

Everyone gave quick assent. And then I prayed.

"Lord, I feel as if we've been on a piece of holy ground tonight. How much I love these friends of mine, and how much I want to reach out and touch each one and pray heaven's blessings upon them. Help us not to worry. Help us to be wise and patient with those issues in our lives that bring us such concern. And help us, Lord, to see each other more clearly and graciously. We pray for Ben tonight and ask that you will give Connie great, great ability to get into his heart and offer him hope. I would pray particularly that you would send some godly men into Ben's life who could provide a source of masculine strength for him. Amen."

Everyone helped with the cleanup that night. It was as if no one really wanted to leave the fellowship of the group. And when we finally had to start saying good night, I was impressed with how much hugging was going on. I took note of this and said to myself, *We New Englanders have a lot more warmth and affection in us than anyone ever realized.*

What about a sermon series on biblical people of the bell curve? It would probably take six weeks. Start with innovators like Joshua and Caleb. Early adopters? Stephen or Aquilla and Pricilla. End with a laggard like Judas Iscariot or Jonah. The idea gets my imagination running.

During the next few days, I heard from individual members of the Discovery Group. Several sent e-mails, while others either stopped in to chat at the church office or bumped into me around town. Each person said pretty much the same thing. They had never been part of a meeting like the one we'd had last Tuesday night.

Evelyn summed up the things people in the group were saying in her note to me: "I want you to know how thankful I was to be part of the group last night. I have known most of them for years, but I never heard any of them talk so openly about what they have been going through. I love them a lot more now. Thank you, Gordon, for bringing us together like this."

That seemed to be the prevailing mood that others were trying to express. May I confide a private thought? I found myself wondering—pure speculation, of course—if some of the reason we had the experience we did was not only because of how Connie handled herself in the opening moments with Ernie, *but because John was not there.* What would have been his reaction to the things that unfolded? Would he have ruined the atmosphere with some reactionary word? There! I've said it. And you mustn't tell anyone.

I don't want to rag on John Sanders. But he does typify what I think of when I see those laggards on Everett Rogers's bell curve. I wonder about their defeatist spirit. Do they cast something almost like a negative spell over groups, over congregations? Is there something that gets stymied in our genuine quest for renewal and progress when we tiptoe around the laggards and let them pin us down, intimidate us? I'm reluctant to come to these kinds of conclusions, but the truth is that, in the wake of John Sanders leaving us, the Discovery Group had begun to move on to be a totally different kind of people. God was doing something in their hearts. They were facing the truth about themselves, and—I loved them for this—they were taking a fresh look at the world beyond themselves.

I've heard it said many times that groups and churches grow *first* by subtraction. Was John's leaving an example of this principle?

In the early days of the church there was a married couple, Ananias and Sapphira, who tried to put on a show of generosity but misrepresented their true intentions in the process. The church's leader, Peter, was harsh with them, and they ended up dying (it's a story with which I am not comfortable). *Dying!* Why? I can only assume that the greater message was that people sometimes cannot move forward until some in the group have stepped away. So again I ask, was it necessary for John to disappear for the Discovery Group to take a step forward? Go figure!

On Sunday I ran into various members of the group, and each in his or her way made sure I knew that he or she was looking forward to Tuesday night. This is probably one of the greatest indicators of the health of any group in a church: are its members anticipating their next meeting to such an extent that nothing will stand in the way of their being there?

I need to mention that as I roamed the church halls between services greeting people, I noticed that Ben, dressed exactly the same way as the week before, was surrounded by several of the men in the Discovery Group. Ernie, Stan, Ted, and Russ were there, and I saw the hint of a smile on Ben's face. I breathed a little prayer in which I said, "Lord, look at them; those guys are getting it." And I breathed the hope that Ben would be responsive to their efforts to make him feel as if he belonged.

Tuesday night came and everyone was there *early*—another of those indicators. When I arrived all the tables and chairs were set up and refreshments, thanks to Russ, were laid out. On Sunday I'd asked Yvonne to be prepared to pray, and she was ready as soon as we were all seated.

"Father, we are so happy to be here tonight. I thank you for my friends, and I thank you for what you're teaching us through one another. We're grateful that you've given Connie a good several days with Ben and that he enjoyed church on Sunday. I pray for Ernie as he takes Ben to the UNH hockey game on Friday night. Give them a good time together. Help us to learn tonight from whatever the pastor has to tell us. In Jesus' name, amen."

"The things I learn when people pray," I said when Yvonne finished. She was more up-to-date than I and had more information. "So what can you tell us, Connie?"

"About Ben? Well, Ernie and Russ invited Ben to go to dinner with them last Friday night, and he had a good time with them. Turns out that he likes hockey, so Ernie invited him to a game in Manchester this Friday. Ben was really thrilled. I think he needs some strong, older men in his life. And . . . then he enjoyed being at church Sunday because the men around this table included him in the coffee hour. Oh, Ben got hired at Home Depot, thanks to Winn, and he starts next week. And I think that his mood or his depression is lifting a little. It's like he has a fresh start. I am so thankful. My brother and his wife are beside themselves with appreciation."

There was some further chatter about Ben as Ernie and Russ talked about their Friday evening with him. We were all inspired by what we heard. I couldn't help but think of the change I was seeing in them all. A few months ago this was a self-absorbed group for the most part. But now they were taking delight in someone who was different than they were; they were caught up in the dream of helping someone find new life. They were like a team in this effort. And it was spontaneous.

When they were finished, Gail, who was sitting to my right, said "I'm wondering if you would all think back to the first time you met around this table. I wish you'd pick some words that you think might describe what this group was feeling that first night."

There was silence, of course, as people tried to remember back those several months. And then the logjam broke, and the descriptive words began to flow.

"Nervous."

"In the dark—"

"Feeling left out . . . or left behind—"

"Angry . . . mad—"

"Scared—"

"Scared? Of what?" Gail asked.

"Scared that your husband was going to tell us off," Lillian said. "We knew that we were standing in the way of some things he wanted to see happen, and we expected him to make us feel bad or guilty about it."

"So did that happen?"

"No, Gail, truthfully, it didn't. I guess we were all impressed that he listened to us."

"Any other words that describe the feelings you had when you met that first night?" Gail asked.

"Put out to pasture . . . discarded," Clayton said. "I don't want to sound like I'm whining, but you have to understand that some of us at this table used to run this church. We were the people who made things happen. Now our opinions don't count for much. We're not asked to be on boards. Other people are in control. And sometimes it's hard to face that. So 'put out to pasture' describes it well for me."

"Clayton's right," Stan said. "I sometimes feel that the church is saying, 'Give us your money, but don't get in our way. It's not your church anymore.'"

Then Gail asked, "What words describe your experience together last week? I wish I could have been here. All week long I've heard that you had quite a time."

Again, a bit of silence. Then:

"Openness."

"Love."

"Care."

"Surprise."

"Vulnerability."

"Sorrow."

"Forgiveness."

"I can't put it in one word . . . but an awareness that we all have things to cry about." This was from Mary Ann, and when she said it, many heads began to nod.

"Want to know my word for last week?" I asked. Everyone looked in my direction. I said, *"Generative."*

"Genitive?" Ted asked.

"No, *generative*," I replied.

"You always go for the unusual word, don't you?" Ted said. "Gen–er–ative. So what's it mean?"

"Well, Gail's set me up real well with her two questions. And your responses are a perfect lead-in to something I think it's time to think about.

"*Generative.* You've all heard the word *generator* because so many of us have them in our homes in case the power goes out. A generator produces power. And a generative group could be said to produce spiritual power. In my book a generative group is the very best kind of group there is because it makes an impact. It doesn't squander its potential."

"And the opposite of a generative group? What would you call that?" Arlene asked.

"Well, if you're talking about kinds of groups, I'd call the opposite of a generative group a *toxic* group. Toxic usually refers to something that's poisonous, something that can kill. You can have toxic air, toxic chemicals, and toxic soil to name a few. And I think you can talk about toxic relationships or groups.

"Let me add a third kind of group that sits between these two opposites. For this group I chose the word *habitual*. I thought we might talk about the three groups for a little while. I'd love it if those three words really meant something to you when we go home tonight."

Most of the group members immediately opened up notebooks of varying kinds. As the weeks passed, taking notes had become a trademark of our discussions. Two of the men, Winn and Stan, used PDAs to record their thoughts, but the rest were still into paper and pens.

When everyone was ready, I began.

"Let me start with an idea that's been banging around in my head for a while. Most people experience their best personal growth and their most satisfying fellowship in groups of about fifteen. You can go two or three numbers below that and above it. But fifteen seems a wonderful number. And that's about the size of this group, isn't it?

"It's been customary to think that Jesus picked twelve disciples to correspond to the twelve tribes of Israel. But I think Jesus knew that a group about that size was the perfect learning group. And what he did with those twelve (I guess they later became eleven) was turn them from a toxic group to a generative team. There are a million books on how he did it. But I'm interested in outcomes.

How had that cluster of men changed when Jesus finished with them? And I like the word *generative* in reaching the answer.

"The first mark of a generative group is so obvious that some of you will want to stop writing. It's *a strong sense of mutual purpose*. Rick Warren wrote about this in his famous book, *The Purpose-Driven Life*. *Purpose* is where it all begins.

"Now getting a bunch of people to agree on a compelling purpose is no small matter. Think back to the first night we got together and how many different ideas we all had about *why* we were meeting or *why* we would keep on meeting. But little by little we have been building a group with a purpose that keeps us showing up each week."

Connie interjected, "We're here trying to discover what our church is supposed to be like and how it needs to keep changing if it's going to get God's work done in our little part of the world."

"Where did you come up with that?" Clayton asked Connie.

"It came to me when I started looking at our church through my nephew Ben's eyes. Ever since I got out of business, I've lost touch with what people outside the church are really like. Then Ben came a couple of weeks ago, and it didn't take long to see human brokenness right up close. I've watched some of you men get involved with him, and I'm saying to myself, so this is what Gordon's been trying to tell us every one of these Tuesday nights."

"Makes sense to me," Clayton said. And several others agreed.

We talked about how people get excited about working together when a great purpose captures their imaginations. A few in the group wondered if our church knew what its purpose really was or if we had lost it. And someone—I think Kenneth—suggested that it would be interesting to ask the elders of our church when the last time was that anyone had discussed this.

When there was a break in the conversation, I suggested a second mark of generativity.

"A generative group is *synergistic*," I said. "The word means that everyone's effort counts, and this combined effort accomplishes things bigger than any individual could have. There are no benchwarmers in a generative group. Everyone has a piece of the action. One of the things I've loved about you is the way you have all pitched in every week to make our meetings happen. You responded to Arlene's organizational skills and did whatever was necessary to get our meetings going on time, keep us fed—you know what I mean. No one has exempted himself or herself from the action. The result? Great meetings.

"A third mark. In a generative group, each person grows in one way or another. Some like the word *mature* better. Whatever word you like—*mature, grow, develop*—it's usually happening to members of a generative group. People grow spiritually stronger rather than becoming depleted. They grow in their love for God. They grow in their understanding of God's purposes. And they often grow in their awareness of giftedness.

"And I just want each of you to know, I've seen every one of you growing. Attitudes, openness, changes of perspective, care for each other. Growth all over the place."

"Not bad for a bunch of old fogies like us," Clayton said.

"Speak for yourself, Clayton," Arlene said.

We took a brief break for coffee and refreshments.

WHEN WE RETURNED TO THE TABLE, I said: "I've got two more marks of a generative group. A generative group is never afraid of conflict. That doesn't mean they love it, but they know that conflict is a part of real life. In a generative group there is a caution sign out whenever there's conflict, but people go out of their way to make it a positive, creative situation. We all become better and closer through our conflicts if we're a generative group.

"Connie and Ernie, you handled a potential conflict beautifully last week. You were both able to speak truth in love to each other. And we're a much better group today because of it.

"The last characteristic is simply that a generative group inspires other people who are looking on. Folks see a generative group in motion and they would like to become a part of it or figure out how to make one of their own."

"And you think we're generative?" Yvonne asked.

"I think we're well on our way . . . no . . . we're probably there," I answered. "I was worried about us in the beginning, but I think God has done something in all of our lives. He is teaching us that we can become something a lot better than we might have been.

"If you think about it, there are several generative groups in the Bible. I think it's fair to call the Jerusalem church a generative group. Can you think of their purpose?"

"I guess more than anything they wanted to preach the gospel in the streets and wherever they could get a crowd," Ernie said.

"Yes, but they also had a strong sense of unity. Wasn't part of their purpose to serve each other and give to one another?" Connie said thoughtfully.

"Here it is in Acts," Evelyn broke in. " 'They devoted themselves to the apostles' teaching and to the fellowship, to the breaking of bread and to prayer' (2:42). That sounds like purpose to me!"

"Were their achievements synergistic?" I asked.

"Of course," said Ted. "They obviously worked together, and thousands came into the church rather quickly as a result. Their love and their generosity attracted a lot of attention."

"Do you think people grew in that church?"

"Sure they grew—they had to," Ernie said.

"The apostles were certainly growing," Clayton said. "They went from being wimps to being about as bold as anyone could be. And look at Stephen. He started out as an administrator and ended up preaching to the leaders in Jerusalem. There were growing people everywhere in that church."

"What about conflict?"

"They had at least one or two big conflicts, but they resolved them rather well," Arlene answered. "Why not? None of them came from New England."

"And would you call them an inspiring group?" I asked.

Several people said quiet yeses around the table. We were in agreement.

"Well, I see almost all those characteristics in the kind of group you've become right here. We've learned a lot, and we're growing. Now—and here's the big question—would you say that we are a generative church?"

Yvonne spoke almost immediately: "I'd rather not answer until I know what the other two groups on your list are like.

"OK," I said. "Let's go to the very opposite end of the continuum."

"The toxic group," Stan said.

"Yeah, toxic. A *toxic group* is filled with people who don't know how to bend in the process of conflict and usually operate from a *me-first* spirit. They measure every initiative on the basis of 'What's in it for me?'

"Second, their group is marked with *low morale*. There is almost no sense of a bright future or vision. And they are territorial—they hold on to things from the past.

"Third, their general method of problem-solving is to *blame* others. Blame other group members; blame the larger organization; blame something going on in the world. Almost all the energy goes into conversations about who's at fault. For some that's easier than going to work to resolve the issue."

"I've been in groups like that before," Lillian said. And several others agreed. One or two started to tell stories. But I asked if I could get through my points before they went any further.

"Toxic groups, fourthly, tend to *drag down* the larger organization around them. Lots of energy is spent trying to resolve their problems and do damage control. For that reason, toxic groups are a danger to younger people and to new Christians. They send the wrong messages about Christ and the gospel.

"And there's one more mark you need to write down. Toxic groups *destroy people*, one after the other. People get cynical, burned out, slanderous, bitter . . . and finally they determine that they'll never again be part of something like this. More than a few of them simply drop out of their church or go somewhere else."

"Think of any biblical churches like this?" I asked.

No one spoke, and so I asked, "What about the church at Laodicea? Listen to this." I opened my Bible to Revelation 3:15–16. "'I know your deeds, that you are neither cold nor hot. I wish you were either one or the other! So, because you are lukewarm—neither hot nor cold—I am about to spit you out of my mouth.' Pretty tough words, huh?"

"There have been times in our church when we've been toxic," Connie said. "I guess we hear about churches like that all over the place."

You could feel the deeper thinking that was going on around the table as people were reminded of situations where a description of toxicity fit.

"So let me take you to the middle position for a moment. I call this the *habitual* group. In a habitual group, activities are *repetitive*. Things are done because they're always done that way. Remember the bell curve from a few weeks ago? These are groups (and churches) that do things over and over again even though they've forgotten the real reason why. They choose to do the things they do because they're comfortable with them and don't want to face the challenge of changing or even risking failure."

"You're thinking about worship at our church, aren't you?" Arlene said. "You think our resistance to new ways is because we want to be comfortable?"

"You're putting words into my mouth, Arlene," I said. "But let's for the moment agree that it's a sometime possibility. I mean, I have a comfort zone too."

I pressed ahead. "When you're in a habitual group, you'll note that there's a lack of passion to be together or to do extraordinary things. So whatever achievements there are take little courage or sacrifice. Making things happen is just not exciting to people in a group like this. They don't want to take risks."

The group was writing all these things down. And, again, you could sense an uneasiness around the table. Was this getting too close to home for some? But if there was uneasiness, I have to credit these dear people that they were not resisting. They were listening, and, in most cases, examining their hearts.

"Habitual groups can be exhausting," I said. "People in these kinds of groups do not go away energized or anxious to expend themselves for something greater than themselves. And that's sad, because I think God wired us to do just that: invest ourselves in something that's bigger than we are. Think of how you all felt last week when you left here. I mean, you were wired, ready to go. And you went out and did things—particularly for Ben—that you would never have done a day or two before. A habitual group never would have done that.

"What saddens me is the number of people I see in their later fifties and sixties who suddenly surrender to an organizational heaviness of some sort. They quit wanting to grow, to make this or that happen. They let their marriages drift, their friendships go shallow, their skills get stale and dull. Somehow all they want to do is duck their heads and run away from the challenges."

"That's what you call retirement," Winn said, "and I for one want nothing to do with it."

There was a bit of nervous laughter, and I decided that we weren't going to go down that road right at this moment.

"One or two last points. Habitual groups try to deny or ignore their problems. They sweep things under the rug and play 'nice' to each other. Nevertheless there is always a little fever of conflict about trivial things. Lots of energy expended, little accomplished."

"This last group describes the church that Mary Ann and I left to come here," Kenneth said. "You've hit the nail on the head, and that's why we had to get out of there. We were growing old in that church, and it would have been better to stay at home."

"OK. Do any of you think *we're* a habitual church?" Winn asked the Discovery Group.

"I think we're going to have to consider the possibility that some parts of our church are," Connie said. "Maybe the younger families see the church differently. Some of them are pouring themselves into various ministries in and out of the church. But us? We're going to have to think pretty carefully about the fact that we're more *habitual* than anything, and that we've been something of an obstacle to those who want to be genitive . . . I mean generative."

Connie's comment was pretty frank, I thought. I'm not sure I'd have said it. I tried to ameliorate her words so that no one would become defensive. "I think there is a certain tendency in every church, every group, every marriage for people to migrate from generative to habitual to toxic. You have to take a regular look at all the relationships you're in and see if there's any slippage.

"Corinth was in serious danger of being a habitual church for many reasons. Remember Paul's words in 1 Corinthians 3:1–3? 'I could not address you as spiritual but as worldly—mere infants in Christ. I gave you milk, not solid food. . .' That's a church moving away from generativity. It's got *habitual* written all over it. And *toxic* is not far behind."

"So what I hear you saying . . . or trying to get us to say . . . is that if we folks around this table don't get our act together, the future is not good." These were Ted's words, and by the time he finished them everyone was deathly silent, looking at me.

I had the feeling that we were at one of the most important moments of our group's life. What I said next might send us in one direction or its opposite. I couldn't afford to blow this.

"I invited you all to be a part of this Discovery Group, first, because I really like you. And second, because I know that this church owes a lot of its existence, humanly speaking, to you and your spouses. But I also know that it is not—nor has it ever been—your church. Nor mine. We have our money and our sweat equity in it, but it's not ours. Not ours—it belongs to Jesus. Remember? He died for it and all other congregations like it.

"If we try to exert ownership and freeze the church into conditions that are comfortable for us, we're going to become hopelessly toxic and lose everything we tried to make happen. Look at what has happened in the last few days with the coming of Ben into our little world. He's forced each of us to look a little differently at a person most of us would like to have avoided. Sorry, Connie."

She murmured quietly "That's OK . . . go on."

"What you have seen in Ben's response to you is what ought to be going on every week among us."

"We have got to understand," I continued, "that this isn't about us in the church. It's about unchurched people that Jesus called 'lost.' *We find them; they don't normally look for us.*"

"So everything is about them—the Bens out there—not about us?" Russ asked.

"That's a strong statement, Russ. I wish you wouldn't force it to sound like that. But the truth is that it is far more about them than us. It's what Jesus meant when he said to the disciples, 'Open your eyes and look at the fields! They are ripe for harvest' [John 4:36b]. He was talking about people—then and now. So the most important question we face as long-term Christians is this: what does it take to engage with people whose lives could be transformed by Christ's love?"

This was hard stuff to internalize for the dear people of the Discovery Group. They couldn't deny that they'd seen just a hint of possibilities in the way Ben had responded to some of the men. And it was beginning to dawn on them that they might have looked at things from too selfish a perspective. But they heard me asking them to surrender familiarity and safety, control and recognition. And that was tough. They might get there, but it would not be without a struggle.

When it came time to go home, I invited people to pray sentence prayers. And this is what I heard.

"Lord, forgive me for being selfish—"

"Father, you know these things come hard for me. Help me."

"God, if we are a habitual or toxic group, show that to us and change us."

"I'd like to pray for John and Whitney. I'd give anything if they'd come back."

"Lord, give us the courage to think differently."

"Bless Ben, Lord. Help him to give his life to Jesus."

"Amen."

Note to myself: do a sermon on how to pray for one another.
Thoughts: We need to feel freer to ask each other for prayer support.
We must not be afraid to lay hands on one another as a symbol of
God's empowerment. And we need to follow up on things we've
prayed for. Did God answer (and how did he?) our prayers? How
do we celebrate answered prayer and reinforce what God wants to
do among us?

J ust before everyone started to leave the Commons on Tuesday night, Ernie asked the men if they could gather together with him. We all joined him, and Ernie brought up his Friday night hockey date with Ben Jacobs.

"I hate to admit this," he said, "but I'm really beginning to wonder what I've gotten myself into. It was one thing when Russ and I were with Ben at dinner last week, but this time it's just him and me. And I don't talk to that many people half my age, especially someone like Ben who's all inside of himself. I keep worrying that I could say something stupid and do more harm than good. I guess I need a lot of prayer and any advice you guys have to give."

Clayton said, "Well, Ernie, you could solve part of the problem by getting tickets for all of us, and we'll go to the game with you." Clayton was grinning when he said this, but for a second Ernie thought he was serious.

"I've only got two tickets. It's a big game against Boston College and—"

"Ernie . . . I was just kidding."

In one way or another, the men all told Ernie they understood and that they would have the same feelings if it were any of them who were going to spend the evening with Ben.

I love what happened next. Winn said, "Ernie, this isn't rocket science. The kid needs an old guy like you to make him feel like he's somebody. Ask him all kinds of questions until you find something he's comfortable talking about. Then listen a lot and keep asking more questions. And whenever you can, tell him something about yourself and how you feel about things. If you can, tell him your story. You've gone through enough stuff in life that there will be something he can connect with. Remember: he needs a father. You're a good father. You can do this."

I was so glad I had kept my mouth shut, because Winn had said what I would have told Ernie, but it sounded a lot better coming from him than from me. Winn was absolutely right. All too often the younger generation feels fatherless, feels that no one listens to them or talks to them about what's down the road in life. Maybe the Bens of this world don't need all the sermons preachers like me want to preach.

What they do need is to know that they belong somewhere to someone. And they need assurance that someone feels they've got some promise in them. And I guess they need to know they're loved. So Winn's counsel was a great start. Ben needed a man who would be a father to him.

I was also fascinated with how carefully Ernie listened to Winn. In a tiny way this was evidence of that *generativity* I'd talked about that night. One member of the group was speaking supportively to another, and everyone else was there to press strength into the one who was about to go into action.

One or two others added thoughts to Winn's comments, and then Stan said, "Could I lead us in prayer for you right now, Ernie?"

Ernie said he'd love that, and we moved in close, put our hands on Ernie's shoulders and listened to Stan pray: "Lord, thanks for giving our friend Ernie the signal to get involved with Ben Jacobs. As the two of them get together on Friday, Lord, we pray that Ernie will be free of the jitters and that he'll know exactly how to be a father to Ben. Lord, we pray for Ben, that he'll feel special and that something will be said that night that will point him in Jesus' direction. He needs you, Lord, and we'd like to see Ernie be your main man in this situation. Amen."

When Stan said, "Amen," we all joined in. One by one we all gave Ernie a masculine version of a big embrace, which usually includes lots of loud back-slapping.

While this was happening I caught a glimpse of the women of our Discovery Group standing across the room watching in respectful silence. I wondered if they'd ever seen anything like this. Maybe not.

On the way home, when I was stopped at an interminably long red light, I took out my PDA and entered the words "Ben and Ernie—Friday night" into the calendar. I checked off "repeat" in the detail box so that for the next three days I would be reminded each morning to fulfill my commitment to pray for Ernie. And I did—whenever the PDA chirped, I lifted Ernie Yost, the HMO manager, and Ben Jacobs, the "crash-landed" nephew of Connie Peterson, to God.

On Saturday morning when I awakened, the first thing that came to mind was Ernie and Ben. *What kind of time had those two guys, with such different personalities and life outlooks, had?* I wondered. I waited until eight, a reasonable morning hour when the whole world should be out of bed, and called Ernie's home.

When Gretchen, Ernie's wife, answered the phone, I asked for him. She said that he had already left the house to go to the dump.

"Nuts!" I said. "I was dying to know about his evening with Ben at the hockey game last night."

"Well, I can tell you this much: he had a very interesting evening," Gretchen responded.

"What's *interesting* mean, Gretchen?"

"Well, Ernie felt they had a great time. But let's just say that Ernie found out how much he has to learn about younger generations. He got home long after midnight, and he kept me awake for an hour talking about Ben and the complications in his life. Ernie kept worrying about whether or not he had anything to offer Ben beyond a dinner and a game. But you need to hear the story from him. He'll be home within the hour. I'll have him call you."

Now I was really curious, and I decided to call Connie.

When she answered, I said, "Connie . . . it's Gordon. Are you in a position to talk or is Ben with you?"

"Ben's down at Home Depot for a training session. I can talk. Something wrong?"

"Not at all, Connie. I just want to know what happened last night. All Gretchen would tell me was that Ernie and Ben had an interesting evening."

"I'd say it was a very interesting evening. In fact, I'd call it a fantastic evening from Ben's point of view. He told me all about it at breakfast."

"So what can you tell me?" I asked.

"Well, Ben said a fascinating thing. He said that the game was nice, but what really meant the most to him was the ride to the arena and back. Apparently he and Ernie had incredible conversations, and after the game was over, they stopped at a Dunkin' Donuts and talked for at least an hour. Ben didn't get in here until twelve thirty."

"I got the feeling from Gretchen that Ernie may have felt he didn't get very far with Ben," I said.

"Just the opposite. Ben loved Ernie's transparency. He told me that Ernie is old enough to be his father and that their conversation was like the one he'd always wished he could have with my brother. Apparently Ernie got him to open up about the last few years in Virginia and all the things that have happened. And there were several times Ernie was able to identify with Ben's feelings. He said enough about his own life that Ben realized that Ernie really understood him. Let me tell you how special the evening was. Ben said to me this morning, and this is a quote: 'Ernie Yost is the first older man I've ever had a serious personal talk with.' Gordon, it makes me wonder where in the world my brother has been all these years. I mean, I know Ben is not the most attractive young adult in the world, but I already have seen enough to love him. I would love to have had him as a son."

"I'm astonished that Ernie could have connected with him so powerfully."

"Why are you surprised? Didn't I see you men praying the other night? Maybe this was God's answer to whatever you were all praying about."

When I hung up the phone, I thought about Connie's words. Ernie: the guy whose prayers seem slow and interminable. The one who isn't sure he's made a good choice in life by going to work in the health insurance world. I would never have predicted that Ernie Yost might be the guy who could reach into Ben Jacobs's soul—this twenty-eight-year-old who was close to being a drop out in life.

Just about an hour later, Ernie called me.

"Gretchen said you phoned," he said when I answered. "You should have called me on my cell."

"I was just wanting to hear about last night with Ben."

"I think it went OK. I'm not sure. When I got home I talked with Gretchen for a long time—maybe she told you—about what it was like. Gordon, he's a pretty complicated guy. He's lived a lot more life than I have, and I'm way beyond twice his age."

"I'd like to hear everything about the evening."

"Well, Gretchen has some plants for Gail that she wants to bring over to your house this afternoon, and if you're going to be there, I'll come over with her and fill you in."

Preachers usually like to keep Saturdays free to polish sermons, but this was something out of the ordinary, so I told Ernie to come ahead.

WHEN ERNIE AND GRETCHEN SHOWED UP after lunch, Ernie and I left the women outside and went into the house where we could talk.

"Last night," Ernie said, "I found myself saying thanks a dozen times for the Discovery Group meetings."

"How so?" I asked.

"Well, I've been listening to you push this issue of church change for quite a few weeks now, and you probably sensed some times that I've been a reluctant *buyer.* Common sense has always told me that you've got to tweak things now and then in a church's life. But now I'm seeing that we're not talking about tweaking. We really are talking *reinvention . . .* that word you've used a few times to describe a total overhaul in the way a church does its ministry."

"Can you tease that out a little bit?" I asked.

"Well, for me it's all become a lot clearer since we saw Ben Jacobs for the first time. I just gotta tell you that the first time he came in the church—you know—I was really turned off. I mean, here was this weird kid (I guess he's older than just a kid) with the gummy hair, the ring in the eyebrow, and that surly face. I mean . . . you see guys like that around but never on your own turf, close up. And it shook me. You know, I've seen a lot of mixed-up people in Colombia when we've visited Amy, but I've never had to deal with them up close myself. And what's worse is that I made a total jerk of myself in front of Connie when I said—"

"Yes, but in the end you handled yourself really well."

"Connie gets the credit for being gracious. Anyway, the more we talked about Ben, the more I began to realize that God might be answering my prayer."

"What prayer?"

"Don't you remember a couple of weeks ago? You asked me to pray, and in the middle of my prayer I heard myself praying that God would use me to help somebody find Jesus. At the moment I really meant that. I just didn't figure that God might have Ben Jacobs in mind. So anyway, a day later Russ and I were talking about Ben, and he had this idea that we should find an excuse to stop by Connie's and see if we could bump into Ben. And that's exactly what happened. We talked him into going out to eat with us, and that went pretty well. And that's how I ended up inviting him to the hockey game last night. The rest is history."

"Gretchen's words were that it was an interesting time."

"I guess I'd call it a mind-boggling time. You know, I think the most important parts of the evening were the drives to Manchester and back. We talked the whole time; in fact, when we got back into town, we stopped for doughnuts and hot chocolate and kept right on talking. Gordon, the guy told me a lot about himself; all I had to do was ask questions and listen. It was like a dam burst inside of him. It was like he'd been waiting to say some things for a long time, and I just happened to be the one to listen. Winn was right the other night. It wasn't rocket science."

Now Ernie got . . . well, let's say, really earnest.

"Gordon, I just can't believe all this young man has gone through. His family life was a disaster . . . I don't know if Connie knows this but—"

"Oh, I think she does, and I think I know what you're going to tell me."

"Ben's father just didn't know how to make it with his son. The man was a workaholic, I guess. And Ben's mother wasn't much different. The way Ben described his life, he was alone all the time . . . or with friends who weren't doing him any good. He told me that he started going to church with a friend and that he really liked it. Then one day when he was about eleven or twelve, I think, a man who worked with young kids in that church drove him home and on the way tried to get him to do some sexual stuff. Ben was terrified, and he never told anyone what had happened . . . until last night. *Until last night, Gordon!* That's close to fifteen years he's been living with that memory locked up inside . . .

never told his father or his mother . . . no one. I can't believe it . . . never said a word about it."

"So no one ever did anything about this man at the church?"

"I guess not. Ben never told anyone. He just never went back to that church or any church, for that matter, until the last couple of weeks when Connie made it one of the conditions for staying with her. But he told me that when he came into our church the first time, memories of that experience came flooding back to him as if it had happened yesterday."

Ernie told me about the other things he and Ben had talked about. Ben had talked about his life in drugs, his desperate attempt to find himself in relationships with women, his failure to keep a job, his disastrous six-month marriage.

"Sounds like you got the full biography, Ernie. What did he learn about you?"

"Well, I suppose he knows a few things. I tried to relate wherever I could by talking about the places where I've struggled and done some stupid things. I told him a bit about what marrying Gretchen had done for me and, even more important, what being a follower of the Lord has meant. I don't know if any of it registered or not."

"Ernie, apparently it all registered. He told Connie this morning that his time with you could not have been better. You were the first man who ever treated him with respect and dignity. You listened to him . . . and you trusted him with your story."

"My story?"

"Yes, the very things you told me that you told him."

"But I wasn't sure that any of it would be interesting to him."

"Interesting? That's the greatest gift men our age have to give to these young men. Whatever you want to say about the homes we grew up in, the fact is that most of us had adults who were basically available to us. But Ben is a good example of a generation that feels fatherless . . . sometimes even motherless. Too many of them have never heard their parents' stories. No one was around at the right times to take on their questions and help them figure out how they were going to make their way in this world. So they had to figure it out for themselves or get insights from their peers. Last night was an important evening for Ben. An older man took him seriously."

"You know, Gordon, I found myself actually liking him. I mean, at first I felt a bit self-conscious being seen with Ben when Russ and I took him out last week. I wondered what other people were thinking when they saw us with this strange-looking guy. But then there came a moment last night when I stopped caring about that. I thought about the times when the Lord hobnobbed with the riff-raff of his time. And I said to myself, *If Jesus did it, if Amy and her husband do it in Colombia, why can't I?* And the moment I got to that thought, I felt a growing affection for Ben. I began to imagine Ben committing his life to Jesus and starting to grow to be whatever Jesus wants him to be."

"You're not saying that you were hoping that Ben would come to a moment when he cut off the dreads and got rid of the ring in the eyebrow, are you?"

"Well . . . I probably started out with those kinds of thoughts. But then it hit me that what Ben looks like is God's problem, not mine. And then I began wondering what church would be like if there were a lot of Bens around—rings and hair and black clothes and all. And I decided that maybe it wouldn't be so bad . . . maybe it would be good for old guys like myself. It would make honest men out of us."

THE NEXT TUESDAY AT DISCOVERY GROUP, we started off the evening with Connie and Ernie telling everyone the story of Ben's experience the night of the hockey game. Two or three times Connie—good, old, tough, New England Connie Peterson—showed emotion as she described what it meant to her that Russ and Ernie had reached out to her nephew.

And then Ernie related his version of the evening. I had cautioned him ahead of time not to disclose certain sensitive matters, and Ernie handled himself wisely. When he was through, everyone had gotten the message that the key to the evening had been Ernie's questions that drew Ben into conversation and Ernie's willingness to lead with his own story and what God had done in his life over the years. Oh, I think there was one more message—that the group's prayers had resulted in God's blessing. In a sense it had been a team effort like in that great Old Testament story of Israel's battle with the Amalekites. Aaron and Hur had held up the arms of Moses while he prayed for Joshua and the soldiers.

When he was through, I said to the group, "I don't think you have any idea of how valuable each of you could be in the lives of younger people if you were willing to be spiritual parents to this new generation. Not all of them of course, but a substantial number, are looking for people with gray hair who will treat them just like Ernie treated Ben."

"But we don't all have hockey tickets," Stan broke in, saying it with a grin. "Maybe if Ernie got us all tickets—"

"Oh good grief! It's not about hockey tickets," I said laughing. "It's about what happens on the drive back and forth . . . when you open up your life and tell the truth about yourself and where Jesus has touched your life."

"You know," Lillian said, "we got just a hint of what you're saying the night we met with Jason and his worship team. I had the feeling that we could have become a lot closer to those young people if we had just tried to listen to them and let them know something of where we were coming from. But it's so hard for me to believe that any of them—Jason, the girls, that drummer, Ben—would be interested in an old woman like me or any of us for that matter."

"You'll never know until you try, Lillian," I said.

That night I talked about Ben's generation and those who were just a few years younger.

Various people around the table began to make comments about things they'd seen in grandchildren or nieces and nephews. By the end of the evening, we had covered a host of topics concerning the behavior and attitudes of the younger generations and how poorly prepared our church was to make them a part of our congregational life.

It was Mary Ann Squires who brought the evening to a wonderful conclusion with a fascinating idea. "Lillian, you mentioned Jason earlier. I hardly know him at all, but I ran into him at Staples," she said. "And I asked when his team was going to lead worship again. He said a week from Sunday, and that they'd be practicing next Saturday morning in the sanctuary."

And here was Mary Ann's idea: "Why don't we ask Jason if we could have a lunch for them after they finish practicing? If we all showed up, it could be our way of encouraging them . . . letting them know we're behind them. We would be saying thanks. Perhaps we'll get to know them a bit better during lunch and do something like Ernie did with Ben the other night."

Only one person, Russ, couldn't commit to Mary Ann's idea because he and Maggie, his wife, were going to be away for the weekend. But for everyone else in the Discovery Group, it was a best seller of an idea.

"Let's call and see if they can do it," Ted said. A minute or two later we had the phone number for the Calder home, and Ted thumbed it into his cell phone. When he reached Jason he told him what the Discovery Group had in mind, and Jason said he was sure he could get everyone on the worship team to be there.

When the evening ended, we had a plan. Our closing prayer was a conversational one.

Kenneth: "Lord, I'm so proud of what Ernie was able to make happen last night."

Arlene: "I agree with Kenneth, Father. And I pray for Ben that he will see the love of Jesus through Connie and her hospitality and men like Ernie who care that much."

Lillian: "Lord, I'll bet that Ben is living with a lot of anger in him. I pray that you will use people like us to help him find a new way to see things and to live."

Stan: "Help us to see our church as a big family that reaches out to people like Ben, . . . a family that treats lost people, broken people—old and young—in the same way you've treated us."

Winn: "Father, please forgive us for being so self-centered . . . so rigid . . . so unkind in our remarks and our attitudes. We really have a lot to learn."

Connie: "You know, heavenly Father, how long I've known most of the people in this room. But I've never loved them as much as I do now. I . . . am . . . . so . . . grateful . . . I—" And with that Connie had to stop praying.

Ted: "I pray that we'll have a great time with the young worship team next week. Help us to be spiritual mothers and fathers to all of them."

There were other prayers, and when it seemed timely, I gave a closing word: "Well, Lord, we've certainly become a discovery group. We're discovering a lot of things about ourselves and about others. We couldn't be more thankful."

And then we straightened up the Commons and headed to our homes.

From my pastoral notes:

Note to myself: if churches have used sports as a way of attracting and sustaining the interest of youth, why not use technology the same way? Young people are into videos and filmmaking. They're flocking to Internet sites like YouTube and MySpace and connecting around home-grown films. We could have a tech lab at church and get younger and older people to mix around film editing, videography, music productions.

A t 11:30 on Saturday morning, Jason Calder and his worship team came into the Commons after having practiced in the sanctuary for two and a half hours. Unlike the first time when the team showed signs of anxiety at meeting with these older people, this time they were a little bit more relaxed. The same was true of the Discovery Group members.

Two nights before the Saturday lunch, Arlene and Jason had talked on the phone because Arlene wanted to know how many people they should prepare for. Would Jason give her the names of everyone so that she could make place cards again?

Jason began giving her the names: himself, Colin, Bethany, Cheryl . . . He named a few more and then said, "Oh, and Ben."

"Ben?" Arlene asked. "Ben who? There wasn't a Ben when you were last with us."

"Ben Jacobs," Jason said. "He's a bit older than all of us, but he's on the team. He's our new PowerPoint guy."

Arlene was stunned.

Later we learned how this had come about. The night that Ernie had taken Ben to the hockey game, he discovered that Ben knew a lot about video production and PowerPoint technology. One of Ben's past dreams was to become a videographer, and he'd taken some courses at a community college in Virginia. Sadly the dream fell apart when he began fooling with drugs.

Ernie talked to Jason about Ben on Sunday, and before the end of the day, Jason had reached Ben and asked if they could talk about the team's need for someone with his expertise.

Ben met with Jason at church on Tuesday. The two took a look at the technical equipment and the ways the team had been presenting its worship material on the screens. It wasn't long before Ben was making suggestions to Jason about how they could improve the quality of the presentations. By Saturday's practice Ben had brought a decidedly new look to the things the congregation would see a week from tomorrow. It would be an understatement to say that the team was ecstatic.

When Ben came into the Commons for lunch after the practice, you could see something new—a glow?—on his face. In just a few days, he had made some new friends—both considerably older and younger, and it looked as if he was in the beginning phase of getting his own "family."

Although Arlene, Connie, and apparently Ernie were aware of Ben's involvement with the worship team during the past week, they had decided to keep it quiet until there was time to know whether or not this was really going to work.

Now Ben was sitting at lunch with the Discovery Group. He would have to leave by one thirty, he said, because he would be working the afternoon shift at Home Depot. I noticed, by the way, that Winn, who also works there, made sure that Ben sat next to him at the table.

When lunch ended, Jason asked if he could say a few things.

"We've been planning next week's worship," he said. "And we wanted to talk with you about some ideas we have. Bethany, could you lead off?"

Bethany Childers took out a small pad. She said, "We have a few questions, and then we want to ask you to help us. First the questions. We're all pretty young on our team, and we realize that when we go to the Bible, we only see things that interest young people. And we asked ourselves what parts of the Bible would some of you like to hear read in a worship service? What verses mean most to you?

As usual there was a moment of reflective silence, and then various people began to speak. Kenneth said he loved John 14 where Jesus talks about going back to heaven to prepare a place for his followers. Lillian talked about Revelation 21 where there is a beautiful description of heaven as a place where there is no crying or pain. It reminded her, she said, of her mother and father and the place where they were now. Stan preferred Isaiah 40 and the words of hope and comfort. Connie liked Philippians 3 where it talks about preparing for the return of Jesus. And while Ted didn't mention a particular Scripture, he said he loved Bible readings about courage and faith, about God's presence and protection.

"When you're my age," he said, "there are moments when life kind of gets scary. You have health issues, and you think about losing people you love very much. And it's important for me to hear assurances that God knows all things and has everything under control."

"I don't think any of us would have thought of that," Bethany said. "Thanks very much."

Bethany had another question. "Tell us about prayer. What do you like to hear people pray for? When we pray, we pray for school and being strong testimonies for the Lord. We pray for someone who has just broken up with her boyfriend or someone who is not getting along with his parents. But what do you like to pray for?"

I couldn't believe that these kids were asking these things. But it made perfect sense if two generations wanted to get to know each other.

Ernie said that his constant prayer was for his grandchildren and the dangerous world they were living in. Stan said that he loved to hear prayers about current events in the world. Lillian talked about friends who were unable to leave their homes because of aging and health issues, about friends who were living alone and felt terribly lonely. The discussion continued for several more minutes, and it grew very serious as some of the Discovery Group members became increasingly vulnerable about issues in their lives that needed prayer. The worship team listened carefully and Bethany scribbled several pages of notes.

Then Jason said, "When we were with you several weeks ago, you named some songs in the hymnbooks you really loved. We know that Pastor Mac loves 'Come Thou Fount of Every Blessing,' and I think it was you Mr. Patton—"

"Hey, please call me Ted."

"OK . . . Ted. I think you said that you love 'Crown Him with Many Crowns'?"

"Someone's got a great memory," Ted said.

"Well, we took those two songs and rearranged them a little bit. And we're going to sing them as part of the worship set next week. And Ben downloaded a video off the Internet that will be playing behind the words when we sing them. The video really blends beautifully with the songs. You won't believe it when you see it!"

As Jason said this, I recalled the morning I'd met the worship team at Panera Bread. We had talked about "Come Thou Fount of Every Blessing" that morning, and Jason had said, "I don't know if this makes sense, but I can't even sing a song like that. The music is so different from our music that it sounds as if it came from some foreign country. I just want to run from it."

Apparently Jason and the others had pushed themselves to learn and adapt a song that they had disdained. On the other hand, I thought some of the Discovery Group members were going to have something akin to a charismatic experience as they listened to Jason's plans. Both groups had come a long distance—*toward each other.*

"One more thing," Jason said. "Mr. Patton . . . I mean Ted, since we're doing one of your favorites, we were wondering if you would do something for us."

"What could that be?" Ted responded.

Cheryl said, "We would like you to tell the congregation about how and why 'Come Thou Fount' was written and what it's supposed to say. You could explain the meaning of *Ebenezer* for everyone."

Ted took a little persuading from both the worship team and the Discovery Group, but he found it hardest to say no to Bethany and Cheryl, who were sitting on either side of him. Everyone cheered when he finally said he would do it.

And that's the way our Saturday lunch went. During the next hour the Discovery Group folks shared with the worship team some of their experiences as choir members and soloists many years ago. Here and there were remembrances that were extremely funny as people recounted times of embarrassment or mistakes that had, at the time, been humiliating. And the youth worship team felt freer to talk about their nervousness and their feelings of intimidation when they led an adult congregation into the presence of God.

Occasionally I would look over to where Ben was seated. He was very quiet, but he was listening, taking in every word. And I thought I saw his face beginning to soften. I tried to imagine what was going on in his mind, and I decided that Ben was probably feeling more and more that these were people to whom he could belong.

And that's one of the first things that has to happen in a *reinvented* church. People of all kinds—the young, the old, the "Bens"—have to feel that they belong. And somewhere along the way, if they are convinced that they have a place in the fellowship, it's quite possible that they will come closer and closer to the day when they will believe in Jesus the Savior. And something told me that such a day was coming for Ben Jacobs.

Whose idea was it to take young people out of the country to places where they can see a brand of faith that puts ours in a better perspective? Convince them to do more trips with older and younger traveling together. Get this congregation out of this building . . . away from here . . . let them see the promise of the kingdom in other parts of the world.

Eight days after that delightful lunch, our church gathered for its weekly worship time. That Sunday was one of the more memorable experiences of my pastoral life. If you had been there with me, I think you would have concluded that, for a New England church, we had something special going on.

The first thing I noticed when Gail and I entered the sanctuary (we sit together in worship on the front row) was that most of the Discovery Group members were sitting in the second row right behind our usual places. I need to tell you that I don't think that any of those folks had *ever* sat in the first half of the sanctuary in their lives. But here they were up front—evidently to cheer on Jason and his team. I wouldn't have dared to think they were there to hear me preach.

Worship started with a bang. Jason and the worship team were radiant with youthful joy, and the congregation picked it up instantly. Right from the first note, the singing was electric. Bethany and Jason took turns introducing each song. With an economy of words they told us why each song had been picked and, where it was helpful, pointed out key words or phrases so that, as we sang, we did it with meaning and heartfelt sincerity.

I have to comment that there was a genius to the selection of their songs. Everybody noticed the mixture of both modern and classic praises, and we were all made to feel a part. I thought about how many times I've looked around while a congregation was supposed to be singing, and most people were just standing silent, blank expressions on their faces. Not this Sunday morning! Everyone was involved up to their eyebrows.

The high point of the music part of our worship came when the worship team welcomed Ted Patton to the front of the sanctuary, and he told the story of Robert Robertson's hymn, "Come Thou Fount." Of course he talked about the significance of the word *Ebenezer*. It was clear that Ted and the worship team had talked about the importance of explaining this word and that Ted had done research on the 1 Samuel passage in which it is found.

"When you sing this word in the second verse," Ted told the congregation, "think of Samuel, the prophet, raising up a monument to God and crying out 'Thus far the Lord has helped us!' And then think of us doing the same thing this morning. That's what we're all here for—to thank the Lord for helping us thus far. Say the word with me—*Ebenezer!*"

And the congregation shouted back to Ted: "Ebenezer!"

Let's just say it was one great moment. Everyone broke out into laughter and applause. These crusty New Englanders had stepped out of their skins and were caught up in genuine praise. Ted said to the congregation, "Say it again . . . louder!"

And this time the response of everyone was thunderous. "Ebenezer!"

And Ted proclaimed once more: "Thus far the Lord has helped us!" And he headed back to his seat in the second row with a huge smile.

When he got there I thought the whole Discovery Group was going to give him high fives. They were as excited as a high school football team scoring a winning touchdown.

There was more to our worship that morning than just the singing. When Bethany led the congregation in prayer, a deep reverential quiet came over the people. Bethany had prepared an incredibly thoughtful prayer. She managed to acknowledge the presence of every generation and their issues through the topics she chose to pray about. You could easily say that we all felt lifted into the presence of God by this young woman's prayer.

I'll not forget the special moment when Kevin, the bass guitarist, read from the Bible. He must have practiced his reading over and over again, because he read the Scripture slowly and with incredible feeling. The congregation picked up the nuance of every word. I had a pinch of regret as I thought about how many times I've read the Bible or heard it read and paid scant attention because it felt as if we were just going through motions. Not this time! Kevin delivered a scriptural word from God, and we knew it had reached our hearts.

I made a mental note: *Bring back the grand event of Bible reading into worship.*

When it came time for the offering to be received, Colin, the drummer, stepped forward to make a comment.

"Last summer most of the members of our worship team went to the Dominican Republic on a missions trip. While we were there we attended a church service that was filled with really poor people. They weren't dressed up like a lot of you are. And we saw how they lived, and it was pretty difficult.

"For me, the thing I'll remember most about that meeting was the offering. People lined up to give their offerings. There were no ushers passing offering plates like ours. These people had to go up to the front and put their money into baskets. Some didn't even have money. They gave . . . maybe . . . eggs or potatoes or something they'd made with their own hands. When we talked about it later, we all agreed that we'd never seen anything like that before. And every time we take the offering here at our church, I think of those people. They gave as much as they could, I guess. And here was what I wanted to say to every one of us: *I never saw such excitement as I saw with those people when they gave their offering.* When we talked about it later, every one of us said that they'd seen the same thing. And Jason showed us in the Bible where it says, 'God loves cheerful givers.' So I'd just like to say to you all today, be really happy when you give. That's all . . . shall we pray?

"God, we want to give you gifts today like our music and our praise. And we want to give you something that each of us has earned. So we pray you would accept our gifts, the big gifts and the small gifts, as a sign of our love to you. Amen."

I didn't look around, but I imagined a lot of happy faces when people put their offerings in the plates. The Monday morning financial reports showed one of the larger offerings of the year.

I need to say in addition that the visuals that we saw on the screen were amazing. In just a few days time, Ben Jacobs must have studied every song Jason's team planned to sing and matched them with an appropriate artistic background. If we sang about the glory of God, Ben used pictures that gave us a perception of splendor. When we sang about the love of Christ, Ben projected symbols of love that grabbed all of our hearts. (Later, after the service, I noticed that, back in the tech booth, the regular tech crew were all around Ben asking questions and discovering that they had a real "pro" in their midst. Suddenly Ben's dreadlocked hair and eyebrow ring were no longer important. Ben was gaining friends and teammates by the minute.)

When I got up to preach, I was so full of joy I could hardly contain myself. I felt full of God's love and presence because the worship had been so powerful. All I could say to myself was that God had given us a tiny glimpse this morning of what can happen when we all overcome our small differences and decide that we're going to get involved with God and his work—*together.*

If someone had indeed stolen the church, this Sunday morning suggested that it was being returned to all—all!—of us.

I'VE TAKEN A TINY SLICE OF OUR CHURCH LIFE and shared it with you during the course of this book. You must have asked yourself from time to time, what did the elders of our church think of all this? What was going on with other people who led worship on other Sundays? With young people who were not part of Jason's team? And with the younger adult leaders of the church who were doing the lion's share of the church's ministry?

Well, the answer is simple. They were all doing their thing, and little by little they were starting to get results. The Discovery Group people began making it a point to let all these people know they were loved and appreciated. Again and again I saw my Tuesday night group volunteering for the small, behind-the-scenes tasks that make a church run smoothly. Soon I felt that our church was indeed getting reinvented. We were no longer headed over the top of the S-curve into oblivion.

In the weeks and months that followed, we began to see strangers come through the door and find places to belong in our various ministry ventures. Most visitors weren't as unique as Ben Jacobs, but each had his or her own adjustments to make as they came to understand the implications of following Jesus.

Our experience leads me to say that if you want to be part of a church that is radically different from anything you've ever known, then plant one—start one. You can create new programs, new rules, and new structures. And you'll have about a one-in-five chance that it will survive. And if that's your call, go for it. There's a lot of nobility in planting churches. It's happening all over the countryside.

But if you are willing to be patient in one of those old churches (like ours) that is pretty high up the S-curve, then put your head down and go to work. Be patient, be prayerful, seek allies, build alliances with other generations. You'll probably have to convince a lot of people, and they'll come dragging their feet like the members of our Discovery Group. But as time passes, somehow the Spirit of God will grab at hearts, and you just may see a miracle—a hundred-year-old church that acts with the spirit of an enthusiastic teenager. That's what happened to us.

But before I end this story about church change, I need to tell you one more thing that absolutely tickles me to death. About a month after that wonderful Sunday morning, I told the Discovery Group that I would have to bring my regular times with them to a conclusion. They protested, mostly out of affection, but everyone knew that this could not go on indefinitely. So we set a date for a last meeting, and Arlene insisted that it be another one of our dinners. She made sure the date was consistent with Gail's calendar, because they all wanted her to be there.

It Was a Dark and Stormy Night . . . Again

*When that Tuesday evening came, guess what? It was a dark and
stormy night. And just as we had done the first night we'd met, we
all found ourselves soaked as we jumped the puddles between our
cars and the side door into the Commons. But once inside we
found the Commons all decorated and lighted only by candles.*

Arlene had arranged for a magnificent catered dinner.
Everything from the appetizers to the desserts was served with
elegance. Throughout the evening we all recounted the discussions we'd had and what we'd learned during the months we'd met.

I was surprised at how much these lovely people had retained. And
I was just as surprised as they spoke of new convictions and new hopes
they had for our church. The conversation was no longer centered on
things that had defined the church twenty or thirty years ago. Now the
talk was about present-tense things that were happening and about
things we all hoped would happen as the church saw more clearly the
challenge of serving in the community in ways that would authenti-
cate the name of Jesus.

When everyone had said something, Connie stood and asked
Winn to join her. It was obvious that the group had planned something that neither Gail nor I knew anything about.

"Gordon, Gail," Connie said, "the group has wracked our brains
to figure out what we could give you that would serve as a memory of
these wonderful times together. We wanted it to be something that
would send a message to you that we are different people than the
ones you met with that first Sunday night. And then we found the
perfect gift for your home.

"Remember the night you brought that thick black book with the long title into our meeting? That was the night you showed us the bell curve and had the nerve to hint that we might all be on the back end. I remember that the word you used was *laggards*. And who knows? Maybe we were exactly that—laggards, every one of us. Well, we hope that this gift will suggest that we now see ourselves as something else."

Having said that, Connie presented Gail with a beautifully wrapped box. And when Gail opened it, she found a magnificent brass bell. Inscribed on it were these words:

> To Gordon and Gail
> Thanks for changing us from
> Laggards into
> Innovators and Early Adopters.
> The Discovery Group

I get tears even writing about that very special moment.

Then Winn spoke. "Gordon, you'll probably never forget the first Sunday night that we all met. That was the meeting that led to all these gatherings. I suspect that if we'd known that we were going to get ramrodded into endless Tuesday evening meetings, we wouldn't have shown up. But we're all glad we did, because you've helped us change our whole view of the church. You've helped us come to love the church even as you had to learn how to love it."

"Amen and amen," Ernie said.

And Winn continued. "When we met that first night, we had just come through a church business meeting where a lot of people stood against a proposal to upgrade our sanctuary. And almost every one of us in this room was among the naysayers and foot-draggers. The truth is, Gordon, that we were laggards. And later on we gave you and the elders a real rough time on the name-change issue. Tonight we'd like to tell you that we regret those moments. And we've asked ourselves how we might make up for time that's been lost because we stood in the way.

"A couple of weeks ago, we had a little meeting without you, Gordon and Gail. The Discovery Group invited the elders and the technical team and the worship leaders to join us. And we all decided to go back to the church and pitch that

$150,000 renovation program again. And just to make it really interesting, we told the leaders that the Discovery Group would provide the first $60,000 toward the total amount. George Huntoon told me Sunday that the elders approved the idea, and they will be announcing another business meeting next Sunday to get the church's yes. We have no doubt—all of us—that the proposal will sail right through.

"And then we have one more thing to tell you about. When we look back across the months that we've been meeting together, we keep on agreeing that one of the most important moments for us all was when you invited Jason and his worship team to come and talk with us. None of us will ever forget that evening when each of the young people told us about their experiences at that church in the Dominican Republic. And we have come to realize that if they had not made that trip, neither they nor we would be where we are today.

"So we decided two things. First, for the next few years, as long as we're able, we are going to make sure that every young person that qualifies for one of our church mission trips will get the funding he or she needs. We'll make sure that if any of them is having difficulties getting the finances together, it will be taken care of.

"And second, we asked ourselves why they should have all the fun. So we've all decided that each year three or four of us are going to go with the mission teams and get the experience of serving."

DURING THE NEXT YEAR the Discovery Group continued to meet without Gail or me. They read books about church innovation and change. They even took a trip together—most of them anyway—and visited some churches that were doing some unusual things.

Some of the husbands and wives of Discovery Group members joined the fellowship as well as a few others in the church. They became a vigorous prayer team, a go-to gang you could depend on when someone needed to be lifted to God.

And I should add that when summer came, Arlene, Winn, Connie, and Yvonne went to the Dominican Republic as part of a mission team. When they came home, let's just say they were different people.

About six months after that last meeting, I married Clayton Reid to Sara Hughes. Three months later I buried Lillian Seamands (cancer). John and Whitney Sanders moved to Florida.

One day Kenneth and Mary Ann Squires received a phone call from their "lost" daughter, Mimi. She was connected with some Christians in Indianapolis who'd formed a church with one of those weird names. She wondered if she could come home, visit, and reestablish contact.

Jason Calder went to college that fall and became a music major. I dream of bringing him back to our church someday as a member of our staff. He's a gifted leader even at his young age.

Ben Jacobs? Many months later Ben made a decision to bow his knee and organize his life around Jesus. He and Ernie Yost had attended a men's retreat, and the speaker said something that put it all together for Ben. Soon after that, Ernie and he began talking about a mentoring program to bring the older and younger men in our church together. Ben did well at Home Depot, and he still works for the company today.

A few months after he first came to us, Ben moved out of Connie's house into a small apartment of his own. I think he's seeing someone. Oh, since you might be curious, I was able to arrange for him to get some excellent counseling from a Christian therapist who seems to have helped him resolve what happened to him as a boy.

And Yvonne Padula? The one who launched this whole story with her irritable comment "Who stole my church?" She stopped me in the post office the other day and said, "I thank God every day that I got my church back."

PREFACE

1. Discuss some of the things that make some people feel like strangers in their own congregations.

2. What does it mean to say that some leaders have no idea what they are getting into when they engage in "growth talk?"

3. Discuss possible thoughts or feelings people might have when they fall "out of alignment" with their church.

4. List some of the unfortunate responses that people pursue when they feel disconnected to their church.

INTRODUCTION

1. As the pastor arranges the tables and chairs in the Commons, he seems uneasy about what might happen that evening when the people gather. What might he gain or lose when he meets with those who are coming?

2. List some common experiences you think people like those who gathered that evening might have had.

3. Name some characteristics that you associate with the *builders* generation.

4. The pastor offers sample comments made by people who feel uneasy about growth in their church. Try to add other similar opinions you have heard or can think of (p. xvii).

5. Identify the principle objectives the pastor shares as he talks about his approach to leading this congregation.

6. The pastor names some groups who seem to have disengaged from the church. How do you relate to his analysis of these people? Are there other reasons that he didn't mention?

CHAPTER 1

1. Express your thoughts on how the pastor opens the conversation on that first evening. Discuss what you think he is trying to do.

2. What are your own responses when you read what the group says in response to the pastor's invitation to express their feelings about what is happening in their church? Which of the comments do you identify with most? If you were there, what might you have added to the questions that were raised at the table?

3. What kinds of thoughts or emotions are expressed as these people talk to the pastor?

4. How are you affected by the pastor's candid admission that he is disappointed that no one spoke of things which had happened during his tenure at the church? What does it say about the group? Or the pastor? Is the pastor being fair in his conclusions?

5. Is Yvonne's comment ("Someone stole my church") something with which you can identify—either as your response on occasion or that of people you know?

6. How do you react when you hear about people "walking out" of a church? Is there something missing in our notion of "church" when people find it easy to drop out?

Chapter 2

1. How does the pastor get this meeting of the Discovery Group under way so that people quickly engage with each other? Discuss what might be learned here about how groups of people launch into substantial conversation.

2. Does the pastor's description of the negativity of conversation about the church in his seminary days have any similarity to conversations sometimes heard in today's churches? Why do some people feel so disappointed in their churches?

3. What impressions come to you as the pastor remembers the encounter with the professor at the seminary? (Look together at Acts 20:28.) What do you hear and how are you affected by what the pastor is trying to say to the Discovery Group?

4. When the pastor speaks of criticizing the church, talk about some of the right and wrong ways to do it. Perhaps you might add to his observations.

5. What is your reaction to Clayton's comment that there are times when he does not feel safe among church people?

6. Read Yvonne's comments (aloud) beginning on page 20. What do you hear her saying and how do her words affect you?

Chapter 3

1. Describe the mood of the group as it gathers for this meeting. What do you imagine is beginning to happen to them? What is causing this?

2. Read Ernie's prayer carefully. Discuss some of the things he's trying to say *both* to God and the group.

3. What reaction do you have when you hear Connie read the Scripture where Jesus walked out of the temple? Try to respond to these words as if you are hearing them for the first time.

4. Someone says of the temple, "It's all about dead religion." List some of the characteristics of dead religion.

5. Do you think Mary Ann Squires's analysis of the disciples' reaction is valid (p. 27)? What can you add about your impressions of the disciples' response to the moment?

6. Contrast the way Jesus saw the temple with the way the disciples saw it.

7. What do you think are some of the root causes of some churches dying?

Chapter 4

1. Get into the head of the pastor as he looks toward the next meeting of the Discovery Group. Why is he struggling?

2. What impresses you about Yvonne's opening prayer?

3. Have someone read aloud the exchange between the pastor and John Sanders. What do you think is going on in terms of content *and* attitude (p. 34)?

4. In the conversation between Jesus and the disciples on the mountain, what is Jesus trying to get at?

5. Describe the differences between life at the temple and life in the early Christian church. Why is this important for the Discovery Group to consider (p. 37)?

6. Who are the major figures in church history that the pastor mentions, and what is significant about each one of them? How do they illustrate the concept of reinvention?

7. What is your response to Yvonne's comment that Jesus is calling the disciples to danger and discomfort? Talk about what this observation seems to be doing to her.

CHAPTER 5

1. Given the information you have, how do you "read" Evelyn Moody? Discuss your impressions about the way this conversation at Borders got started.

2. As the pastor recounts some seventeenth- and eighteenth-century Christian leaders, what observations can you make about them?

3. List some of the technological innovations that began to affect the twentieth-century church positively or negatively. Are there others?

4. What of the pastor's description of some of the recent changes in the church (p. 49)? Again, are there more that he did not mention?

5. Respond to the pastor's comment concerning five generations in the church. Why is this significant (p. 51)?

6. How would you describe Evelyn's conclusions when the conversation at Borders comes to an end (p. 52)?

CHAPTER 6

1. Respond to how the pastor handled Clayton's reluctance to pray. Name some of the values of "out-loud" praying (p. 54).

2. How would you sum up the pastor's comments on the nature of historic change (p. 56)? What is he saying that, perhaps, many people have never considered?

3. How do Russ and Clayton reflect the sorts of changes that people are facing in the market place of our time (pp. 56–67)? What is "change" doing to people in the larger world? Why do many of the same people struggle with changes when they come into the life of the church?

4. Talk about the difference between "suitable adjustments" and "total reinvention" (p. 58).

5. As the group expresses consternation about things that have happened in the church in recent times, which of their comments resonates with you? Would you add to their list? If so, how (pp. 60–61)?

6. Do you agree with the pastor's suggestion that there is a revival of sorts going on today (p. 61)? How does he compare and contrast life in the world today with Biblical times (p. 62)?

7. Read through the pastor's description of how evangelism may be changing (p. 63ff). Express your thoughts and responses.

Points to Ponder

CHAPTER 7

1. What are your observations about the common ways people come to faith in Jesus Christ? Do you have any sense that this process is changing? If so, in what way (p. 68)?

2. *"People want to see evidence that what you believe has legs—that it does things"* (p. 73). Comment about your reaction to this sentence and its surrounding paragraph. Does this match anything in your experience?

3. How is the pastor using the word *belonging* (pp. 74–75)? Describe your church's view of this concept. Are changes necessary in your church congregation when it comes to the need to belong?

4. *"There's very little belonging in most churches until you believe."* How does this observation settle with you (p. 75)?

CHAPTER 8

1. When the power went out in the worship service (pp. 77–79), the pastor convinced the congregation to sing songs that did not require words on the screen. What kinds of songs were they most likely to sing, and why?

2. Identify the sequence of inner thoughts and feelings the pastor admits to having during his seemingly never-ending "Sunday." What's going on in his heart? Do you find his reactions comprehensible? Which one speaks most to you (pp. 76–79)?

3. Think of an organization or church that you know enough about that you could identify the need or the opportunity that it called into existence (p. 80).

4. Can you describe a situation in which someone stepped forward with a vision that compelled people into action? Alternatively, can you think of a situation where the lack of vision diminished the spirit of people (pp. 80–81)?

5. When asked how long programs can last, the pastor responds, *"But only as long as they meet the need and fulfill the vision"* (p. 84). Compare or contrast this answer with the way you see churches you know about dealing with their programs.

6. Discuss Stan's comment (p. 87) that the time to begin new things is when other programs are running smoothly. How ready are most people to accept this principle?

CHAPTER 9

1. Respond to the pastor's statement (p. 90) about doctrinally-defined movements where personal relationships are so easily dissolved. What do you think he's trying to say?

2. On pages 90–91, the pastor speaks of a time when music unified people. Why would this unifying action happen at one time in the life of a church and yet cause just the opposite reaction at another time?

3. As this meeting of the Discovery Group moves ahead, people start identifying songs that have marked their lives. What songs (both secular and sacred) have marked yours, and why (pp. 92–93)?

4. The pastor reviews some times when music strengthened biblical people (p. 94). Identify times when music did the same for you.

5. What impresses you about Mary Ann Squires's story and how the group responded to her? Are there events that might have had a similar impact on your life (pp. 98–99)?

6. How do you see the Discovery Group changing as they gather each week in the Commons? How would you describe them as a group the first time they met? What is different about them now? What has caused these changes?

CHAPTER 10

1. The pastor makes some comments about his perspective of the Discovery Group. What does he say that interests you? Is there anything going on in the group that offers insights into the way all groups which regularly meet should carry on their life together (p. 103)?

2. On pages 104–105, various members of the group reflect on the previous meetings. Discuss any statements which you think bear further conversation.

3. Restate in your own words what you think Martin Luther was saying as recorded on page 106.

4. On page 107 the pastor asked members of the group to think about whether they would have embraced Isaac Watts's music when it was first sung. How would you answer that question for yourself?

5. Review the various periods of music development the pastor speaks about (p. 107ff). What are the characteristics of each period in terms of style and content? What impresses you about this process of change through the years?

6. How did you react when you read Sankey's description of his experiences in leading and singing music during the Moody years (p. 110ff)?

7. *Genuineness* and *authenticity* (p. 116)—what do these words mean to you when you sing Christian songs written in the past few years? How do you see this happening in the worship that occurs in your church?

CHAPTER 11

1. Is the pastor's description of music and worship changes going on in the church typical from your vantage point? What aspects of his account attract your attention, and why (p. 118ff)?

2. What interests you about the young people's reaction to the pastor's attempt to raise their interest in certain old hymns (pp. 120–122)?

3. After the pastor invites the young worship team to meet with the Discovery Group, he begins to have second thoughts (p. 124). Why do you think he would fall prey to sudden caution about such a meeting?

4. The pastor describes (p. 124) what happened at Matt Redman's church when he and his pastor temporarily suspended music from the worship experience. Why did they do this? How would you have responded to this action if you had been there?

5. Talk about how the church leader prayed for the "preliminaries" (p. 125). What does it say about his view of worship? And how is his view different from the way people look at worship today?

6. On pages 125–126, the pastor describes changes in many churches over the past thirty years. What words or sentences does he use that get your attention? Any surprises in what he says?

CHAPTER 12

1. *"Here's your chance to ask any questions you like (about young people)"* the pastor writes to the Discovery Group (p. 128). If you were meeting with a young worship team, list some questions you might bring to the meeting.

2. *I wonder if, in the life of our church, there had ever been a gathering quite like*

this," the pastor writes (p. 128). Why might there be a scarcity of such meetings?

3. Look at the pastor's observations about how some young people appear in the eyes of an older generation. Is he accurate, fair, or appropriate in his remarks? How do you think the younger generation appears in our world today (pp. 128–129)?

4. Think about Clayton's prayer—his way of praying and his comments in the prayer (p. 130)?

5. Detail the highlights you see in the description Jason Calder and his friends offer about worship in the church they visited in the Dominican Republic (p. 131ff).

6. By contrast, explain what Jason and his friends experience in worship in their home church (p. 132ff)?

7. Describe what happens in the process of conversation that begins to draw the two generations together (p. 134ff).

8. Discuss what you think about the way this evening ended.

CHAPTER 13

1. As the pastor recounts the earliest events that surrounded the name-change issue in his church, what jumps out at you as significant or provocative (pp. 139–143)?

2. On page 143 the pastor shares some of his notes about a leadership discussion. Which of these comments is most important to you?

3. When Lisa Benedict and Rich Fisher speak to the group about their thoughts and discoveries, is there anything they say that you'd not thought about before? What in their presentations provokes further thought in you? (pp. 144–146)?

4. When the leadership suddenly finds agreement on a proposed new name, various members of the group begin to speak more openly about their attitudes concerning church names. What do you hear them saying (p. 147)?

5. Describe your thoughts or feelings when you read the pastor's description of what happened after the leadership recommended the new name to the church congregation (p. 148ff)? Differentiate between the attitude of the leaders and the various parts of the congregation. What is going on here?

CHAPTER 14

1. Talk about any changes you discern in the attitudes of Discovery Group members when they meet a few weeks after the business meeting. What comments are made that are worth noting (p. 152ff)?

2. Express what you think is happening in the group as Kenneth Squires offers his perspective on name changers. How are people being affected (p. 154ff)?

3. Think through the "blow up" that occurs when John Sanders loses his temper. What are we learning about John's deepest attitudes? What role did Winn Rilkey play in this process and what do you think about it? Could anything have been done to avert John's exit (p. 156)?

4. Discuss your combined thoughts about the pastor's comments regarding people who leave the church in stressful times (p. 157).

5. Respond to Arlene and the way she handled herself during and after the meeting. Describe how she differs from John Sanders (p. 156ff).

6. Are there any lessons in leadership to be learned by the way the pastor handled himself in this meeting? If so, what are they?

CHAPTER 15

1. When people leave a church, they do it in different ways. What's to be learned as one observe the various behaviors? And what are your thoughts about people leaving a church?

2. Describe what you hear the pastor saying as he shares his own thoughts and feelings about people leaving. Are there any insights here that might help us appreciate how church leaders and pastors feel when there is stress in a congregation (p. 161ff)?

3. Discuss how the pastor's letter to John Sanders (pp. 164–165) is instructive concerning our efforts toward reconciliation.

4. When you have finished the chapter, what do you now know about John Sanders that you might not have known otherwise? Is he a "strong" Christian man, or is he something else? Is John Sanders an example of some people who have spent years in the church but failed to grow into spiritual maturity? Do we have other versions of "John Sanders" in most churches? If so, what do they look like? And how might they have become this way?

CHAPTER 16

1. How do you react to Arlene Lewis and her way of doing things (p. 168)?

2. Explain what we can learn from Ernie Yost's prayer? What hints are there that he is growing in his spiritual perspectives (p. 171)?

3. Winn Rilkey to the pastor (p. 172): *"Maybe you're making the wrong assumption. Maybe you're assuming that everyone in the church is good friends with each other . . ."* Read Winn's complete comment (and Stan's follow up) and decide whether or not you agree with their thoughts. Is much of the talk in many churches about intimacy and community simply not true? Respond.

4. Draw your own version of Everett Rogers's bell curve (p. 174ff) and try to identify where you think you are. If you are meeting in a group, challenge each person to put his or her initials at an appropriate place and explain what causes them to come to that conclusion.

5. What can be said about the Discovery Group as the evening progresses? Describe their relationships. Are there any emerging leaders? Are there key comments through the chapter that show people strengthening and encouraging one another?

CHAPTER 17

1. List character traits of Connie Peterson that impress you (p. 179ff). What does she have to teach all of us? Is she a model of a mature Christian? If so, what convinces you of this?

2. Describe what kind of a person Ben Jacobs "seems" to be? Does he have a chance of fitting in at most churches (p. 181ff)?

3. When Ernie Yost made his boorish comments regarding Ben to Ted Patton and they were overheard by Connie Peterson, what might have gone wrong if Connie had not handled the moment so well? And what is your reaction to the way she did handle things (p. 184ff)?

4. How does the group respond when Mary Ann Squires prays? What can we learn from these exchanges that help us to understand how young Christians are encouraged (p. 185)?

5. When Connie Peterson interrupts the pastor (p. 185ff) and begins to speak, what do you learn about her deepest thoughts and convictions? How does she affect the perspective of the entire Discovery Group?

6. Express what happens to the Discovery Group as a result of Connie Peterson's disclosures about her family and her own sense of God's direction in her life (p. 188ff).

7. *"Shame on us. We're talking about the wrong things,"* Ted Patton remarks on page 191. What do you hear him trying to say?

CHAPTER 18

1. What is your reaction to the pastor's comments regarding John Sanders's exit from the Discovery Group and the difference it may have made? Is he suggesting that there may be occasions when such departures are beneficial (p. 193ff)?

CHAPTER 19

1. Discuss what happened during the evening that Ernie Yost and Ben Jacobs spent together. What might each of us learn from their encounter (p. 208ff)?

2. In your opinion, what was the most important thing that Ernie gave to Ben in the course of their time together (p. 209ff)?

3. On page 212, the pastor tells the Discovery Group: *"I don't think you have any idea of how valuable each of you could be in the lives of younger people if you were willing to be spiritual parents to this new generation."* Discuss the implications and importance of what he is saying to them. How would the life of an average congregation change if such a thing were to happen?

4. Address both the spirit and the content of the prayers of the Discovery Group as the meeting ended (pp. 213–214).

CHAPTER 20

1. How was Ben Jacobs drawn into the church's life? What does this say about the nature of belonging (p. 215ff)?

2. How do Jason Calder and his team build a bridge to the Discovery Group and get them involved in a joint venture of worship? Note the subtle ways attitudes are changing (p. 216ff).

3. Discuss the mood throughout this meeting. Would you have enjoyed being there? Why or why not?

4. How do you see this meeting affecting Ben Jacobs? Imagine together what is going on in his mind.

CHAPTER 21

1. As the pastor describes his own impressions of the beginning of Sunday's worship experience, what stands out to you as evidence that things are changing (p. 220ff)?

2. Discuss different characteristics of the worship service that draw your attention (p. 221ff).

3. As the story of the Discovery Group reaches its conclusion, what is slowly changing in this church so that everyone feels a part of things (pp. 221–224)?

4. As you reflect on this book, what are the ways the Discovery Group has changed in terms of its quality of relationships, its view of the church, and its reaction to the challenge of reinvention?

5. As you read the *Epilogue*, express together what effects it had on your own perspective of the church, and what is possible when people love the church that God our Father loves and for whom Jesus, His Son, gave his blood.

Notes

Chapter 4

1. William Barclay, *The Mind of Jesus* (London: Arthur James Limited, 1997), 97.
2. Peter Drucker, *Post-Capitalist Society* (New York: HarperCollins, 1993).

Chapter 6

1. Peter Drucker, *Post-Capitalist Society* (New York: HarperCollins, 1993).

Chapter 10

1. Kenneth W. Osbeck, *101 Hymn Stories* (Grand Rapids: Kregel Publications, 1982), 14, 122.
2. Ira D. Sankey, *Sankey's Story of the Gospel Hymns* (The Sunday School Times Co., 1906), 19.
3. Ibid.
4. Ellen Koskoff, *Music Cultures in the United States* (New York: Routledge, 2005), 131, 206.

Chapter 11

1. *Wow Worship: Blue,* special edition CD disc 2 "Come, Now is the Time to Worship" Integrity Media, 2007.
2. *Wow Worship: Blue,* special edition CD disc 1 "The Heart of Worship" Integrity Media, 2007.
3. Matt Redman, *The Unquenchable Worshipper* (Ventura, CA: Regal Books, 2006); available in the UK from Kingsway.

Chapter 16

1. Everett M. Rogers, *The Diffusion of Innovations,* 5th ed. (New York: Free Press, 2003).